BILLY MITCHELL

Crusader for Air Power

D0882130

BILLY MITCHELL

Crusader for Air Power

■

ALFRED F. HURLEY

Indiana University Press
Bloomington and Indianapolis

This book is a publication of

Indiana University Press
601 North Morton Street
Bloomington, Indiana 47404-3797 USA

http://iupress.indiana.edu

Telephone orders   800-842-6796
Fax orders   812-855-7931
Orders by e-mail   iuporder@indiana.edu

The paper used in this publication meets the minimum requirements of
American National Standard for Information Sciences—Permanence
of Paper for Printed Library Materials, ANSI Z39.48-1984.

Manufactured in the United States of America

Cataloging information is available from the Library of Congress.

Library of Congress Cataloging in Publication Data
Hurley, Alfred F
Billy Mitchell, crusader for air power.

Bibliography
Includes index.
1. Mitchell, William, 1879–1936. I. Title.
UG633.M45H8 1975 358.4'13'320924 [B] 74-22831

ISBN 0-253-31203-5
ISBN 0-253-20180-2 pbk.

2 3 4 5 6 11 10 09 08 07 06

All photos courtesy U.S. Air Force

Contents

Illustrations follow page 38 and page 72.

Introduction

REVERED by many Americans as a martyr, Brigadier General William ("Billy") Mitchell has been one of the least understood public figures of recent times. Mitchell was the dominant figure in American aviation from 1919 until his court-martial in the fall of 1925 and his subsequent resignation from the United States Army in 1926. His pioneer role in aviation, as well as the dramatic ending to his career, have understandably made him an exciting subject for biography, the movies, television, and the press. These portrayals of Mitchell, however, have always been one-sided, with little or no effort made to balance his side of the story with any other point of view. All of Mitchell's biographers have tended to overemphasize one or two sensational elements in his story, particularly his court-martial. Those writers, it seems to me, have not made it clear that, to Mitchell, sensationalism was only a means to an end.[1] Thus, his deliberate provocation of his court-martial was but another tactic to draw attention to his ideas about aviation. Only when Mitchell is considered in the light of those ideas and in the context in which he progressively acquired, applied, and publicized them, does a balanced appraisal of the man become possible. This emphasis on his ideas is the approach that I have followed in this book.

When Mitchell is considered in terms of his ideas, he emerges as one of the significant figures of the years between World Wars I and II. He foresaw, to an impressive degree, the direction of aviation development and its role in World War II and subsequent military policy. He was the trailblazer in preparing the American people to accept the role of aeronautics in their nation's military and diplomatic policies. Further, he was an important agent in the growth of United States naval aviation and one of the founding fathers of the United States Air Force. Indeed, Mitchell's ideas lend perspective to many of the problems facing mankind in the nuclear age. Many of his ideas span an era which will not end until the missile displaces the airplane as the primary carrier of the nuclear weapon. Mitchell's role in that era can be both inspirational and instructive, not only for the airmen of the world today, but also for everyone who is concerned about current military affairs.

This book, therefore, is the first documented, critical, and, hopefully, balanced study of Mitchell and his work. The reader should be aware at the outset that I am a professional officer and navigator in the United States Air Force. I believe, however, that my training as a historian has given me the tools to evaluate even one of the founders of my own service with a measure of objectivity. Of course, the views that I express in this book are mine alone and should not be construed as carrying the official sanction of the Department of Defense, the Department of the Air Force, the United States Air Force Academy, or of the publishers.

* * *

The foregoing words introduced the 1964 edition of this book. Today, I would modify that introduction in only two important respects. In 1967, Mr. Burke Davis neatly reversed the trend toward sensationalism among the full-scale biographies of Mitchell and published *The Mitchell Affair,* a straightforward, although uncritical, account. Also, I previously anticipated that the missile might replace the airplane as the primary carrier of the nuclear weapon. During the past decade, the soundness of Mitchell's emphasis on the flexibility of the airplane has become all the more apparent. That flexibility has assured the long-range bomber, along with land-based and sea-based missiles, of full membership in the TRIAD, the national strategic team.

In revising this book, I have drawn upon criticisms of the first edition, the perspective gained from another decade of Air Force service, and a broader and deeper study of the sources of air power, including materials closed to me in 1963. The newly opened materials were the transcript of the Mitchell court-martial and the reports of the various U.S. Army attachés assigned to Italy in the years 1919–39. The changes in this edition include this introduction, a revised epilogue, and the addition of a fully documented appendix, "New Insights" on Mitchell and his ideas.

I am indebted to Professors Robert H. Ferrell and Robin Higham, and my colleagues, Lieutenant Colonels David MacIsaac and Philip D. Caine for their excellent criticisms of the 1964 edition. For the shortcomings of this edition, however, only I bear the responsibility.

United States Air Force Academy   A.F.H.
January 1975

BILLY MITCHELL

Crusader for Air Power

CHAPTER ONE

"A Fair Foundation"

BRIGADIER GENERAL William ("Billy") Mitchell was really a latecomer among the pioneers of American aviation. When he entered that field in 1916, the first powered flight of the Wright brothers was more than twelve years past. That he still became the most prominent figure of the next decade in American aeronautics was due to something he called the "fair foundation" upon which he built his aviation career. That foundation had several key elements: his own remarkable personality, his distinguished family background, and his long service with the United States Army as it changed from a force of Indian fighters into the world-ranging arm of a new great power. The most important element in that foundation was his education in the problems that the United States faced in the twentieth century.[2]

1

I

Mitchell's life began in a successful setting of financial and political achievement. His grandfather, Alexander Mitchell, was a millionaire banker and railroad king, as well as a significant force in Democratic national and Wisconsin state politics. Billy's father, John Lendrum Mitchell, was a longtime public servant and eventually a United States Senator from Wisconsin. Billy had many of the characteristics which propelled his grandfather from the obscurity of a Scottish immigrant in 1837 to financial prominence a half century later. The drive, ambition, courage, and occasional ruthlessness of the nineteenth-century entrepreneur were qualities which, in large measure, described Billy himself. His own frequent encounters with controversy were in the tradition of his family. His grandfather's victory over the early Wisconsin reformers who sought to regulate his railroads followed one of the classic battles of that state's history. His father also had been one of the few men in the Senate who dared to oppose the imperialist mood that swept the nation into the war with Spain in 1898.[3]

The wealth of the grandfather enabled Billy's father to study at a series of European universities where he acquired a lasting taste for the cosmopolitan life. Thus, John Mitchell and his wife were temporarily residing in Nice, France, when Billy was born on December 29, 1879. Three years went by before the Mitchells brought their son back to their estate at "Meadowmere," near Milwaukee. It was there that the boy developed an enduring love of hunting and horsemanship. By the time he was fourteen, horsemanship for the Mitchell family had taken on a highly practical aspect. John Mitchell had turned to raising horses as an additional source of income after the panic of 1893 had closed the family bank and forced him to pledge over a million dollars of his personal assets to reopen it. To what extent John Mitchell ever recouped any losses is not clear. The financial crisis, however, may have set into motion a decline in family fortunes which his death in 1904 accelerated.[4]

In that financial adversity, Harriet Danforth Becker Mitchell, mother of Billy and six other children, doubtless played the key role in sustaining the family's spirit. Mitchell's consistent tone of intimacy toward his mother, his extraordinary frankness to her about his aspirations, and his evident desire to please her suggested her continuous influence on him until her death in 1922. Above all, it was Harriet Mitchell who stoked the fires of her son's ambition to match previous family achievements.[5]

In preparing for that goal, Mitchell received a broad liberal education both at home and in school. After a brief period of private tutoring, he spent six years in an Episcopalian preparatory school, Racine College of Wisconsin. Academically, Mitchell lacked his father's studiousness, but he held his own as a student at Racine. He had the normal boy's share of minor disciplinary problems. One school report stated that Mitchell had been in trouble for "talking before grace in the dining room, boisterous conduct at table, disorder in dormitory, and offences of that kind." Outdoor sports absorbed as much time and perhaps more than he could afford.

His already evident charm made him a popular student. His reputation among his peers was even strong enough for him to survive playing the female part in one school play. As his final year of preparatory school approached, Mitchell grew restive under Racine's rigid discipline, complained to his parents about what he thought was shoddy teaching there, and asked them to transfer him to Columbian Preparatory, in Washington, D. C. John Mitchell was then in the Senate, and the normal desire of the parents to have their son nearby probably resolved the issue. Although he had talked about applying for Princeton or Harvard, Mitchell entered the college division of Columbian (now George Washington University) in the fall of 1895, having graduated from its preparatory school the previous June.[6]

Mitchell's enthusiasm for the outdoors, however, made prolonged college study a trial for him. In fact, this passion for sports had become so ingrained in Mitchell that he could not envision a happy life without "horses and guns." An unexpected chance for such an active life appeared in April, 1898, when the United States declared war on Spain. Although Mitchell was only eighteen and a junior in college, he promptly enlisted as a private in the First Wisconsin, a volunteer regiment. His father's influence soon asserted itself, and in three weeks Mitchell had accepted a second lieutenant's commission in a volunteer signal company.[7]

II

Mitchell quickly adjusted to military life. Although the chaotic expansion of the Army from a constabulary to a tropical expeditionary force was something of a national disgrace, Mitchell adopted a positive attitude about things. He kept his discomforts to himself, tried to learn as much as he could, and noted that the frequent illnesses of his fellow volunteers often were due to their own neglect. They ignored many commonsense precautions for taking care of their health, he explained in a letter home; they were "drinking all kinds of stuff, eating warm watermelons when they are hardly able to sit up, and not taking off their clothes for weeks at a time." In writing this, Mitchell was doubtless trying to reassure his parents, but he still spoke like a youth at ease in the outdoors. His skill with "horses and guns" made it easier for him to imitate the regular or professional officers whom he encountered. Their acceptance of him was heady wine for an eighteen-year-old. Equally exhilarating were his occasional chances to lead small groups that included some men older than he.[8]

At this time, Mitchell demonstrated a flair for ready rapport with political and military leaders. The famous politician, William Jennings Bryan, also in Florida with a volunteer regiment, and Major General Adolphus Greely, the Chief Signal Officer of the Army, were the earliest of a long line of such figures to be attentive to Mitchell as the scion of an important family. Yet he was still realistic enough to appreciate the ease with which he had obtained a commission, for he had had no formal training. "Influence," he once wrote, "cuts a larger figure in this war than merit."

Nevertheless, when he learned of the promotion of several other second lieutenants who did not "know how to keep themselves warm," Mitchell was quick to ask that his father put in a word for him.[9] The promotion eventually came, and Senator Mitchell duly thanked General Greely for giving this "new responsibility" to his son. However, the Senator added quite correctly that his son was not without genuine military aptitude. He also might have pointed out that Billy had campaigned as vigorously for arduous duty as for promotion. Billy was "disgusted" when Spain sued for peace before his regiment could be called into action from its Florida base.

Most of his fellow volunteers wanted to go home, but Mitchell begged his father to use his influence to keep the regiment on active duty for occupation service in Cuba. "The most difficult work has just begun," he argued, and periodically sought his father's help in getting him to Cuba. His regiment finally sailed to Cuba in December, 1898, four months after the fighting had ended.[10]

Mitchell began his Cuban service in time to witness the formal surrender of the island by Spain to the United States. Seeing the ceremony in Havana was one of a series of personal experiences that made him appreciate America's new worldwide role. The winning of Cuba, he wrote, marked "the beginning of a new policy on the part of the U.S., that of territorial expansion and showing himself [sic] to the world as one of the greatest of nations."

The occupation force required an extensive communications system to be set up by the Signal Corps, and Mitchell had ample opportunities for the creative but concrete type of work he most enjoyed. Within four months after his arrival, he had supervised the stringing of 136 miles of telegraph wire in Santiago Province. But, after this initial spurt of activity, his life seemed to settle into an incessant round of hunting in the Cuban countryside and attending parties in Havana. In fact, he had so many invitations that he had to restrict himself to accepting just three an evening.[11]

About this time, Mitchell wrote: "I am just as much at home wherever I am now as any place." This realization helped spur his interest in a military career. His commander, Colonel Joseph E. Maxfield, was a professional officer who had encouraged him, praising his work and inviting him to seriously consider a career in the Signal Corps. But Mitchell preferred the Cavalry and its promise of a life on horseback, fearing that Signal Corps duty would be too confining in peacetime. Still, the Signal Corps offered him the rank of first lieutenant while only a second lieutenancy was available in the Cavalry, and Mitchell speculated about transferring later to the Cavalry in the higher grade. Such planning, however, had to wait until later since Mitchell could not legally apply for a career appointment for two more years, when he would be twenty-one. Moreover, his parents doubtless were opposed to this, for he had told them he wanted to try a military career for a brief period only and then resign.[12]

At any rate, his parents were clearly against Billy's desire to serve in the troubled Philippine Islands. The Filipinos were bitterly resisting U.S. annexation, and the struggle was soon to involve 100,000 American troops. But Mitchell, toying with the idea of a military career and attracted by the prospect of adventure for its own sake, could not ignore what American professional soldiers have always described as the "sound of the guns." Despite his parents' objections, he first volunteered for duty in the Philippines, then simply presented them with his transfer orders. While they agreed that he should not shirk this hazardous duty, his father comforted Mrs. Mitchell with the thought that the worst part of the campaign would be over before Billy reached the islands in October, 1899. The Senator's judgment was based upon the first optimistic reports from the Philippines that the Army could quickly defeat the rebels in conventional warfare. Soon, however, the rebels' leader, Emilio Aguinaldo, repudiated this belief by adopting guerrilla tactics and prolonging the conflict.[13]

Thus Mitchell's arrival in the islands actually coincided with the opening of a two-year campaign. He quickly went into action, finding more excitement than he ever had experienced back home in Milwaukee. Billy had visited there while en route to the port of embarkation in San Francisco and all his old friends did, he wrote, "was sit around, talk and play golf" at the country club. In the Philippines it was a matter of survival. His request for a Christmas present of a "Mauser automatic or any other *good* automatic pistol with 500 rounds of ammunition for same" betrayed the terribly personal nature of guerrilla warfare.

In Billy's view, "all the laws, usages, and precedents of our nation or any other" established that the Filipinos had been beaten, but they did not seem to know it. Their guerrilla tactics exasperated the Army generally, and Mitchell in particular. The formula for victory became the application "of the fire and the sword" and the use "of any manner known for extracting information" from the uncooperative. By his own testimony, Mitchell freely used this formula.[14]

Mitchell's service in the Philippines reinforced his growing conviction that he could do outstandingly well in military life. While he believed that he could have won great distinction as the commander of a cavalry troop in combat, his record as a signal officer with General Arthur MacArthur's division won the warm praise of his superiors. And, when not in the field, Billy once again made the most of every moment to hunt or participate in social life. He had come to "know pretty nearly every officer in the American Army" and the good fellowship they so readily extended to him impressed him mightily. Serving in a situation where there was a cycle of combat and then a lull enabled him to appraise Army life further. He decided that his temperament could never abide the inactivity of garrison duty. Even in the Philippines, where fighting could break out at any time, most of the Army in the peaceful areas "had nothing to do except fight chickens, play poker, and drink whiskey when they can get it or vino if they can't." Because the specter of doing this in a peacetime garrison made him cautious about embarking on a full service career, he anticipated only five or perhaps six years of service during which he would complete his formal education. Then he planned to "quit, have a home, some settled aim, business and association and try to earn one's self respect and of one's neighbors." [15]

As matters turned out, the exigencies of the twentieth century were to prevent the stagnation Mitchell had feared. If America's decision to retain the Philippines had put her among the great powers, it also had exposed her to the troubles besetting such nations. Some American diplomats and military men saw dangerous portents in Germany's desire to increase her holdings in the Pacific. Indeed, there had already been friction between Germany and the United States over the control of Samoa in 1889, and German heavy-handedness in the Philippines after Dewey's destruction of the Spanish fleet in Manila Bay had concerned a widening American diplomatic and military audience. In a letter to his mother in June, 1900, while she was vacationing in Germany, Mitchell remarked that a career commission in the Army would be especially valuable because "there will be a big stir up somewhere one of these days and not far away and probably with the country in which you are now in, among others."

In any case, America's new world position offered sufficient reason for modifying her traditional practice of maintaining the smallest possible professional army. An increased Regular Army was in order and four months before the enlistments of the volunteer regiments stationed in the Philippines expired, Congress passed the Army Act of February, 1901. This legislation authorized a career force of 100,000 men, a fourfold increase over the standing Army of 1897. The officer corps expanded accordingly, and Mitchell's aim of obtaining a regular or permanent commission was made easier. On April 26, 1901, shortly after he had returned to the United States from the Philippines via Europe, he accepted an appointment as a first lieutenant in the career Signal Corps.[16]

A numerical increase in the standing Army was one thing; its actual fitness for its new tasks was another. The assassination of President William McKinley, some four months after Mitchell had begun his career, rescued Vice-President Theodore Roosevelt from political exile. Roosevelt's realization of the crucial relationship between a meaningful foreign policy and significant military power prompted him to spur the modernization of the Army and Navy. His agent in the improvement of the Army was Elihu Root, the Secretary of War inherited from McKinley. When McKinley appointed Root in 1898, the President had denied that he wanted a Secretary who "knows anything about the Army." Rather, he sought a lawyer of Root's talents to supervise the administration of the territories acquired from Spain. Root rapidly discovered that he could not separate the problems of colonial administration from those of the effectiveness of the Army. Moreover, he recognized his ignorance of military affairs and drew upon the ideas of others— principally those of the late Major General Emory Upton. Twenty years before, Upton had studied the problems of creating a modern army in the light of previous American military history and of his firsthand study of the leading armies of Europe and Asia. Before giving up his office in February, 1904, Root managed to secure the adoption of two of Upton's most important recommendations—the creation of a general staff, and the improvement of the Army's educational system. He did not seek the adoption of still another one of Upton's far-reaching recommendations, the Continental Army Plan or a federalized militia system, based on conscription, which would train a force in peacetime that could quickly increase the standing Army in the event of war.[17]

Upton's death in 1881 prevented him from completing his *Military Policy of the United States,* the work in which he focused on the Continental Army Plan. Root found the unfinished manuscript and had it published in January, 1904, as an official document. Reprinted four times between 1904 and 1917, the book dominated the intellectual climate of the Army until America entered World

War I; it also served as a symbol of the military progressivism encouraged by Roosevelt and Root. This progressive spirit was taking hold of the Regular Army just as Mitchell entered it. A man of his personality and background could readily accept that spirit.[18]

III

Mitchell's duties in the next ten years preserved his interest in a military career. The Army sent him overseas three times on the field duty he preferred, while its educational system fostered his professional development. These experiences were the basis for much of his later thought, for they developed his world view, an appreciation of the increasingly technical nature of war, and an active interest in national military policy.

After the Philippines, Mitchell's next major assignment was Alaska. The discovery of gold in Canada's Klondike area in 1896 reminded the U.S. government how isolated Alaska was. The Signal Corps drew the task of ending that isolation by building a communications system throughout Alaska and connecting it to existing links between Canada and the United States. In the summer of 1901, Mitchell was delighted when General Greely, the Chief Signal Officer, relieved him from a tedious assignment at Fort Myer, Virginia, and ordered him to survey the work accomplished so far in Alaska.

Upon completing the survey, Mitchell volunteered his services for the construction project. They were accepted and, together with two other Signal Corps officers, he spent two years supervising military-civilian teams in the erection of a 1,700-mile telegraph line. While Mitchell still preferred a Cavalry assignment, he had to admit that the Signal Corps had at least given him responsibilities in Alaska that few civilians in their twenties could ever hope for. Moreover, he soon had his first taste of publicity when the *National Geographic Magazine* published his article on his Alaskan experiences. At one point in his Alaskan tour, his sense of importance carried him too far. He telegraphed Greely that "if he would give me what I wanted, I could complete the whole Alaskan telegraph system" inside eighteen months. Mitchell conceded to his mother that he was uncertain whether Greely thought he was putting himself "forward too much or not. But after all what is there in it unless one can get forward as much as possible." [19]

Mitchell also gained the advancement he had been looking for. At twenty-four, he became the youngest captain in the Army. To do so he had to take the stiff mandatory promotion examination. After studying harder than he ever had before, Billy passed it. As the most technically oriented of the Army's branches the Signal Corps required its officers to be familiar with subjects ranging from aeronautics to electricity. During Mitchell's early career, the Signal Corps made use of a long list of inventions including the balloon, the telegraph, the telephone, the dirigible, the camera, the automobile, and the airplane.

In November, 1903, a chance loomed for Mitchell to study many of these technical developments at first hand. After his return to the United States, Greely promised him a tour of duty at Fort Leavenworth, Kansas, where the Signal Corps was going to carry on much of its experimental work.[20] But this assignment did not take place for another year and a half.

Meanwhile, Mitchell met and married Caroline Stoddard, a Vassar graduate and member of a prominent Rochester, New York, family. The ceremony took place on December 2, 1903. The marriage had been encouraged by the mothers of the bride and groom, who had been longtime friends. After a honeymoon in Cuba and Mexico, and brief duty tours in Colorado and Virginia, Mitchell received his Leavenworth assignment.

At that time, Fort Leavenworth, Kansas, was the "intellectual center of the Army." As early as 1881, the post had been the site of the Infantry and Cavalry School, providing theoretical instruction for the junior officers of those branches of the Army. After the Spanish-American War had temporarily ended all such activities, military education came into its own at Leavenworth with the reestablishment of the Infantry and Cavalry School in 1901, the creation of a Staff College in 1904, and of a Signal School in 1905. Mitchell served as an assistant instructor in the Signal School and as the commander of the Signal Company attached to the post. His unit was a team of enlisted technical specialists in "field telegraphy, telephone, and field communications," which assisted the various resident schools during their field exercises and tested new developments in Signal Corps equipment.[21]

As Mitchell soon came to realize, duty at Leavenworth was a professional plum. He had a command which won General Greely's plaudits as the "best company" in the Army. His associates were some of the outstanding men in the service, including the brilliant inventor, Major George O. Squier, who was the commander of the Signal School. The testing facilities for new equipment prompted Mitchell to try his own hand as an inventor. One of his devices, a horse-borne pack for carrying telegraph wire, drew some attention. The best indication of the breadth of his activities at Leavenworth, however, was a lecture that he presented to the Signal School and then published in 1906. Its unwieldy title demonstrated the range of his work: "The Signal Corps with Divisional Cavalry and Notes on Wireless Telegraphy, Searchlights and Military Ballooning." [22]

Mitchell's analysis of military ballooning in this lecture was especially significant. Although the Signal Corps had used balloons during the Civil War, military interest in them had lagged until 1892. Only a single balloon was used in Cuba during the Spanish-American War. When Alberto Santos-Dumont, the Brazilian aeronaut, and Thomas Baldwin, an American, later began experimenting with dirigibles, new military possibilities in lighter-than-air craft arose. Mitchell and his fellow Signal Corps officers had to study all of these developments in preparation for their promotion examinations. It was common knowledge that European inventors were suggesting that the dirigible had potential reconnaissance, transport, and even strategic uses. [23]

Mitchell's views on the subject included ideas that he later advocated vigorously. The dirigible, he predicted in his 1906 article, might "course at will over a battlefield, carry messages out of a besieged fortress, or sail alone above a beleaguered place, immune from the action of men on the earth's surface." In fact, Mitchell foresaw the possibility of the dirigible's offensive employment. "By towing another balloon, loaded with explosive, several hundred pounds of guncotton could be dropped from the balloon which it is towing in the midst of the enemy's fortifications." Because objects deep in the water could be seen from a dirigible's cruising altitude, he thought that dirigibles might act as "scouts for the Navy to detect the presence of submarine vessels."

Mitchell closed his article with a prediction that "conflicts, no doubt, will be carried on in the future in the air, on the surface of the earth and water, and under the earth and water." But Mitchell also recognized the existing technological limits. For example, no one had learned how to compensate for the dropping of a "pound or two," so as to prevent the dirigible from rising so fast that its envelope would crack. Until this problem had been overcome, there could be no talk of bombardment from a dirigible.[24]

Mitchell had no direct connection with the Signal Corps' early aviation work, which was formalized by the establishment of its Aeronautical Division on August 1, 1907. In fact, there were few opportunities for assignment to flying duty. The Aeronautical Division did not get its first airplane until 1908, and by 1913 it had only six. Moreover, there was only one dirigible in the Division's inventory during this period. Mitchell himself never expressed any ambition to fly before 1916. Thus, his remarks about military ballooning suggested no more than the range of his active mind at a time when a fast-moving technical revolution was challenging the entire Army, and the Signal Corps in particular.[25]

Leavenworth was also the site of Mitchell's only formal military schooling. After brief tours of duty away from that post—one at the scene of the San Francisco earthquake in 1906, and another later that year in Cuba during a period of unrest—Mitchell entered the School of the Line (formerly the Infantry and Cavalry School) in 1907. His selection as a student marked the first time that a member of the Signal Corps had been given such training. Out of the thirty-nine officers completing the one-year course, Mitchell was one of twenty designated as "Distinguished Graduates" and one of twenty-four selected to attend the Staff College for the next year. Mitchell's training at both schools showed how far Root's educational reforms had changed the Army's thinking from what it had been in the Indian-fighting days. The two-year curriculum, climaxed by the Staff College's annual ride through the Civil War battlefields, emphasized the preparation of the student body for mass warfare.

The research problem assigned to Mitchell and a group of his fellow students at the Staff College indicated the mood of the Leavenworth faculty. It was nothing less than producing an organizational plan for a 500,000-man force, deployed to meet a hypothetical invasion of the east coast. The last part of the problem was a reminder that this after all, was 1909: "Show the number of horses and mules required." Mitchell's solution has not survived, but it may well have depended on ideas gained from his military history course at Leavenworth, which had been by far his favorite. The course that year had treated many examples of the battles of the age of mass warfare, including the struggles of the Napoleonic era at Austerlitz and Waterloo, the Civil War experiences at Donelson and on the Peninsula, the Franco-Prussian encounter at Metz, and the Boer War engagement at Paardeberg.[26]

With this important preparation behind him, Mitchell made his long-considered move to transfer from the Signal Corps into the Cavalry. He doubtless was gambling that he could make greater progress in a command rather than in a staff position. The leadership positions in the Army and opportunities for distinction in war were far more accessible to the cavalryman than to the technical specialist.

Accordingly, Mitchell succeeded in locating a Cavalry officer who was willing to trade branch assignments with him but, even though Billy used political pressure, Chief of Staff Major General Franklin J. Bell refused to approve the proposition. Everyone concerned with the transfer offered different reasons why it failed, but perhaps the one Mitchell himself stressed was the most cogent. He claimed that General Bell balked because the change would give Mitchell an unfair advantage in rank over his peers in the Cavalry who had not enjoyed his opportunities for promotion.[27]

Swallowing his disappointment, Mitchell now began to use his Leavenworth training for broader purposes than Signal Corps work. During his next tour—two years in the Philippines—Mitchell carried out a successful undercover reconnaissance of Japanese activities in the islands lying between Formosa and the Philippines. He also visited the battlefields of the Russo-Japanese War and studied the various Chinese armies, as well as the Russian and Japanese forces. After returning to the United States, he reported on these experiences to the War College Division of the General Staff.

Mitchell's major point in these reports was that war with Japan was inevitable and that the Philippines were consequently in great danger. This happened to be the extreme side of a common view held among many American military men and diplomats at that time. The Japanese victory over Russia in 1905 had amazed them and now it made their earlier predictions of trouble with Germany in the Pacific seem trivial.

While Mitchell's predictions about Japan were significant primarily as landmarks in his personal development, some of his thoughts deserved consideration in Washington. American diplomatic policies in that area of the world, Mitchell stressed, were not isolationist. Mitchell warned that the constant display of American interest in Korea, Manchuria, and China ran counter to Japanese plans. Moreover, the United States had chosen to antagonize the most advanced of the Oriental nations—Japan—through a policy of discrimination against her nationals who had immigrated to America. American persistence in such policies, not to mention the "Open Door" policy in China, made it imperative that America make military preparations to back up her diplomacy.[28]

The key to those preparations, Mitchell felt, was the creation of a force much like that desired by Upton and then under consideration by the progressives of the Army led by Secretary of War Henry L. Stimson and Chief of Staff Major General Leonard Wood. These men wanted an Army of the size Mitchell had studied at Leavenworth—one that included a regular component of 100,000 backed up by a trained reserve. This reserve was to be, in Mitchell's version, composed of volunteers who had served two years on active duty, who were organized in divisional strength, located in the centers of population, and who were controlled by the federal government. As Mitchell doubtless knew, substantial political considerations argued against such a plan. When Stimson and Wood tried to consolidate the then-existing forty-nine Army posts scattered throughout twenty-four states as the first step in creating divisional units, they ran afoul of vigorous congressional opposition. Even though these posts were relics of the Army's constabulary days, they were still important economically to the districts in which they were located. Yet to be fully tested were other issues, such as the federal control of any militia. The previous pattern of American military policy had emphasized a minimum standing Army, state-controlled militia, and volunteers recruited after a crisis had begun.[29]

Mitchell's harmony with current General Staff thinking may have figured in the announcement in March, 1912, of his selection along with twenty other officers for duty with that organization. He thought his paper on his Far Eastern trip had been a factor, as well as his good record and Leavenworth training. A source of particular pleasure to him was that the appointment had come on merit and without the use of any influence. General Staff duty, he knew full well, could be the stepping-stone to great things from his present rank of captain. "If fortunate," he confided to his mother, "I may be a general before many years have passed." [30]

In looking forward to his tour on the General Staff, Mitchell correctly noted that he had developed a "fair foundation" in fourteen years of army life. He now possessed many of the credentials for becoming an outstanding twentieth-century professional soldier —his patrician background, the sponsorship of a politically potent family, an engaging personality, the zeal for distinction and preference for field combat service that marks most military leaders, and a sincere desire to serve his country. The Army had furnished him with a worldwide viewpoint and an appreciation of rapid technical advances that was rare among his civilian brethren; his service had trained him to think in terms of mass warfare, but had hardened him in the most bitter form of modern war—guerrilla combat. Above all, Mitchell's service had taken place in a progressive climate favorable to educating the American people as to the military implications of the new century.[31]

IV

In February of 1913, Mitchell went to Washington determined to make the most of his General Staff assignment. If this were to be a successful turning point in his career, he believed that he had to develop the political and social contacts that Washington and the east coast in general offered him. This meant full participation in the horse shows, polo matches, and club life both of Washington and of the even more fashionable Long Island society. Billy's natural gaiety and superb abilities as a horseman and dancer stood him in good stead, but at the same time he soon learned that the social whirl was too ambitious for his captain's pay. In fact, Mitchell frequently had to turn to his mother for financial assistance, and each time he did so, he confided to her what he was trying to do. Other than Fort Leavenworth, he told her, only Washington, D.C., was a professionally worthwhile post in peacetime, and the costs of such duty had to be judged accordingly.

Now that he was thirty-four years of age, Mitchell felt fully committed to an Army career. If he ever were to match the record of his grandfather and father, it was in the Army that his reputation had to be made. He had to prepare himself in every way, especially on the chance that there might be a war. And, were he successful in war, there could be "no limit in the gift" of the American people.[32]

Mitchell made some promising contacts in Washington, and also in New York society. He began an enduring friendship with another Wisconsinite, Joseph E. Davies, who soon became the head of the Federal Trade Commission. In addition, he came to know such prominent men as Henry T. Breckenridge, the Assistant Secretary of War; Willard Straight, the banker and Far Eastern expert; and James Hay, Jr., the son of the powerful Chairman of the House Military Affairs Committee. Mitchell's political ties with his home state of Wisconsin were also evident. When the crisis with Mexico over the recognition of a government acceptable to the Wilson Administration verged on war, Mitchell sought a colonelcy and the command of a Wisconsin volunteer cavalry regiment. He anticipated that success in such a post could do much for the family's political chances in their onetime stronghold. President Woodrow Wilson, however, managed to avoid a war, even though on several occasions during the four-year dispute a conflict seemed certain.[33]

Meanwhile, Mitchell did not neglect the more immediate concern of building his reputation within the Army. In an article for the *Infantry Journal* in the fall of 1913, he publicly allied himself with the advocates of the Continental Army idea. Although the piece was the most detailed he ever published, well grounded in history and balanced in its judgments, it nevertheless covered familiar ground. Since the article included the drafts of bills that might be put in the congressional hopper, it was likely that his work benefited from some collaboration or at least a bit of legal advice. In any case, Mitchell happily reported to his mother that the article "was commented on everywhere and made a great deal of an impression in Congress." [34]

This interest in general American military policy dominated his outlook during the years 1913 to 1916. His technological background made him realize that the United States could no longer completely trust in the protection of the great distances separating her from the rest of the world. The rapid advance of science "as exemplified in transport methods and means which daily bring us closer to prospective enemies" had already made it necessary to measure distance in time, rather than in miles. Still, as important as these technical advances were, the American people, he believed, must not forget that "only human blood and bone" were able to do the job in modern warfare. The contemporary European conflict had already made it clear that victory would only go to the side which could "supply for the longest time, well-trained and disciplined officers and men for its field armies." [35]

Such ideas lent perspective to Billy's occasional contacts with aeronautics as the only Signal Corps officer on the General Staff. Yet Mitchell at this time still treated aviation as essentially just another element of the Signal Corps. He wrote but infrequently on the subject and only when one of his superiors directed him to study some aeronautical problem or other. While Mitchell was aware of the strides aeronautics was making abroad, his principal duty on the General Staff was to collect all the information coming into the War College Division initially about the Balkan Wars and then the great European conflict.[36]

His reaction in 1913 to the earliest major attempt to put aviation into a separate organization was consistent with his membership in the Signal Corps. Some of the flyers in the Aeronautical Division maintained that more progress could be made if they had an organization of their own. Yet Mitchell and other future aviation leaders, including Lieutenant Henry ("Hap") Arnold, testified before a congressional hearing that the Signal Corps and aviation perfectly complemented each other. Aviation, Mitchell said, was at best a reconnaissance device; hence, it was an integral part of his branch's communication system. "The offensive value of this thing has yet to be proved," he argued, and added: "It is being experimented with— bomb dropping and machines carrying guns . . . but there is nothing to it so far except in an experimental way." In fact, he made clear his own lack of an active interest in aviation by insisting that it was a young man's field and "no man should be taken in, who is more than thirty years of age or married to start with." Mitchell claimed that Congressman Hay had let him draft the resulting legislation in July, 1914. It was evident that the main features of the law tallied with his testimony. Congress kept aeronautics in the Signal Corps (although in a new Aviation Section), restricted flight training to bachelor lieutenants under 30 years of age, and made minor improvements in the status of the flyers and their equipment.[37]

Of more concern at the moment to Mitchell was the outbreak of the war in Europe at the end of July. Recalling how General George McClellan's service as an observer in the Crimean War had helped his claim to a key position in the Civil War, Mitchell was anxious to go to Europe in a similar role. He preferred an assignment with the Russian army "as they have a problem to handle much like ours would be under the same conditions." However, neither the Wilson Administration nor the belligerents wanted more than a few American observers in Europe. Actually, Mitchell shared the Administration's initial isolationist attitude toward the war, but thought its policy on observers was "shortsighted." Although he also believed that his civilian superiors took a dim view of statements or articles by professional military men about the conflict, he circumvented possible disapproval on several occasions. At first, he was an unidentified "military expert" for the *Chicago Tribune,* and then he wrote at least one unsigned article on military preparedness for *World's Work* magazine.[38]

The crisis with Germany over her submarine campaign of 1915 brought home to a great number of Americans what Mitchell and other publicists were trying to say. All questions of intervention in Europe aside, the United States was plainly too weak to back up any meaningful diplomatic action in behalf of her interests. In this respect, the submarine crisis had educated President Wilson, who also saw how preparedness had become a political issue. He reluctantly swung the Administration in the direction of preparedness by ordering the service secretaries to initiate studies of the country's military needs. The Army General Staff was more than ready with proposals. The core of its ideas, as finally presented to Congress, was a threefold request for an increase in the Regular Army, the creation of the Continental Army, and the elimination of the National Guard as a factor in any future mobilization.

Mitchell must have been happy to note that his *Infantry Journal* article was among the literature on the Continental Army question cited during the congressional hearings. His arguments and those of better-known proponents could not, however, match the political power of their opposition. A mixture of National Guard lobbyists, states rights advocates, pacifists, and those who thought any increase in military strength meant militarism, thwarted the General Staff's proposals. Moreover, the controversy led to the resignations of Mitchell's friend, Assistant Secretary Breckenridge, and of the Secretary of War, Lindley M. Garrison. The eventual legislation—The National Defense Act of 1916—almost doubled the Regular Army over a five-year period, but retained the National Guard as the main reserve force. The federal government would control the National Guard to a greater degree, although professional officers such as Major General Hugh Scott, the Army's Chief of Staff, privately doubted that any element of state control was sound. More significantly, the long-range view of this legislation, evidenced by the five-year plan for increasing the Regular Army and matched by a three-year program of naval expansion, meant that the nation would not be ready for any immediate crisis, and only possibly for those crises stemming from the outcome of the European war.[39]

Mitchell's minor role in the "Preparedness Controversy" had some results which he probably could not have foreseen. The General Staff's response to Wilson's request for proposals on preparedness included some thirty studies on specific areas of national defense. Mitchell appeared to have drawn the assignment of preparing one of the studies, a survey of America's aviation needs. The unsigned report, published by the War Department in November, 1915, has the distinction of being one of the earliest comprehensive statements of American military aviation policy and an excellent statement of aeronautical thinking at this time. If the report were his, Mitchell succeeded in producing a full-scale treatment of aviation as it had been developed by others in the United States and abroad. The author of the pamphlet remained firmly committed to an Army support role for aircraft under the control of the Signal Corps. He theorized that aviation would be a particularly valuable adjunct to the Army—a "second line of defense," if the Navy, "the first line of defense," should fail to stop an invasion of the United States. Specifically, aviation attached to harbor and mobile coastal defenses within the continental United States and its overseas possessions would be useful both for reconnaissance and for preventing similar enemy activity. As spotters over an invasion force, they would enhance the accuracy of coastal artillery. Offensively, aircraft could destroy an invader's aircraft, attack his submarines, and disrupt the work of his minelayers. For these purposes, the author saw the urgent need to increase Army aviation beyond its strength of 46 officers, 243 enlisted men, and 23 aircraft of varying utility.[40]

Congress attempted to solve some of the problems raised in the General Staff study. The shortcomings of the squadron of eight planes supporting Brigadier General John J. Pershing's pursuit of Pancho Villa into Mexico in the spring of 1916 were most apparent when Congress was considering military aeronautics. Pershing's aircraft were only training ships, not suited for field service. They simply fell apart. Their wooden propellers cracked in the dry heat of the southwest and their engines could not perform efficiently over the mountainous terrain. This debacle inspired an emergency appropriation of $500,000, followed by a gigantic $13,281,666 for the Aviation Section which was nine times the total of all funds allotted for Army aviation to date.

Aviation also benefited from a provision of the National Defense Act which ended the old restriction of flight training to bachelor lieutenants under thirty. This major policy change arose from another incident while the National Defense Act was under congressional study. The aviation legislation of July, 1914, had not pleased the junior airmen in the Aviation Section and their obstreperous conduct came to the attention of President Wilson and his new Secretary of War, Newton D. Baker. They removed Colonel Samuel Reber, the head of the Aviation Section, and ordered Mitchell's onetime associate at Leavenworth, Lieutenant Colonel George O. Squier, to take Reber's place. Pending Squier's return from attaché duty in London, Mitchell temporarily left his General Staff duties to head the Aviation Section. By changing the law to permit maturer officers to enter aviation, Congress prevented the recurrence of such incidents and also presented Mitchell with a new opportunity.[41]

Mitchell never commented directly on his General Staff experiences other than to remark privately that the constant office work had been so confining as to weaken him physically. He suffered from eyestrain at one point during his Washington tour and, at the end of 1915, spent five weeks in the hospital with what was probably rheumatism. Added to this physical wear and tear was his constant anxiety over his financial position. Even more to the point was the judgment of his superiors on the General Staff that he was temperamentally far better suited for active field service than in any staff appointment in a war. Since most Signal Corps work was essentially staff-oriented and particularly so as an officer's rank increased, only the Corps' Aviation Section offered the chance for the field service that Mitchell had always wanted and that his superiors thought best for him. Thus, after finishing his General Staff assignment in June, he returned to the Aviation Section as Squier's deputy.[42]

Mitchell won promotion to major in July and characteristically threw himself into the job of building up Army aviation. One of his biggest assignments was to step up flying training, and it quickly led to an incident symptomatic of his stormy future in aeronautics. As small as American aviation then was, there were already interested parties involved in it. The foremost of these was the Aero Club of America, the pioneer organization for promoting flying. This group wanted the government to focus on the flying training of National Guardsmen, while Mitchell and his associates basically wanted to step up the training of active duty personnel. A squabble followed that finally brought Newton Baker to Mitchell's support. Indeed, Mitchell was especially sensitive about the flying training issue. In the fall of 1916, he himself had begun pilot training in his off-duty time at the Curtiss Aviation School in Newport News, Virginia. His fifteen hours of instruction and thirty-six flights taught him the rudiments of a "controlled-crash" type of flying. Although Mitchell tried to bill the government for his training, the Comptroller of the Treasury ruled eventually that Congress had authorized officers like Mitchell to fly, but had not appropriated funds for their instruction. What was more, he did not receive his wings as a Junior Military Aviator until September, 1917, after he was in France. This new knowledge cost Mitchell the sum of $1,470, but there was an immediate dividend. In January of 1917, the War Department decided to send an officer to Europe as an aeronautical observer. Presumably on the strength of his flying knowledge, Mitchell got the job and left the United States for France on March 19, 1917. He departed at a moment when German-American relations were rapidly disintegrating because of the unrestricted submarine warfare campaign which had been under way since February. Two weeks later, on April 2, 1917, President Wilson decided that he had to act and asked Congress to declare war on Germany.[43]

CHAPTER TWO

"No Decision on the Ground . . . Before a Decision in the Air"

BILLY MITCHELL's arrival in Europe was timely. He reached Paris on April 10, 1917, only four days after the United States had declared war on Germany. Reporting to the headquarters of the American Military Mission, he joined the handful of officers who had already begun to lay the groundwork for the American Expeditionary Force. An extended interval seemed certain, however, before even the vanguard of the AEF would arrive. Mitchell made the most of that time by taking an intensive course in aeronautics taught by the top Allied airmen. What they had to say and even more, what they were doing, converted him to a theory of air power still unappreciated in the United States.

I

Major Mitchell began serious work at once in the French capital. His knowledge of the language (acquired during earlier visits to

France), his ease in Parisian political and social life, and his role as a symbol of coming American aid opened doors usually closed to a major. Using his own money, he quickly set up an unofficial aviation office. The Paris branch of the American Radiator Company gave him a room, while a group of American expatriates and French volunteers made up his "staff." [1]

After talking to several French experts, Mitchell soon came to believe that the United States should buy its aviation equipment from France until its own industry began full-scale production. That time would come more quickly, he also learned, if American manufacturers used French designs. Washington made no reply to these suggestions when Mitchell passed them on. Nor did they reply to any of his messages, including his urgent request for $50,000 to run his "office." Actually, Mitchell's letters were only a fraction of the 40,000 messages swamping the War Department each day. In addition, as his superiors later explained, they did not think Mitchell's few days abroad had made him an aviation expert. [2]

Only two weeks after reaching Paris, Mitchell toured the French sector of the battlefield for ten days. The French had just launched the Nivelle Offensive against the ridge of the Chemin des Dames, northeast of Paris. This was another all-out drive to end the three-year deadlock on the western front. Mitchell painfully watched the futile efforts of the French infantry to breach the German defenses. Within a few more weeks, this bloodbath drove some French units to mutiny, impairing the usefulness of the entire army for the rest of the war. Presumably, the sight of this slaughter changed Mitchell's mind about the supremacy of "blood and bone" in mass warfare. [3]

Certainly the aerial side of the fighting was a revelation to Mitchell. The performance of the French pilots, aircraft, and supporting units deeply impressed on him the tremendous tasks facing American aviation. The pressures of combat had forced the French and the other participants to push aviation development at a rate impossible in peacetime and to a level unknown in America. In 1914, the best European airplanes were of a single type, the observation ship, and they operated at speeds of 65 mph for an unreliable range of 200 miles. After three years of warfare, however, the aerial inventories of the European powers now included fighters and bombers. The best fighters approached 120 mph in speed, while the best bombers flew at 85 mph. In prospect were bombers capable of reaching Berlin from bases in England. By contrast, the aircraft used by the U.S. Army's Aviation Section were comparable only to the 1914 European models. Mitchell, with his limited training in the inferior American models, needed more flying training at Le Bourget Airport outside Paris before he could fly the fast Nieuport fighter-observation ship the French gave him. His hosts also gave him his first lessons in a theory of aerial warfare that went far beyond mere reconnaissance.[4]

At the front, the role of aviation had markedly changed from simple observation by single aircraft in the early days of the war to a vastly more complex one involving hundreds of airplanes. Reconnaissance had quickly proved its value, but the rapid evolution of the fighter plane had given both sides the chance to block one another's aerial view of the ground situation. For a force to be able to operate with full freedom on the ground, control of the airspace above the front was mandatory. The French airmen, as well as their British counterparts, had learned that this control or "command of the air" could not be won merely by positioning fighters within a particular segment of the airspace. By their very nature, airplanes could not be stationed like artillery pieces zeroed in on every yard of a valuable piece of terrain. The only solution, the airmen thought, was to seek out the enemy wherever he could be found, both over and beyond the front. After wearing down his strength, they expected in time to win free rein for their reconnaissance and to exploit the possibilities of attacking the enemy, especially his army. To gain this end, the French had concentrated hundreds of fighters and bombers, called *aviation de combat,* under the direction of the two Army Groups at the front. Observation units remained under the local control of the individual regiments and divisions, but the higher level control over the *aviation de combat* enabled it to range over a major sector of the front. The airmen compared their *aviation de combat* with cavalry and dreamed of a role similar to that which Marshal Murat and his famous horsemen had played under Napoleon. Still ahead, moreover, lay the enticing possibility of penetrations by that "aerial cavalry" deep into enemy territory. Occasionally, the French had tried unescorted bomber raids on targets in the Ruhr, but as yet their bombers were no match for German fighters.[5]

As Mitchell soon realized, the French airmen had suffered a

major setback during the Nivelle Offensive. They had begun their part of the operation with the claim that "victory in the air must come before victory on the ground." Despite severe losses and increasing cries from beleaguered ground commanders for air support, the airmen stuck to their theory until the collapse of the offensive forced them to assist the infantry. The Army's High Command finally broke up the *aviation de combat* and gave control of the aircraft to the lower echelon units. Although Mitchell witnessed this aerial defeat, he still preferred the goals of the French airmen.[6]

Mitchell further strengthened this newfound preference when he visited the British sector of the battlefield in May. As much as he liked the French, Mitchell was more at home with what he thought was the British way of doing business. In questions ranging from their grooming of horses to their world view, Mitchell believed the British to be vastly superior. In aviation, the French had produced no one of the stature of Major General Hugh Trenchard, the Commander of the Royal Flying Corps in France and a real power in Britain's highest military and political circles. Trenchard's aviation career began like Mitchell's. Trenchard was thirty-nine and a major in the army before he had taken up flying in 1912, in response to a call for mature professional officers to direct aviation. Shortly after the war began, Trenchard was in France first as a wing commander and then as leader of the RFC. With only limited materiel and personnel, he soon shaped the RFC into an instrument that was a model for the world's airmen. His distinctive achievements had won him the rank of a major general and the full confidence of Field Marshal Douglas Haig, the commander of the British army in France.[7]

The first meeting between Trenchard and Mitchell set the tone for their future relationship. Trenchard, famous for his brusqueness, quickly challenged Mitchell's demands on his time. But Mitchell's reply that Trenchard could well afford to ignore RFC business for a little while because he had organized it so well broke down Trenchard's reserve. The RFC staff answered Mitchell's many questions about the routine phases of their operations, including their organization, training, and maintenance. Yet it was Trenchard himself who talked to Mitchell about the role of the air weapon of the present and of the future. Trenchard's intense belief in the air offensive was his trademark. He insisted that command of the air over the battlefield was possible only through a "relentless and incessant offensive." He thought it best "to exploit the moral effect of the airplane on the enemy, but not to let him exploit it on ourselves . . . this can only be done by attacking and continuing to attack." Ground commanders who wanted the RFC merely to hover over their positions, in order to protect them from aerial observation and attack, had taken strong exception to Trenchard's views. General Haig quickly overruled them, and the air offensive became established RFC policy.[8]

During their initial talk, Trenchard also told Mitchell about the RFC's General Headquarters Brigade, a force much like the *aviation de combat* in its purpose and in its control by the highest level of the army. A small-scale brigade had been operating since 1916, but there were not enough surplus aircraft to achieve Trenchard's goal for the unit: to destroy the German army's "means of supply, subsistence, and replacements." Further, Trenchard predicted that his aircraft would someday bomb Berlin itself, but there was no early prospect at present of getting the necessary crews and airplanes to do so.

As Mitchell well knew, the doctrine of the offensive had almost drained the resources of the RFC. British losses in the air had mounted until they reached their highest point in April; some pilots were even going into combat with only seven hours of flying experience. Materiel was also at a premium. In 1916, the RFC had asked London for ten bomber squadrons, but during Mitchell's visit it still had only two. Even fighter production barely covered losses. The vital difference between the British and French airmen in their struggle to carry on the offensive was Haig's backing of Trenchard.[9]

One reason why Trenchard enjoyed this support was doubtless his own determination to assist Haig in winning the war by achieving a breakthrough on the western front. Trenchard must not be included in the "considerable section of British military opinion" whom Mitchell found interested "in a radical air strategy." Only the radicals argued that a strategic bombardment campaign against Germany would end the war more quickly than a continued stress on ground operations. Among these radicals were some of the younger airmen around Trenchard who were trying to interest him in such a viewpoint. At about this time in London, two of the leaders of British aviation, General David Henderson and Sir Sefton Brancker, sought such a policy. The clearest exponent of it, however, was General Jan Christian Smuts, the soldier-politician whose report to the British government on strategic bombardment on August 17, 1917, was significant in the formation both of the Royal Air Force and of the nucleus of a strategic bombing effort the following spring.[10]

Mitchell's actions, shortly after he had completed his first round of visits to the British and French sectors, left no doubt that the Allied airmen had influenced him greatly. According to Mitchell, he collaborated with the staff of the French Army Group of the Northeast on a crucial letter to the Minister of War. The letter, dated May 6, 1917, described the aeronautical contributions which the United States should make in time for the spring offensive in 1918. The French planners sought the creation of an American force of some 4,300 bombers and fighters for offensive operations, replaceable at the rate of 2,000 planes per month.

The French Premier Alexandre Ribot apparently used substantially these figures in a message that reached Washington about May 23. The "Ribot Cable" won immediate acceptance in the United States as the basis for a 640 million dollar aircraft production program. For some unknown reason, Ribot's request omitted any specific data on the types of aircraft needed. Conceivably Mitchell might have saved the situation. On May 17, he had sent his own message which contained the data missing from the "Ribot Cable." He had also emphasized what the Allied airmen had taught him: that only an enormous bomber and fighter force could win control of the air. Without that control, the Allied armies could not operate successfully.

Unfortunately, Mitchell's report met the fate of his earlier efforts. He still was not an expert in the eyes of his superiors and, even then, his message did not reach Washington until June 4, almost two weeks after the Ribot Cable arrived. The defective Ribot Cable and the failure of Mitchell's message to win attention were poor omens for the success of the American aviation program. The Washington authorities relied upon their old ideas and gave reconnaissance aircraft a higher priority than the French and Mitchell wanted. That decision started the production program in the wrong direction at a time when every moment was too precious to be wasted.[11]

As for Mitchell, his education continued into early June with a visit to the Royal Naval Air Service Unit at Dunkerque. Its commander was Wing Captain C. L. Lambe, whom Mitchell had known since they had played together in the International Polo Matches at Hong Kong in 1910. Lambe and his airmen were primarily engaged in raiding German shipping and attacking the occupied ports on the Belgian Coast. But they also had a more unusual mission— the bombardment of German inland targets. This objective bore the imprint of Winston Churchill's service as First Lord of the Admiralty. In 1915, Churchill had encouraged the naval airmen to attack the sheds housing the airships that were raiding England. A year later, this work temporarily expanded to include strikes on German targets from a base at Luxeuil, in eastern France. The naval airmen were experimenting with bombs and hoped for new aircraft with the range to carry them into Germany. One of their number, Commander Spenser Grey, showed Mitchell their most potent weapon, a 1,650-pound bomb. Others showed him their Handley-Page bombers, then too slow at 65 mph and still too limited in their 200-mile range for anything but night attacks on targets close to the front.[12]

This gulf between the dreams and the actual performance of the naval airmen illustrated much of what Mitchell had learned from his first two months in France. He consistently imagined AEF aviation as a force of airplanes borrowed or copied from the French and utilized in keeping with the most promising of the British ideas. In his more realistic moments, however, Mitchell knew that his country lacked even a respectable reconnaissance capability. How much more Mitchell could do as a new lieutenant colonel (his rank since May 15, 1917) remained to be seen.[13]

II

The arrival in Paris of Major General John J. Pershing and the AEF staff on June 13, 1917, abruptly ended Mitchell's two months of independent study. Pershing faced one of the toughest jobs ever assigned to any American commander. The United States had plunged into history's greatest war, three thousand miles from her own territory. Her Army had no definite war plans and she had not yet mobilized manpower or industry at home. The National Defense

Act of 1916 had been enacted too late to meet the immediate needs of the AEF and especially its aviation requirements. Pershing thought the American people should have been "mortified" by the poor condition of their aviation. Despite his unhappy experience with his aviation support in Mexico, he fully realized its importance and felt certain that an army without aviation "was doomed to failure against one with it." Also, the Mexican experience had convinced him that aviation had to develop on its own in an arm separate from Signal Corps control. Nor did the general leave any doubt about his belief that AEF aviation would serve the ground forces in a decisive campaign to force the Germans out of the trenches and defeat them.[14]

Pershing then made Mitchell the Aviation Officer of the AEF because he was the senior flyer in France. Billy immediately sought the general's approval for "tactical" and "strategical" aviation based on the lessons he had learned from his British and French teachers. The "tactical aviation" would supply each Division, Corps, and Army with its own observation and fighter units with the latter using the offensive tactics which Trenchard had thought so essential. The "strategical" arm resembled the General Headquarters Brigade or even *aviation de combat*. Under Pershing's immediate control, that force could fly "into the enemy's country," attacking German aircraft and materiel "at a distance from the actual lines." Mitchell supported the proposal for strategical aviation with a copy of the letter from the Army Group of the Northeast that had inspired the Ribot Cable. Once again, Mitchell made clear the specific types of aircraft the French wanted: the United States must create thirty pursuit and bomber groups. In addition, Mitchell repeated the French beliefs that "no decision on the ground would be reached before a decision in the air" and that strategic aviation was becoming the "new cavalry" of the war. He even dared to tell Pershing that strategic aviation could have "a greater influence on the ultimate decision of the war than any other arm." [15]

Pershing referred the points Mitchell had raised to a board of officers—including Mitchell—whom he instructed to produce a "complete aviation project for the U.S. Army in France." That panel endorsed Mitchell's proposal for strategic aviation, as well as another far-reaching point. One of the board members, Major Townsend F. Dodd, a veteran pilot and the Aviation Officer before

Mitchell, had also surveyed aeronautics in Great Britain while he was en route to France. After comparing notes in Paris, Dodd and Mitchell jointly argued that the British Air Board, operating at the highest governmental level, coordinated their aviation development better than the United States. The AEF committee agreed and asked Pershing to recommend the establishment of a stronger version of the Air Board in the United States with a cabinet post for the head of the "American Air Service whose assistants were to be the Chiefs of the Army and Navy Air Services and a member of the Munitions Board or corresponding organization."

So far as is known, however, Pershing never acted on this and also ignored the question of strategic aviation for several more months. Mitchell later blamed Pershing for being too cautious about aviation, but then Pershing was cautious about every aspect of the AEF. Understandably, Pershing was feeling his way as he built a gigantic military organization with which neither he nor any other American had had experience. Mitchell did not concede, moreover, that when Pershing created the Air Service of the AEF in June, he had at least taken aviation away from the Signal Corps. In making aviation a service branch, like the Infantry or Cavalry, Pershing had duplicated the existing Royal Flying Corps organization. A year passed, however, before President Wilson finally ordered the complete divorce of the Air Service from the Signal Corps both within and outside the AEF.[16]

The creation of the Air Service of the AEF was in itself ambitious, but efforts to equip it had been unsuccessful. In agreeing to the Ribot Cable, Congress had appropriated the money for an intensified production program, but the Army had a confused picture of what to do next. Any real hope for immediate improvement of that program rested upon the recommendations of a mission that had been sent to study European aviation in mid-June of 1917. Led by Major Raynal C. Bolling, this group included aviators, aeronautical engineers, and craftsmen. Had the Bolling Mission, as it was called, gone to Europe a month earlier, its members probably could have based their recommendations primarily on the basis of the combat experiences of Allied airmen. Now, however, they had to work through Pershing and his staff. Mitchell compounded their problem by urging Pershing's staff to keep the members of the Bolling Mission under firm control. The mission had come to France unannounced.

To Mitchell, and possibly also to Pershing, its coming meant interference by Washington in a purely AEF matter.[17]

Actually, several members of the Bolling Mission reacted much as Mitchell had in their initial contacts with Allied aviators. General David Henderson of the British Air Board had urged Bolling, a U.S. Steel executive in civilian life, to forget about producing a balanced observation, fighter, and bomber force, and to concentrate on bombers. Others of the Bolling Mission—Captain Edgar Gorrell, a veteran pilot, and Captain Virginius E. Clark, one of America's few aeronautical engineers—quickly became bombardment enthusiasts after visiting Italy, where they saw Caproni bombers staging attacks on Austrian targets. The manufacturer of these planes, Gianni Caproni, also happened to be a salesman for the views of his longtime partner, the aviation theorist, Colonel Giulio Douhet. When the Bolling Mission visited Italy, Douhet was still in a military fortress after being court-martialed for criticizing his government's conduct of the war. While in prison, he had meditated on Allied strategy and by June, 1917, had perfected a clear-cut argument for strategic bombardment. He believed that the power of the enemy's defenses ended any hope of a breakthrough by the Allied armies; a better course, in his opinion, would be a crusade to seize command of the air and then to destroy the "vital centers" of the Central Powers. These "vital centers," Douhet believed, were both tangible and intangible: the enemies' sources of supply and the will of their peoples to resist. Although Caproni even went to Paris during the winter of 1917 to try to interest the French government in such ideas, he and Douhet could not get sufficient support.[18]

The Bolling Mission at first recommended the Caproni bomber as the model for American production but, after lengthy talks with the AEF staff, they assigned all bombers a priority below observation and fighter aircraft. In November, three months after submitting this report, Bolling personally appealed to Howard Coffin, the Chairman of the Aircraft Production Board in Washington, to put bombers first. By then, questions of aircraft types were becoming academic. Organizational and technical problems were bogging down any real production. The best hope for aviation equipment was the purchase of European materiel, of which the French, for example, had promised delivery in the spring of 1918.[19]

Although armed only with an idea, Mitchell made what specific plans he could. He corresponded with Caproni, presumably about the production of his bomber. He asked AEF Intelligence in August to collect information on possible strategic targets, and he later received from French sources a list of German industrial targets in the Ruhr.

Mitchell's career position continued to improve with his promotion to full colonel in September. Pershing had marked him for a combat or a training command after their first meeting. In October, he made Mitchell commander of the Air Service in the Zone of the Advance, the final training ground before combat, and in January, the Chief of Air Service, First Army, the top combat position. Mitchell's assignments thereafter largely matched America's share of the fighting and were his rewards for his services on the Pershing team. Although General Henry ("Hap") Arnold, in 1949, recalled Mitchell's desire to "blow up Germany," Mitchell knew how to trim his sails before the winds blowing out of AEF headquarters. He highlighted this position in a policy statement when he took command of the Zone of the Advance. "The Air Service of an army is one of its offensive arms. Alone it cannot bring about a decision. It therefore helps the other arms in their appointed mission. . . ." In the last analysis, this was the credo that earned for Mitchell the credentials he needed to win an audience for his advanced ideas.[20]

III

The AEF, and especially its aviation branch, were not ready for combat on May 29, 1918, when the Ludendorff Offensive almost ruptured the Allied lines, forcing all the American strength on hand into action. The equipment shortages already noted persisted until the Armistice, while the aircraft production failure in the United States mushroomed into a major scandal. French industry, the other best hope for airplanes, fell behind in promised deliveries. General Henri Petain, then the commander of the French Armies of the North and Northeast, had told Pershing in December of 1917 that aviation was the one category, besides infantry replacements, in which "the United States can bring us the greatest help in 1918." To do this, Petain urged Pershing to bring more raw materials and skilled labor for the French aircraft industry from the United States. The decisive factor, however, was shipping. The compelling need for infantry in the spring and summer of 1918 ate up so much shipping space that between May and July, for example, no American aviation personnel arrived at all. French aircraft production suffered accordingly.[21]

The limited equipment that the Air Service finally did receive was mostly French fighter aircraft. This situation hindered any test Mitchell might have wished to give his ideas. He finally won higher priority for bomber production in the United States, but this achievement only added to the existing confusion in the overall program. A new planning organization, the Strategical Aviation Branch of the Air Service, took over Mitchell's earlier task of gathering target information. Edgar Gorrell, one of the Bolling Mission's converts to bombardment and now a colonel, was made the chief of the new office. With the advice of Gianni Caproni and Commander Spenser Grey, who had previously shown Mitchell the 1,650-pound bomb, Gorrell developed a comprehensive plan for a campaign against German targets. The bomber shortage, however, and the continued opposition of Pershing's staff killed the plan.[22]

The airmen's sometimes radical ideas and the lack of essential equipment were only a few of Pershing's problems with aviation. For a year, he had to experiment with the organization of the Air Service. The managerial skills and experience which aviation needed to be rescued from chaos were beyond the capabilities of many of its leaders, including Mitchell himself. As Pershing succinctly put it, they were "good men running around in circles."

But the general made no mention of another irritating problem—the bitter animosity between the Chief of the Air Service Brigadier General Benjamin Foulois and Mitchell. Foulois, a contemporary of Mitchell in total service, had been one of the Army's first pilots and had been the commander of the abortive air effort in Mexico. He vaulted to general's rank and to the post of Chief of the Air Service, AEF, through an appointment made in Washington and probably without Pershing's consent. Mitchell bitterly resented Foulois' elevation, ostensibly as another example of Washington's interference with the running of the AEF. By his own account, Mitchell complained directly to Pershing about Foulois' alleged inefficiency. Pershing became dissatisfied with Foulois in any case, and soon replaced him with a Corps of Engineers officer, Major General Mason Patrick. Foulois moved down the chain of command to take

Mitchell's latest job as Chief of the Air Service, First Army, and Mitchell dropped to Chief of Air Service, First Brigade. Their close contact inevitably caused a scene which, in Foulois' documented version, could have led only to Mitchell's being transferred back to the United States. Pershing, however, stepped in to save Mitchell, because he did not want to lose a man of Mitchell's fighting abilities. Foulois soon backed down and after seeing Mitchell's performance at the front in July, he realistically, but manfully, recommended that Mitchell be appointed in his place. Foulois' action assured Mitchell of the top combat command, but the incident may have had some connection with the intense enmity some AEF veterans later showed Mitchell. The incident also demonstrated the scarcity of trained leaders in the air arm. If more experienced aviation officers had been available, as one member of the AEF staff later noted, Pershing might well have fired both Mitchell and Foulois.[23]

While this squabble moved to a climax, Mitchell's direction of the first combat operations had given Pershing ample evidence of his tactical ability. Using mostly pilots who had previously served with the Allies, he put the first squadron into the fighting in early April, 1918. Shortly thereafter, the first American-trained pilots began to trickle into the Air Service, AEF. Among them was Mitchell's own brother, John L. Mitchell. No pilot, including Foulois, ever denied Billy Mitchell's flair for combat leadership. Some of the best American pilots during and after the war never rated Mitchell their equal in flying skill, but consistently praised his bravery in an airplane and respected his knowledge of its use in warfare.

Most of the AEF airmen were civilians at heart whose regard for themselves as a class of men apart from all others sometimes knew no bounds. Mitchell's nonregulation uniforms and madcap social life may well have been calculated to match their mood. Among men who were over fifteen years his junior, his methods stirred enthusiasm for a job all too often ending in solitary, flaming death. Mitchell's approach was often pragmatic: "Results are what count in war." But this required a self-imposed discipline of a different order from that derived by the automatic obedience which Pershing wanted and needed in ground warfare. Mitchell, in bearing the burden of the deaths of his pilots, needed considerable self-discipline. Most tragically, many of his pilots, including his brother

John, died not in combat, but in flying accidents. Mitchell's only course was to keep going. As he told his mother: "This is war. It has to be kept up until one or another breaks." [24]

With Mitchell directing the aerial combat, and Patrick giving some badly needed management to the Air Service of the AEF, the air arm rounded into shape. Mitchell never had more than 650 American airplanes at the front, but he was able to draw upon Allied aviation units for the AEF's only two major battles, St.-Mihiel and the Meuse-Argonne.

On its aerial side, the battle of St.-Mihiel was most significant as the scene of the greatest concentration of aircraft during the war. Some 1,481 planes, most of them borrowed from the British, French, and Italians, were to support the American ground forces. Mitchell was, in a loose sense, the commander of the force. In coordinating the aerial effort, he had the assistance of a staff that included representatives of the various Allied participants. Significantly, he could count on the support of a French Air Division, some 500 bombers and fighters concentrated in a new version of *aviation de combat*. French doctrine, fortified by a frontline strength of 2,800 aircraft since July, had swung back to an offensive emphasis with the intention of destroying "enemy aviation so as to win complete mastery of the air." Mitchell's handful of Italian aircraft showed how far Caproni and Douhet's ideas were from fruition. In the fall of 1917, Italian aviation had collapsed after meeting German opposition for the first time. This defeat contributed to the Caporetto disaster, but it also vindicated Douhet's criticisms and restored him to duty, if only in a largely honorary assignment.

Mitchell also had the cooperation of the Independent Force, a new command for Trenchard, after his very brief tenure as Chief of Staff of the new Royal Air Force. The German air raids on Great Britain in the spring of 1918 had led to both the formation of the Royal Air Force, and a reprisal activity, the Independent Force. Even though 1,600 British aircraft were at the front as early as July, 1918, the Independent Force did not have the means to carry on the strategic bombing sought by the radical thinkers. Trenchard could make only scattered raids intended primarily to break enemy morale or to assist such infantry operations as the St.-Mihiel battle. [25]

Bad weather and a planned German withdrawal from the St.-

Mihiel salient prevented any meaningful test of this combined aviation. Mitchell grossly exaggerated what had happened at St.-Mihiel when he claimed after the war that before the battle he "contemplated not only facilitating the advance of the ground troops but also spreading fear and consternation into the lines of communications, the enemy's supply system and the cities and towns behind it which supplied our foe with the sinews of war." Actually, he worked in strict subordination to Pershing's needs in the ground battle. Mitchell's force operated within less than a 35-mile radius of action which tied it to "facilitating the advance of the ground troops." His achievement, however, in quickly gaining air superiority over the weaker German force of 243 planes delighted Pershing and motivated Patrick to recommend Mitchell's promotion to brigadier general.[26]

The Meuse-Argonne campaign, which lasted from September 26 until the Armistice, presented a much severer test than did St.-Mihiel. As he took command of the Air Service, Army Group, on October 15, General Mitchell had his hands full supporting the ground forces. He had drawn a hint of the future on October 9 when he sent two hundred French and American bombers against a German troop concentration behind the lines at Damvillers. The aircraft dropped 39 tons of bombs, followed during the same 24-hour period by British units dropping some 40 more tons on other targets. The 79-ton total was impressive when balanced against the AEF total of 138 tons dropped during the entire war.[27]

The Armistice ended all this. Many of the new methods which had fascinated Mitchell had not been tried. For example, he had proposed to Pershing in October, 1918, that the First Division, the most experienced unit in the Army, be given parachute training for a drop behind the German lines. Also in the thinking stage was an Allied bombardment campaign such as Douhet, Caproni, and Smuts had projected. On October 3, 1918, the Allies had agreed to form an Inter-Allied Independent Air Force, headed by Trenchard but under the Supreme Commander, General Ferdinand Foch, "for operations." The Air Service, AEF, would have participated in such activities since the British had agreed to supply improved Handley-Page night bombers and to train American crews. These bombers, with a range of over 650 miles, would have permitted Mitchell to send aviation "deep into Germany." [28]

The war ended, therefore, on an inconclusive note for the more advanced theories of the Allied airmen. Any claim that aviation was more than a servant to the armies or navies of 1918 lacked the proof which might have resulted from the test planned for 1919. Mitchell had no qualms about the future. Having acquired a sense of the pace of aviation's wartime evolution, he thought of its full development as only a question of time and further effort. In his more exuberant moments, he may even have thought of it as the decisive dimension for future military operations.[29]

Other Americans did not share Mitchell's appreciation of the role the airplane might play in war. The airplane's potential as a bomber raised a moral question for them little noticed in the context of total war waged in Europe. The Wilson Administration, through its Secretary of War Newton D. Baker, refused to avoid the issue. Only a few days before the Armistice, Baker told General Peyton March, the Army's Chief of Staff, to warn the Air Service that the United States would not participate in any bombardment plan that "has as its objective, promiscuous bombing upon industry, commerce or population, in enemy countries disassociated from obvious military needs to be served by such action . . ." What effect this order would have had on the Inter-Allied Independent Air Force plans for 1919 is debatable. The attitude of the Administration and, it might be assumed, the American people, had an undoubted impact on Mitchell's hopes of gaining acceptance in the United States for his more advanced ideas.[30]

IV

Mitchell's success in the war brought him the rank and prestige which had been his goals since he joined the Army. Indeed, he thought that if the war had lasted long enough, he might even have become the chief of all Allied aviation. His evidence for this seemed primarily to have been his rationale that with Foch in command of the Allied armies, an Englishman would head the Allied navies, and an American could expect the aviation post. He had better grounds for thinking that his wartime success had entitled him to the postwar leadership of the Army's air arm. But that did not happen, either, although his orders returning him to the United States in December, 1918, initially appointed him Director of

Military Aeronautics. That spot had been the top military position in wartime Army aviation, but it was about to disappear in a post-war reorganization.[31]

En route home to the United States, Mitchell stopped in London, where he conferred with Trenchard and studied British air organization. On February 15, 1919, Trenchard once again became Chief of Staff of the RAF. All of Britain's military aviation, including even the aircraft of the Royal Navy, now were under his control. His RAF in turn was a part of the Air Ministry, the governmental agency also charged with supervising civil aviation. A similar organizational approach seemed to Mitchell to be the answer to American postwar needs. He could have profitably realized, however, that the British organization had only come about under the pressures of war and that there was no certainty in early 1919 of its surviving in the postwar era.[32]

Yet Mitchell was undaunted. An unidentified American naval officer accompanying him home from England noted that Mitchell "was fully prepared with evidence, plans, data, propaganda posters and articles, to break things open for air power as the sole requisite of the national defense in the future." This was an overstatement to the extent that Mitchell intended to avoid "political maneuvering" for the time being, at least until he had had a chance to get settled in Washington. There could be no doubt, however, as to Mitchell's long-range intentions. An intensive discussion about the future place of aeronautics in the American military establishment was already under way in Washington among the airmen as well as among interested legislators. For example, the establishment of the RAF had already prompted Senator Harry S. New of Indiana to propose in 1918 a separate Department of Aeronautics. Mitchell, inspired by his aeronautical education abroad and equipped with the rank and prestige he had earned in the war, was now in a position to take over the leadership of the work New and others had begun.[33]

Brigadier General William ("Billy") Mitchell.

General John J. Pershing and his staff with General Petain in France during World War I. Billy Mitchell is to be seen just above Petain.

This rare photo shows General Mitchell talking with the Prince of Wales.

Mitchell is shown here on his prizewinning horse "Home Again."

The supposedly "unsinkable" German battleship Ostfriesland. *Picture was taken the day before Mitchell's bombers attacked her.*

The next day, July 21, 1921. Ostfriesland *takes a bomb from Mitchell's Martin bombers.*

A few minutes later, Ostfriesland *starts her final plunge to the bottom.*

Mitchell mission to Europe, February 1922, Rome, Italy.

CHAPTER THREE

"Everything on a Broad Basis and High Plane"

In March, 1919, Mitchell returned to the United States fully determined to bring about a revolution in American military policy by persuasion alone. He apparently assumed that his fellow officers in the Army and Navy and the civilian officials in the government could be as easily convinced as he had been by his vision of aeronautics.

Actually, Mitchell was one of those rare officers who emerged from the war with an insight into its lessons for the next conflict. The total nature of the war had diverted immense national resources into the creation of remarkable scientific advances. Although none of these strides in chemicals, tanks, submarines, and aircraft had been decisive in the war itself, they presented ominous implications for the future. Mitchell could be numbered with Generals J. F. C. Fuller and Giulio Douhet, Colonel Charles de Gaulle, and Captain Basil Liddell Hart in sensing the impact of one or more

39

of those weapons. For Mitchell, these technical breakthroughs destroyed assumptions that had guided American policy makers since the founding of the country. The third, or aerial, dimension to warfare, in Mitchell's opinion, had wiped out the first and foremost of those assumptions: that America could rely primarily upon geographical isolation as a means of defense. An overhaul of the national defense structure was mandatory. In Mitchell's view, room had to be made for aeronautics as an equal partner of the Army and Navy, if the United States were to protect its interests in a world that was rapidly shrinking with every technical advance.

In the tradition of his profession, Mitchell did not recommend any political action to deal with his country's new position in a smaller world, such as American membership in the League of Nations. Indeed, the fate of the chief American advocate of the League, President Wilson, should have been instructive to Mitchell. Both men had the same fatal flaw. Each could stir his countrymen, but, in the end, neither could compromise with them.[1]

For almost two years, then, Mitchell tried to sell his views within the government. To succeed, or even to have a reasonable chance of winning congressional approval on any legislation, he would have to win the backing of the War and Navy Departments. Without the support of the existing services, he could only expect a hearing before the Military and Naval Affairs Committees of the Congress. Their recommendations would be decisive in bringing the legislation to a vote by Congress. If the War and Navy Departments opposed him, then the final hurdle of an almost inevitable presidential veto remained. In contending with these gigantic obstacles, Mitchell might well have accomplished nothing in these years had he not at the same time been the driving force behind an Air Service effort to give America a basis for future aeronautical achievements.

I

When Mitchell reported for duty in Washington as the Director of Military Aeronautics, he found that a new reorganization of Army aviation had eliminated his post. Instead, Major General Charles C. Menoher, a non-flyer and a successful wartime infantry commander, now headed the Air Service organization. Mason Patrick, the more likely and certainly the better qualified man for this command, had remained in France to help Pershing close out AEF affairs and also to serve as one of the military advisers to the peace-makers.

General Menoher gave Mitchell the tactical supervision of the Air Service as the Third Assistant Executive and Chief, Training and Operations Group. Since Menoher openly conceded Mitchell's greater knowledge of flying, Mitchell had a chance to dominate the Air Service. His position was all the stronger because he had carefully selected a team of veterans to assist him in the Training and Operations Group. Among them were Colonels Thomas De Witt Milling and Charles de F. Chandler, and Lieutenant Colonels William C. Sherman, Lewis H. Brereton, and Harold E. Hartney. These officers not only zealously carried out the details of the constructive projects he supervised in 1919–20, but men like Milling, Brereton, Hartney, and perhaps Sherman, also did much to stimulate Mitchell's thinking. A fatal airplane crash in 1919 denied Mitchell the continued advice of the very able Colonel Townsend F. Dodd, who was not in the Training and Operations Group, but elsewhere in the Air Service headquarters.

The views of these men were not always the same as Mitchell's. Milling, for example, thought that a separate service for aeronautics was premature. Just the same, Mitchell was recognizing the influence of all these men when he said in December, 1919: "We have always known exactly what we wanted and have gone right ahead with it." The activities of Mitchell and his followers, especially those favoring a separate service, drew strong criticism within the Air Service from such men as Menoher's Executive Officer, Colonel Oscar Westover. But for most of 1919, this infighting gave way before a common effort to save the Air Service from extinction.[2]

America's return to what its next President, Warren G. Harding, described as "normalcy," almost wrecked the nation's armed forces. Because of the rapid demobilization, the number of Air Service officers dropped from 20,000 to a nucleus of little more than 200 regular officers in 1919. Even the regulars were only "on detail" or loan to aviation from other branches of the Army. Airplanes in the United States were almost entirely of a training variety. Combat equipment was obsolescent. And there were more serious and fundamental problems. Military aviation had no traditional role in national defense. The new domestic aircraft industry had lost its only contracts, those for military equipment, and had little early prospect for a commercial market. The minimum safety devices needed for such development were not available. The instruments and the techniques for weather and night flying were only in the experimental stage. Aviation was still very much a novelty, as Air Service pilots themselves demonstrated when they spoke excitedly about pioneering nonstop flights between New York and Chicago and the "first flight over the Sierra Nevada." [3]

Despite aviation's poor position in the United States, informed congressmen knew what had been accomplished overseas and recognized that there must be room in the national defense structure for the air weapon. The questions were: "Where?" "How much?" and "Under whose control?" Congress delayed action pending the results of its own and other studies both of aviation and the larger problem of the proper defense structure for the future. Meanwhile, temporary legislation halted the disintegration which both Menoher and Mitchell feared by keeping the Air Service alive at mimimum strength levels into 1920. Mitchell used this lull to make his views known throughout the government. [4]

II

The major theme of Mitchell's aviation program was that aerial warfare now ranked with naval and ground warfare in importance. Future military operations could not proceed on land or sea without command of the air by an "air force." While only ground operations in the war offered some evidence for this, Mitchell claimed the inference for sea operations was equally sound. "No difference pertains in the tactics of air units whether they be over water or over the land; the only difference is in the airdromes from which the planes rise." As early as April, 1919, Mitchell discussed with the Navy's General Board the possibility of testing the effectiveness of air attack against warships. For the Air Service's part, Mitchell promised the assembled admirals: "We will get a missile to attack a big ship, whether it takes a ton or two tons." [5]

In extending the idea of command of the air to naval warfare, Mitchell laid claim to another role for the Air Service. The task of the American armed services most consistent with traditional isolationism was defense against external attack. Since America's immediate neighbors were friendly or at least weak, any external attack most likely would be seaborne and could now include airplanes launched by the catapults of capital ships or from aircraft carriers. The latter had made their appearance in 1916 when the British converted a cruiser into the first carrier, *Furious*. To defend the United States against carrier attack, Mitchell wanted to place seventeen of the twenty-nine bases he sought for the Air Service on the coastlines of the country. His proposal challenged the usual shoreline division between Army and Navy responsibilities, but he insisted that land-based aircraft moved this dividing point out to sea, to the perimeter of the airplane's range.[6]

Mitchell's concern with aviation's defensive role also depended in part upon the chance of direct attack through the air by some distant enemy. Although no airplane could do this as yet, dirigibles could. These ships could already carry 25 to 30 tons for 211 hours at 45 mph. Mitchell knew that the Germans had built such a dirigible, the L-72, for use against the United States. In April, 1919, the British were readying another dirigible for a transatlantic round trip. The German Zeppelins had failed in their raids on England during the war principally because their hydrogen-filled containers made easy targets for incendiary bullets. Noninflammable helium could solve that problem, but substantial difficulties remained. American balloon experts optimistically forecast an early solution to the most pressing questions: how to increase the dirigible's pay load and to improve its handling in bad weather and on the ground.[7]

In the view of Mitchell and his followers, the dirigible, like the aircraft carrier, emphasized offensive action as the best defense. In an age of total war, "the entire nation is or may be considered a combatant force." It was criminal, in their opinion, for a "nation not to prepare for the destruction of enemy combatants and property of all classes . . . throughout the enemy's entire territory as well as in the fighting zone." This job belonged to an "air force unaffected by the swaying of the battle line," and capable of sustaining an independent campaign for "the destruction of those industries and equipment that form part of or are auxiliary to the enemy's military establishment." Such an air force, moreover, should operate independently of the Army and Navy and should be subject to the control only of the highest command.[8]

As the foregoing suggests, Mitchell's thinking in the spring of

1919 was already identified with the idea of strategic bombardment. But for many years to come, such ideas would remain the subject of unofficial discussion within the Air Service. He understood that aviation had not progressed sufficiently to make strategic bombardment meaningful enough for America either to use it or to fear its employment against herself. Mitchell and his associates were not certain when there would be a fundamental change in this regard. Perhaps "ten years" would elapse before the change would be realized. An American strategic force certainly would be necessary when technology permitted "one ton to be carried from the nearest point of a possible enemy's territory to our commercial and industrial centers, and to return to the starting point." Mitchell's caution in discussing this question publicly undoubtedly showed a characteristic regard for public opinion. Also, he may have been aware of Newton Baker's previously quoted condemnation of all-out bombing of civilian targets. In public discussions, therefore, he used veiled terms to describe enemy targets as "elements which are further back than his troops are." [9]

The state of public opinion and the inadequacies of the airplane did not stop Mitchell from trying to equip the Air Service with an offensive capability. He asked that the air leadership look ahead to the building of bombers which could cross the American continent, or even the Atlantic Ocean, and return. For the interim period, he proposed that the Air Service be equipped with aircraft carriers and dirigibles. He believed two carriers should accompany the Army units on "offensive expeditions." Both ships should have 900-foot decks, complete maintenance facilities, defenses against air and submarine attacks, and "a very high speed." Although the Navy's General Board had told Mitchell that it was trying to get a carrier for their service, Mitchell urged the adoption of his own idea. Mitchell's intrusion into the Navy's normal sphere of action jolted Menoher, and he returned the proposal to Mitchell for more study.[10]

Mitchell wanted dirigibles "for the direct attack of naval vessels at sea and formations of various sorts on land, and in time of peace, for the transport of troops and material." This dirigible proposal also cut across jurisdictional lines. Although the Army had experimented with dirigibles since 1906, the Navy had an early interest as well. In 1918, the Joint Airship Board of the Army and Navy, formed to prevent any duplication of effort by the services,

had given the Navy primary responsibility for dirigible development.[11]

Despite such roadblocks, the very scope of Mitchell's proposals
made clear not only his ambitious view of aviation in national
defense, but also how he sought to equip the Air Service with an
offensive capability ranging beyond merely defensive needs. Above
all, his proposals showed his awareness that technology had shattered
the old framework of American military policy.

A new framework, Mitchell asserted, must include a Department
of Aeronautics supervising military, civil, and commercial aviation.
The British Air Ministry was clearly his model. A cabinet officer
would run the new agency with the assistance of aviation experts.
In the military sphere, the department would hold equal rank with
the Army and Navy. Those services would draw whatever aviation
and trained personnel they required from the Department of Aeronautics. Remaining under its direct control would be that aviation
intended for independent air operations. In its civil role, the new
department would both foster and regulate commercial aviation.
Also, other government agencies such as the Post Office would
get their flying equipment and personnel from the Department of
Aeronautics. Underlying the civil and commercial functions was
Mitchell's conviction that military aviation could not develop without the industrial and personnel base that the peaceful uses of
aviation ensured. He thought private initiative was too slow and
advocated a system of subsidy, comparable to the government's aid
to the railroads after the Civil War. Mitchell contended that such
assistance had helped only internal development, but aid to aviation
had international implications. If the United States failed to create
its own aircraft industry, then foreign sources might well control it
just as they presently dominated the merchant marine America
used.[12]

Upon their return from France, then, Mitchell and his followers
had firm ideas about the aerial doctrine, types of weapons, and the
organization they wanted. Taken together, these ideas made up
the goals they sought in the years to come.

III

In reviewing what he had been able to do during 1919, Mitchell

could say with considerable justice that: "We have handled every-
thing on a broad basis and high plane." His public role in 1919
generally was restrained and was in striking contrast to that of
Foulois, then serving in his peacetime rank of major. Foulois
momentarily held the center of the stage as the most vocal spokesman for a separate service. Mitchell made no attempt to present
aviation as a panacea. What he sought was above the normal requirements of the Army and Navy, neither of which he believed could
operate without mastery of the air. He argued that the United States
needed more than ever a substantial peacetime military force. In
the past, the American people had "considered themselves so isolated that they did not consider the need of a military organization."
Optimistically believing "most people realize that this time has
passed," he supported a universal military training program to pro-
vide the Army with a reserve of 7,000,000 in ten years. "That," he
asserted, "is what we need in case of war or more than that." [13]

Mitchell erred, however, in believing that his program would win
early acceptance, even though it was "drastic" and required "a great
deal of discussion" first. An array of military experts ranging from
Pershing down through almost the entire membership of the general
officers' and admirals' lists lined up against him. The aura of success
gained in their leadership in the war gave them a powerful voice in
Congress, especially before its Military and Naval Affairs Committees. [14]

The Army's leadership had taken pains to build an impressive
case against Mitchell's ideas. In April, Pershing had appointed
several committees of AEF officers to study the lessons of the war
for the Army of the future. His top panel, headed by Major General
Joseph T. Dickman, considered "the lessons to be learned . . .
insofar as they affect tactics and organization." The Dickman
Board's judgment of Army aviation raised the basic objection constantly repeated against Mitchell's ideas in the years to come. Independence for aviation, the board ruled, was justifiable only if the
air weapon had a capability for decisive action in war like that of
the Army or Navy. The war offered no proof for this, although the
struggle had made obvious the great value of aviation as a servant
of the Army in reconnaissance and ground support duties. [15]

The Navy lacked the Army's relatively intensive aviation experience in the war, but it echoed the Dickman Board. The Assistant

Secretary of the Navy, Franklin D. Roosevelt, became the first government official to attack Mitchell's ideas publicly. Aviation was also an indispensable servant of the Navy, he declared in an article on naval aviation, while dismissing Mitchell's views as "pernicious." Although Roosevelt did not say so, the future of naval aviation was doubtful. One month after his article appeared, Admiral William Benson, the Chief of Naval Operations, disbanded the Division of Naval Aeronautics and distributed its functions among various bureaus of the Navy. Thus, naval aviation had no definite status within its own service.[16]

The leaders of the Army and Navy raised other objections to Mitchell's position, but all were subordinate to the crucial one: "Can aviation independently effect a decision in war?" Thorny organizational matters also arose, such as the problem of coordinating the activities of a new service with the older ones and of allotting the Army and Navy the kind of aviation and distinctively trained personnel they desired. There were other problems resulting either from the reluctance of the older services to make room for a new and very different service or from distrust of the personal ambitions of the airmen. Finally, there was a very real reluctance on the part of men such as Newton Baker to lump all aviation together, and a denial that its civil and military functions were as much alike as Mitchell implied.[17]

Mitchell, of course, had answers to every question. The creation of a new service, he thought, must lead to a "Ministry of Defense" to coordinate the activities of the three services and to assign to each its proper role in war. He insisted that only a Department of Aeronautics could efficiently develop the aviation and train the personnel to be used by the Army, Navy, and other parts of the government. Mitchell refrained at this time from publicly attacking the motivations of his opponents. His approach on a "high plane" continued in his assurances to Congress that his military colleagues were honorable men. There was "a greater sense of responsibility to the State and a greater honesty as a whole among our corps of officers than you will find in any corresponding number of people anywhere." Mitchell's basic answer to his critics was an appeal to look to the future. Only an independent organization manned by airmen could develop the full potential of aeronautics. When one congressional committee asked him about Trenchard's Independent Force, the closest example so far of the kind of independent operation aviation might pursue in the future, Mitchell would make no claim for the force. It was "just beginning. So I say, you cannot look back." Just how far in the future Mitchell meant was not always clear. Some men like Franklin D. Roosevelt could agree about the potential of aviation, but the note of immediacy Mitchell conveyed to his audience disturbed them.[18]

Mitchell's emphasis on the future won some support in the Executive Branch of the government. The Assistant Secretary of War, Benedict Crowell, led an official delegation of Army, Navy, and aircraft industry representatives to Europe in May, 1919, for a three-month study of English, French, and Italian aeronautics. They met many of the same leaders, such as Trenchard, who had infected Mitchell with their enthusiasm. When word reached Baker that many in the group might be succumbing to similar influences, he cabled a warning from Washington that they were only a fact-finding group. They were not to submit any conclusions in their study. The Crowell Mission, however, returned from Europe with a report that essentially supported Mitchell's plea for a Department of Aeronautics —with only the Navy representative dissenting. Baker refused to endorse their unwanted conclusions. He insisted that the Army and Navy had to have complete control over their own aviation. The Joint Board already had sufficient authority to iron out any disagreements or duplications of effort. Baker believed that another government agency should handle commercial air matters. This turndown, one of the Mitchell coterie, Harold Hartney, argued in 1940, gave "American aviation a blow from which it has hardly yet begun to recover." [19]

Perhaps Mitchell's conviction that his program would soon be accepted stemmed from the backing some congressmen gave the idea of a Department of Aeronautics, even though he lacked support from his military superiors and colleagues. During 1919, they introduced eight different measures to establish a Department of Aeronautics. Mitchell pinned his hopes on the legislation introduced by Senator Harry S. New of Indiana, whose proposal was one of two with the most congressional support. The War Department fought the New bill after another board, chaired by Menoher, found the vast majority of top Army officers in opposition. Mitchell unsuccessfully appealed to Pershing, who had returned triumphantly from France in the fall. Pershing's public opposition was for the reasons Mitchell's other opponents had already cited but, behind the scenes, other factors may have been at work. Mason Patrick, once more in the Corps of the Engineers and in his peacetime rank of colonel, made in a letter to Pershing the strongest attack against Mitchell and his followers.[20]

Patrick assailed what he thought were the self-serving motives of both those officers pursuing a separate service and the aircraft industry representatives on the Crowell Mission. The vehemence of his views suggested that both groups had blundered in ignoring him. His friendship with Pershing and his managerial record as the Chief of the Air Service, AEF, were important assets. Also, his later role as a champion of military aviation indicated that he could have been most helpful in 1919. As it was, Patrick had become weary of the Air Service and its feuds. He resented what he thought was the Crowell Mission's indifference to him when it was in Europe. The last straw may have been Benedict Crowell's failure to discuss his group's conclusions with Patrick when both men were voyaging together to the United States from Europe.[21]

Pershing, instead, supported the Army-sponsored Reorganization Act which kept aviation under its control. Mitchell conceded at least a temporary defeat as he tried negotiating behind the scenes to remove the defects he saw in the bill. The legislation that passed in early 1920 as the National Defense Act certainly represented the considered judgment not only of Congress but also that of most of the nation's military experts. Taking the long view, aviation had progressed. The tiny aviation section of the Signal Corps of the prewar era became the Army Air Service, a combat arm with 1,516 officers and 16,000 enlisted men in an overall Army of 280,000.[22]

During the organizational debate, Mitchell kept trying to add to his claims the touch of realism promised by the aircraft carrier and the dirigible. His first carrier proposal never left the War Department. An attempt by his staff in February, 1920, to define the aircraft carrier as an airplane transport, not a working unit in a battle fleet, also flopped. Baker did try to convince Josephus Daniels, the Secretary of the Navy, that the Army and Navy should go their separate ways in dirigible development. The Joint Board, however, reaffirmed the Navy's primacy in dirigibles. Interim efforts to buy a dirigible in England or to get the German L-72 as part of the Versailles agreement also were unsuccessful. Mitchell, then, could only wait while the Navy struggled with the dirigible's many technical defects, highlighted by a series of disastrous accidents. The first was the tragic loss of the ZR-2 during its acceptance trials in England in August, 1921. Other tragedies followed throughout the next decade.[23]

Since his return to the United States, Mitchell had moved on a broad theoretical front that covered the offensive and defensive capabilities of aviation. Until science produced airplanes which matched the dirigible and carrier in promise, suitable offensive power was impossible. The only courses left open to Mitchell were to push aviation development and to exploit the defensive capabilities of the aircraft in the Air Service inventory.

Mitchell was determined to fight on in any case. At work was not only his vision of the future of aviation, but also driving him on was the best prospect he had of matching the achievements of his grandfather and father. "If I can get this on a firm basis within the next ten years," he wrote his mother, "I shall consider my work pretty well done to the country." But this campaign was costly. Duty in Washington was again taking its toll of him. Mitchell's salary plus his flying pay made him one of the highest-paid officers in the American military. The postwar inflation, however, had hurt every serviceman; after all, the basic military pay scale had been set in 1908. Mitchell found it a financial strain even to buy his first home. Washington was to be his permanent residence, he decided, whether or not he stayed in the Army or succumbed to the lure of business or of politics. He was beginning to believe that the only way to live within his means was "to get out of Washington or leave the service and make more money." Were he to remain in the Army, but seek duty elsewhere, he would "break faith" with his followers, as he was "practically the only one that can bring about a betterment of our national defense at this time."

Thus Mitchell chose to keep up his campaign, at least until he was eligible for retirement in 1928. By that time, he might be able to put "our air service on a firm foundation." Eventually, his mother provided financial help and Congress voted a small pay increase to the military to help them meet the inflation. Just the same, the most important personal reason for his decision to stay in the Air Service and in Washington remained his resolve to build an "air force" that would be his monument.[24]

IV

While Mitchell expounded his theories and worked for a separate service, he sponsored many constructive projects to put American aviation on an enduring basis. Many of these projects were spectacular inasmuch as aviation was a novelty in 1919–20, and Mitchell used his gift for making them good newspaper copy. Nevertheless, each of these efforts highlighted a host of technical problems whose ultimate solutions were landmarks in the growth of American aviation; they included problems of engine and airframe performance, navigation, and human endurance. Also, this work took on added importance because so little was being done in the private sector. The Navy, the Post Office, and the National Advisory Committee for Aeronautics, after the Air Service, had the only meaningful aeronautical activities. Mitchell's role stemmed from his position as Chief of the Training and Operations Group of the Air Service. As its tactical leader and its most authoritative spokesman, Mitchell was the driving force behind the Air Service's contributions to aviation development in the early years of the postwar period.

The Air Service-sponsored Transcontinental Reliability Test of October, 1919, was the first air race of its kind in the United States. The participants used airplanes designed for combat in Europe. With less than two and one-half hours' gasoline supply, the airmen had to make as many as forty refueling stops as they crossed the United States in either direction in a little less than forty hours' flying time. The deaths of nine pilots, including two en route to the starting point, prompted speculation as to the value of such events. Mitchell, however, had no doubts. He did not say this, but the race helped to focus congressional attention on aviation at the very moment the organizational battle within the government was coming to a climax. He publicly claimed that the race was proof that American isolation had been shattered forever. Here was the note of immediacy of which Franklin D. Roosevelt complained, for Mitchell pointed out that the distance covered equalled that between New York and Constantinople, or Denver and Berlin. He agreed that there had to be extensive experimentation before regular flights over such a distance could occur. He was no less ready to specify what was needed: among other things, the development of more powerful and dependable engines, the ability to "revital [sic] airplanes in the air," and methods of slowing up landings, such as using external gas tanks which could be dropped before landing. These were goals for the aeronautical engineer to satisfy. Within a year, the Post Office's civilian flyers were following the route blazed by the airmen in the first transcontinental airmail service.[25]

The most substantial project pioneered by Mitchell and the Air Service in these years was the erection of the first airways system in the United States. A mighty obstacle to any consistent flying by day or night and in marginal weather was the absence of well-defined air routes. Just as the motorist needed a road system complete with traffic directions, gasoline and repair stations to travel across the United States, so also aviation needed a series of aerial roads complete with navigational and airdrome facilities along every route. Mitchell established the Civil Affairs Division in the Training and Operations Group to stimulate interest in the airways project on the part of the nation's communities. He supervised the drawing up of a master airways plan for the United States in 1919 which forecast with remarkable accuracy the system of the future. By the end of 1920, the Civil Affairs unit was at work laying the first airway between Washington, D.C., and Dayton, Ohio. There was a solid military purpose behind this activity. While commercial aviation might profitably use these routes in peacetime, military forces could also be speedily shifted along them in case of war. In addition Mitchell proposed airways to Panama, Alaska, and Asia. The defense of the Panama Canal and the advantage of Alaska's strategic position in relation to Asia dominated these extensions of the airways plan.[26]

Alaska's position near the roof of the world, Mitchell saw, had previously kept it far away from the traditional East-West trade routes over which older forms of transportation had traveled. The coming of aircraft made travel possible along the shortest paths between any two points on earth, the great-circle routes. Since Alaska lay astride the great-circle route between the United States and Asia, this generally neglected possession of the United States took on new strategical importance. In July, 1920, the Air Service made the first flight between New York and Nome. Behind the scenes, Mitchell had tried to make it a New York-to-Asia flight by including in the itinerary a landing on the Russian side of the Bering Strait. The State Department ruled out the venture since it believed the flight might further disturb the still unsettled relations between revolutionary Russia and the United States. In any case, the flight drove home the closeness of New York and Nome and so was important in itself. The 9,000-mile trip was a stringent exercise for airmen whose tactical experience had largely been confined to wartime Europe. Achieved without a casualty and over mostly uncharted territory, the flight laid the basis for an airway between the United States and Alaska.[27]

Mitchell was also interested in building an air route to Europe. There was the island-hopping route from the United States by way of Canada, Labrador, Greenland, Iceland, the Faroes, and England to the European Continent, a path which would cross no more than three hundred miles of water at a time. This possible access to and from Europe by air gave the route, in Mitchell's mind, a strategic importance that ranked with that of the Alaskan route to Asia.[28]

Technical progress, however, was a prerequisite to the realization of the possibilities for aviation suggested by these routes as well as by the daring flights of the airmen with inadequate equipment. Mitchell was not, in any strict sense, a scientist or aeronautical engineer, but he was the embodiment of the tactical user of the engineer's product. A more intimate acquaintanceship on his part with the problems the engineers faced might well have diluted the note of immediacy with which he spoke about aviation. Certainly, such knowledge would have tempered his enthusiasm about purchasing aircraft on a larger scale before technical development had slowed down. His prominence in the adoption of the Thomas Morse fighter aircraft, which the Army bought in large numbers and quickly abandoned after they proved unreliable, damaged his reputation. However, Mitchell was a pacesetter, never satisfied with what the engineers had done and always demanding higher standards of excellence. As one aviation pioneer who knew him has said: "No one could be content in his presence."

Mitchell's most solid contact with technical progress from 1919–25 came through his active association with private American aeronautical engineers such as Glenn Martin, Donald Douglas, Alfred Verville, and Alexander de Seversky, and with engineers in the Air Service Engineering Division at Dayton, Ohio. Mitchell never let Colonel Thurman Bane, the Director of the Division, forget that his unit existed only to serve the flyers. The best service could only come, Mitchell impressed on Bane, when the researchers were willing to take risks. A case in point was the production of a giant four-engine bomber. By early 1920, only one had been built in the United States, the LWF. Mitchell found the engineers reluctant to approve its purchase because the plane seemed an accumulation of old ideas. "The fact is," Mitchell pointed out, "that this is the only example of a giant plane that exists in the country." The government should buy it "not to find what it won't do but what it will do." [29]

In outlining requirements for the engineers, Mitchell showed his familiarity with every detail of each aircraft type already in the Air Service inventory or about to be purchased. He frequently followed up his requests with personal inspection trips to the Engineering Division. Normally, either Mitchell or a member of his staff flew the equipment and passed judgment on it. The numerous accessories in the airplanes received similar attention.[30]

His frequent contacts with technical development offered one explanation as to why his predictions on aviation's future had a technical soundness which took him out of the class of a mere commentator on aeronautics. Another reason was his information from such sources as the reports of American airmen serving as assistant military attachés at the major embassies abroad. These men sent Mitchell copies of their regular reports to the Military Intelligence Division of the General Staff, as well as personal letters. Information came, too, from the principal foreign attachés in Washington. Captain Paul de Lavergne of France, Lieutenant Colonel A Guidoni of Italy, and Commodore L. E. O. Charlton of Great Britain were Mitchell's contacts in the international community of Allied airmen that had been formed at St.-Mihiel. The three were personal friends besides being professional associates of Mitchell, and they eagerly solicited his ideas and forwarded information to him in return. Occasional visitors from abroad, among them Caproni, added to Mitchell's knowledge of foreign technical and theoretical advances.[31]

Mitchell, then, was very much in touch with the technical side of American and world aviation. His appreciation of its accomplishments, his part as one of its pacesetters, and his leadership of the Air Service's contributions to aviation's progress in these years are important aspects of the man and his ideas.

V

By early 1920, the magnitude of the problems facing Mitchell was apparent. He had lost his campaign within the government to convince his military colleagues and his civilian superiors of the soundness of his views. The aviation industry was almost at a standstill in postwar America. Other problems were on the way, especially an almost violent reaction among the American people against war and a refusal to appreciate their greater place in world affairs as a result of World War I. To educate public opinion both to appreciate the problems of military policy presented by aviation and to sell their solutions to those problems, Mitchell and his followers plainly needed new tactics.

CHAPTER FOUR

The First Campaign:
"Make Them Either 'Fish or Cut Bait'"

IN EARLY 1920, Billy Mitchell changed his tactics when he began hammering at the idea that aviation could make a distinctive contribution to the defense of the United States. His new approach was notably shrewd. The equipment of the Air Service was primarily defensive in nature, especially since his proposals for dirigibles and aircraft carriers were dead. His defensive emphasis was also in step with the national mood, because isolationism, pacifism, and a public demand for reduced government spending were on the upswing. The National Defense Act of 1920 became, in the perspective provided by the advancing years, the nation's last expression of interest in creating a military policy for some time to come.

This climate especially hurt the U.S. Navy, whose leaders had dreamed for decades of sailing the world's largest fleet. A public reaction from navalism and the battleship in particular as a too expensive symbol of imperialism was mainly responsible for ending that dream. Mitchell's charges that the much more effective and economical airplane had dethroned the battleship as the queen of national power only compounded the Navy's problems. He voiced these claims at first within government circles, but by the end of 1920, he had made them a refrain in the national press. This publicity campaign, climaxed by the bombing tests of June-July, 1921, sparked one of the most bitter controversies in the entire history of American military affairs. While the participants never agreed on the meaning of the results, these tests undoubtedly helped to hasten the refashioning of the American Navy.[1]

I

Despite the publicity advantages Mitchell gained by proclaiming the superiority of the airplane over the battleship, he was raising a substantial question about the impact of aviation upon the navies of the world. The United States Navy's aviators themselves had raised this question ever since they had begun flying in 1909. Their achievements in experimentation and practical demonstrations, such as the first transatlantic flight in May, 1919, compared favorably with those of their Army Air Service counterparts. Far less favorable, however, was the attitude of many of the superiors of the naval airmen. In June, 1919, the General Board, the Navy Department's advisory group, had described aviation "as an adjunct . . . of such vital importance . . . that no inferiority must be accepted." Yet two months later, Admiral William Benson, the Chief of Naval Operations, closed the Division of Naval Aeronautics. His decision denied the naval aviators any effective voice at the policy-making level. Promotion boards mirrored Benson's action by continuing to select only officers who had served regular periods of sea duty. Noted flyers such as Commander John Towers, the leader of the transatlantic flight, suffered because they remained in aviation assignments.[2]

As trying as this conservatism must have been to the naval aviators, most of them would not accept Mitchell's solution of a united aviation service. The RAF control of the Royal Navy's aviation had given Mitchell a selling point, but had also caused frictions of which the American naval airmen were fully aware. Moreover, the ranking naval aviators were especially loyal to their service and were convinced that sea and air war must be integrated. Whatever sentiment there may have been for a separate service was seemingly confined to those younger aviators who were not career officers.[3]

The best known of Mitchell's naval supporters were the three admirals, William Fullam, William E. Sims, and Bradley Fiske. They all agreed with Mitchell that aviation had revolutionized naval warfare, but argued for what Fullam, the wartime commander of the Pacific fleet, called a "three-plane Navy." This view gave proportionate roles to surface craft, planes, and submarines. Sims, the wartime commander of the Navy in European waters, predicted that the aircraft carrier would become the mainstay of the fleet of the future, but nevertheless, the carrier still would be part of a fleet. Fiske, the highest ranking naval officer with aviation experience, had pioneered in the prewar experiments with the torpedo plane. Just the same, he was adamantly in favor of the Navy preserving control over its own aviation.[4]

II

Even before the war, naval airmen had been interested in testing the effectiveness of aerial bombardment on ships. The first substantial discussion in naval circles was the pamphlet by Lieutenant Commander B. G. Leighton, *Possibilities of Bombing Aircraft*, published in May, 1919. Leighton believed that the destruction of ships by aerial bombardment was both practicable and "purely naval work." Another officer, Lieutenant Commander H. T. Bartlett, suggested a few months later that obsolete ships be used for such tests. More than a year elapsed, however, before the Navy acted.[5]

In the interim, Mitchell became the external agent the naval aviators needed to educate their leadership. Two months before Leighton's pamphlet appeared, and as has already been noted, Mitchell had discussed with the General Board the possibility of bombing tests in Chesapeake Bay. With an eye to such an event, he had also asked Army Ordnance to develop suitable bombs. While he did not press the test issue further in 1919, he did continue his study of the impact of aviation upon naval warfare.

In October of that year, he challenged the views of the Army General Staff on coastal defense with a study drafted for him by

Air Service Major Lewis H. Brereton, the lone Naval Academy graduate on his staff. The General Staff believed that only three forces acted in defense of the United States: the battle fleet, the naval coastal defenses, and the Army's coastal network. In the style of much of Mitchell's prewar thinking and training, the staff planners described the battle fleet as an offensive arm which sought out and destroyed the invading force. If the fleet failed, then the naval defensive weapons, minesweepers, submarines, and naval air units were to engage the invader. Final reliance was on the Army, and particularly its coastal fortifications.

Mitchell, however, argued that the General Staffers had not given proper attention to the possibilities of aviation. He insisted that the "air force" now had the preeminent role in defense. If the battle fleet failed under the old system, two lines of defense remained. Unless the United States had an "air force" to find and destroy the enemy's carrier-borne air forces, the enemy would have an air mastery that enabled him to vault the old lines of defense. The result would be "practically unhindered access to this country." The old elements of defense were absolutely powerless to prevent such an attack, limited only by enemy "strength in the air." [6]

By February, 1920, Mitchell had devised a complete tactical plan for a defense against enemy fleets. A three-phase operation, reconnaissance by a dirigible to locate the enemy, then an attack to gain control of the air, and, finally, direct attack against the enemy fleet summed up Mitchell's plan. If the attack against the enemy fleet were by day, the operation would begin with a low-level raid using attack aircraft firing machine guns and cannon. Once the low-level forces had engaged the enemy, then a bombardment with one-ton missiles would start, followed by airborne and submarine-launched torpedo attacks, the latter directed by radio from the air. At night, dirigibles with one-ton bombs would be used after attack forces had knocked out the enemy's searchlights, and a low-level bombardment action had begun. Submarines then would finish off whatever remained. Mitchell concluded this tactical analysis by saying that "an attack carried out" on these lines and with the available means "will render surface craft incapable of operating to the same extent that they have heretofore, if it does not entirely drive them off the surface of the water." He thought aviation in future wars would make existence almost impossible for surface craft. Were aviation given the money used for "construction and equipment of two or three battleships each year," he believed "surface craft would be put out of business in a very short time." During a congressional hearing a few days later, Mitchell formally challenged the Navy to test his claims.[7]

The challenge went unnoticed by the general public, although Josephus Daniels, the Secretary of the Navy, eventually protested to Secretary Baker about Mitchell's statements. By the summer of 1920, Mitchell had become Assistant Chief of the Air Service and was openly seeking public support. The reduction of Air Service appropriations from 60 to 27 million dollars gave him an excellent incentive. Very much in prospect was the possibility that the service which dominated the coastal defense mission would get the major share of a shrinking military budget.[8]

Mitchell began to enlist the help of the American public, when he praised the union of the Aero Club of America and the American Flying Club. He saw the partnership doing "for aviation what the Navy League has done for the Navy and the National Defense League for the Army." When he won the headline in the usually staid *New York Times*—"Declares America Helpless in Air War"— he was definitely in the public spotlight. His first major incursion into national magazines, such as *World's Work* and the *Review of Reviews,* came that fall with a series of articles on the case which had failed to win approval within the government. These failures went unmentioned as Mitchell outlined ideas that leaned as heavily on aircraft carriers and dirigibles as on airplanes.

Mitchell pounded away at the view *The New York Times* had headlined—that a failure in aerial defense meant attacks on the major cities of America. He had one eye on the cutback in government spending when he argued that the cost of one battleship equalled that of one thousand airplanes. This oversimplified argument made no reference to the faster rate of obsolescence for airplanes compared to that of capital ships. Nothing was said of the cost of training personnel and establishing supporting bases. These realities would have made it clear, had Mitchell chosen to note them as he had before, that aviation was no panacea.[9]

Mitchell kept up his clamor within the government for a bombing test, as when he told Menoher: "We must at all costs obtain the battleship to attack and the necessary bombs, planes and so on to make the test a thorough and complete one." Meanwhile, the Navy finally began its own tests and invited Mitchell to see the results. The tests took place in secret in November, 1920, on the battleship *Indiana*. They were mainly of the static variety; bombs of no more than six hundred pounds were positioned in key points on and near the ship and then exploded. Only dummy bombs were dropped from the air. The damage inflicted justified both further aerial tests with heavier live bombs and caution in any public statement about air attack on ships. The Navy was less than candid in a public statement that the tests pointed to the "improbability of a modern battleship being either destroyed completely or put out of action by aerial bombs." The pictures of the extensive damage to *Indiana* that appeared in the *Illustrated London News* gave rise to a widespread suspicion about the accuracy of the Navy's statement. Mitchell only had to keep the furor growing by stepping up his claims about the power of the airplane against the battleship.[10]

By January, 1921, public pressures became very intense for a bombing test handled by the Air Service. *The New York Times* editorialized that the nation could not afford to ignore Mitchell's claims and still expect to have full defense insurance. At the end of the month, two congressmen introduced resolutions in the House and Senate ordering the Navy to give Mitchell the ships he wanted, while Baker sent Daniels a formal request on the same point. Mitchell sensed that success was imminent as he confidently ordered Colonel Bane, the Director of the Engineering Division, to get ready for a test: "We are going to smoke these people out that do not believe in the air business and make them 'either fish or cut bait.' " [11]

Mitchell's confidence was justified. Within a week, Daniels invited the Air Service to join with the Navy in a bombing experiment. His campaign also had a more immediate effect. The naval aviators discovered magic in pointing out to their leaders that it was better for the Navy to have an air arm than to let Mitchell have it. They won their own organization, the Bureau of Aeronautics, which the Navy asked Congress to authorize in February. The Bureau began operations the following August under the direction of Rear Admiral William A. Moffett. He was a convert to naval aviation who proved to be not only a shrewder campaigner than Mitchell, but also one of his most formidable antagonists. Although both men were dedicated to the development of aviation, the united service question divided them, as it divided Mitchell from nearly all the Navy's aviators. Without realizing it then, Mitchell had become the external agent the Navy needed to make it aviation conscious.[12]

III

Throughout the spring of 1921, Mitchell campaigned for the support of the American people. Several friendly congressmen and newspaper publishers, as well as active and reserve Air Service officers throughout the United States and abroad, were part of a network over which he spread his story. He expended most of his energy, however, on an appeal through the nation's press. His staff prepared editorials, letters to editors, and articles for newspapers which would use them. Mitchell's own magazine article production increased markedly after he had won approval for the bombing tests. Many of the mass-audience publications of the day, including that of the newly formed and politically potent American Legion, carried articles by Mitchell. His theme continued to be the economical defense purchasable by the airplane in preference to the battleship. Mitchell stopped hinting and painted verbal pictures of the catastrophes awaiting America's major cities in future wars, if her aerial defenses were ineffective. TNT was not the most formidable weapon that could be used; the world's chemists, he reported, had produced an assortment of gases which could easily break a population's moral and physical resistance. At the very same time, the American press was featuring a story by the British Air Ministry leader, Sir Frederick Sykes, who added to Mitchell's picture with his own lurid descriptions of the air attacks which would begin future conflicts. Since the war, this so-called "bolt from the blue" thesis had preoccupied many British airmen. Their island's exposure to short-range attack gave them much more justification than Mitchell, but he made no allowances for America's rather sheltered position in his articles.[13]

A somewhat better-balanced exposition of Mitchell's views appeared that spring in his first book, *Our Air Force*. In the greater space available to him than in magazine articles, Mitchell made it clear that he was thinking of the future, and asked his readers to gauge that future by a rate of aeronautical advance like that demonstrated in the war. One claim, rather lightly passed over in the book, was his assertion that "a study of aeronautical conditions in the world indicates that a force of 1,200 airplanes might be deployed against us on this continent within two weeks." Great Britain was the only power which could even begin to transport so many aircraft, if she had them, but reports of coolness between that country and the United States gave some plausibility to what Mitchell was saying.

Except for this doubtful point, Mitchell gave his readers a popular but authoritative picture of aviation's progress. As the title implied, he treated American aviation as an entity, and as much as the times permitted, he described aviation's offensive as well as defensive role. Noting that the Allies planned to retaliate against Germany's use of total war from the air just before the war ended, Mitchell suggested that America might be forced to employ such a strategy in the future. His contention that aviation should be in the proportion of 60 per cent pursuit, 20 per cent bombardment, and 20 per cent observation may well have seemed a defensive emphasis. Actually, he was laying down the principle that air mastery was the first condition of successful bombardment. Because control of the air was most difficult to achieve, the greatest amount of aerial strength had to be used to win it. Once obtained, bombardment, as well as reconnaissance, could follow easily enough.[14]

Privately, Mitchell took a long view of his campaign. He had hoped the new Administration would take a more favorable attitude toward his proposals, but by June, 1921, he was expressing surprise at "the stand President Harding was taking." Mitchell denied "that any material damage has been done to our cause" as he believed "the system of education seems to be going successfully and the people on the 'Hill' are beginning to see the practical value of aviation."

While "the system of education" was at work, Mitchell tried to do what he could to keep the Air Service a meaningful force. During 1921, Congress cut the Army from 280,000 to 150,000 men. The Air Service portion of that cut was not so bad proportionately as that which the other arms suffered but its enlisted personnel dropped from 16,000 to a little more than 10,000.[15]

The climate of retrenchment took such a hold that Mitchell failed to arouse any interest in one project that he thought could reduce the shrinkage of the Air Service. When Harding's Postmaster General Will Hays suggested to Secretary of War John Weeks that the two departments might now cooperate more closely in handling the airmail, Mitchell saw an opportunity. He won Hays's support for a virtual integration of the airmail's activities with those of the Air Service. Menoher and his superiors, however, rejected the idea because they feared that Congress might seize the chance to lump airmail and Air Service appropriations together. As retrenchment progressed, this total sum might suffer cuts to a point below the amounts the airmail and Air Service were now getting separately.[16]

The merits of Mitchell's proposal aside, the incident showed the uncertain basis upon which American aviation existed in the early 1920's. Mitchell's campaign, then, had a solid educational purpose to serve insofar as it sought the creation of an understanding by the American people of aviation and the functions it might play in their country.

IV

The bombing tests of June-July, 1921, marked the climax of Mitchell's first campaign and also meant a step forward in the general progress of aviation. Unfortunately, the controversy surrounding the joint Army-Navy project clouded the values of the tests from their very inception. Questions of prestige, the personalities involved, and a disagreement as to the objectives of the tests made a furor inevitable. President-elect Harding's call in February for a world naval disarmament conference foreshadowed the difficulties ahead for the Navy, especially if the tests went badly. Likewise, Mitchell's confident assertions had put his own reputation on the line. His intransigence had its naval counterpart in that of Josephus Daniels, the outgoing Secretary of the Navy, who allegedly had offered to stand bareheaded on the bridge of any ship Mitchell tried to bomb. Most importantly, the differences between Mitchell and the Navy as to what the tests should set out to accomplish were so pronounced as to outweigh other reasons for the controversy.[17]

From the very first, the Navy had laid down certain objectives from which it never deviated. The leaders of that service wanted the tests to be scientific appraisals of the capacity of ships of various kinds to endure gunfire and static explosion as well as bombardment from the air. Destruction was to proceed methodically with frequent delays for construction experts to inspect the damage inflicted. The tests were to take place on the fifty fathom curve in the ocean or as much as sixty miles off the Atlantic Coast. Since the Navy intended to use seaplanes for the aerial bombardment phase, the danger from forced landings was minimal. Also, the Navy's plan to wind up the exercises with gunfire against the targets indicated the doubts of her leaders about the effectiveness of aerial bombardment.[18]

Mitchell and his associates had vastly different purposes and procedures in mind. The objective of the Mitchell group was to climax its publicity campaign with the sinking of each target in as vivid a manner as possible. Relays of pursuit, attack, and bombardment aircraft using gunfire, bombs, and gas were to annihilate their targets according to Mitchell's previously outlined tactical plan. Even domestic animals were to be included as stand-ins for human beings on the decks. Because the pursuit ships had less than two hours' gasoline capacity at high speeds, the targets would have to be closer to the shore than the Navy desired. Furthermore, to send the longer-range land-based aircraft any distance over the water seemed an unnecessary risk to Mitchell. The proper navigation equipment to guide aircraft flying out of sight of land had not been developed. During the Navy's transatlantic flight in 1919, for example, a string of seventy-three ships was required to mark their path across the ocean.[19]

The Joint Board of the Army and Navy quickly tried to resolve these fundamental differences by directing that the tests were to be carried out under naval control and procedures. Furthermore, the Board ruled that the publicity resulting from the *Indiana* tests of the previous November had gotten out of hand. It ordered a complete news blackout on test preparations as well as on any official interpretations of the results. In order to satisfy Mitchell's request for a full test of all types of aerial equipment and projectiles, the Board offered the Air Service an obsolete battleship for a separate test.[20]

Since the joint test was far more elaborate and potentially much more newsworthy, Mitchell had no alternative other than to go along with the Navy's rules for the time being. The Navy had scheduled tests against a wide array of targets, many of them former German vessels obtained in the peace settlement, including submarines, destroyers, a cruiser, and two battleships. Navy and Marine aircraft as well as Army planes would participate. The main events were a search problem and dummy bombing attack on the radio-controlled battleship *Iowa,* followed a few days later by the live bombardment of the ex-German battleship *Ostfriesland.* In keeping with the original plans, the Navy decided to position the German battleship some sixty miles off the Virginia coast. This meant a flight of at least eighty-five miles for the Army bombers from their base at Langley Field. The expected rigid controls were imposed whereby the destruction was to take place in a step-by-step process, with frequent interruptions by a board of naval observers to inspect the damage.[21]

In February, Mitchell had told Congress that the Air Service would be ready "tomorrow" for the tests, but this was not the case. The Air Service generally lacked bombardment experience, particularly in this kind of exercise. In addition to crews drawn from the faculty and student officers at the new Air Service Tactical School at Langley Field, Virginia, other crews and their aircraft came from all over the United States to form a new unit, the First Provisional Brigade. The administrative difficulties in hastily bringing personnel from their home bases soon prompted an Inspector General's investigation. The Brigade had to carry out long practice sessions against mock ships near Langley Field. Fortunately, Mitchell could draw upon the assistance of some leading airmen. Directly under him in the brigade were two of his former associates in the Operations and Training Group, Major Thomas Milling and Captain William C. Sherman. He received technical advice from the Italian and French air attachés Guidoni and de Lavergne, as well as from a new figure in his circle, Alexander de Seversky. The latter had flown bombing missions as a Russian naval aviator against German shipping in the Baltic during the war. He later claimed that he used his experience to advise Mitchell that the best technique for sinking a major ship was not to hit her directly but to drop bombs into the water sufficiently close to cause a mining effect against the hull. Army Ordnance cooperated by rushing the production of 2,000-pound bombs of the size needed for sinking a ship of the *Ostfriesland*'s class. As the frantic preparations moved toward completion, Mitchell took personal charge of the Brigade.[22]

Before the bombing tests began in early June, Mitchell almost lost his post as Assistant Chief of the Air Service. His activities as a publicist spurred Menoher to recommend Mitchell's removal to the Secretary of War, John W. Weeks. The exact charges did not appear in the press at this time when Mitchell was riding the crest of his popularity, but Menoher had privately attacked him with all the ammunition at his command. He accused Mitchell of antagonizing the Navy by "attempting to influence" personnel legislation affecting the new Bureau of Aeronautics, of attracting "unfortunate and undesirable publicity" to his flying exploits during a storm in which another Air Service plane crashed, killing seven persons, and of agitating for a separate service "contrary to Administration policy." Menoher concluded by complaining of Mitchell's "persistent publicity" to the detriment of his own prestige. This publicity, Menoher conceded, had not been pushed by Mitchell himself but had gone on with his tacit consent. Weeks, however, chose to support Mitchell by dismissing his activities as indiscretions and persuading Menoher to back down. Weeks' exact reasons were unclear. As a brand new Secretary still familiarizing himself with his job, Weeks may have been reluctant to make so drastic a decision so soon, especially just before the bombing tests. Mitchell brushed off the affair as "departmental politics" and accused the Navy Department and the tiny but already influential National Advisory Committee for Aeronautics of plotting his proposed ouster. His accusation against the Navy, at least, had some validity, since Moffett had presented charges against Mitchell to his own superiors that were quite similar to those Menoher had made.[23]

When the bombing experiments finally began, Mitchell reluctantly agreed to the Navy's general rules, but he steadfastly refused to permit his airmen to drop only dummy bombs on *Iowa*. Navy sources afterwards charged, and with some merit, that Mitchell feared that his aircraft lacked the equipment even to locate *Iowa* during the initial search problem. In succeeding weeks, however, the remainder of the tests against the submarines, destroyers, and cruiser targets proceeded smoothly enough.

But the climactic event, the attack on *Ostfriesland* on July 21 and 22, was another matter. When Mitchell got his chance to use 2,000-pound bombs against that target on the second day of the tests, he reasserted his original plan to sink the battleship in as spectacular a fashion as possible. Nothing could stop him until his crews had dropped six 2,000-pounders and within twenty-one minutes had plunged *Ostfriesland* toward the bottom of the sea. The Navy protested Mitchell's violation of their rules in pressing the attack so vigorously that their construction experts were given no opportunity to inspect *Ostfriesland*. Accordingly, the naval officials denied that the test was conclusive and argued that the experiment was not under service conditions. If, for example, *Ostfriesland* had been manned by a crew, was under way and had been firing antiaircraft guns, the ship might have stayed afloat. Mitchell replied that if *Ostfriesland* had been under way and her magazines had been full, she would have made an easier target. The dispute, however, could not get away from the basic fact which had deeply impressed itself on the public's mind—Mitchell had sunk a battleship, as he claimed he could.[24]

The Joint Board's evaluation of the experiment could not ignore that fact either. The Board looked to major changes in the direction of American naval policy, but not the complete revolution Mitchell had sought. It recognized that "aircraft carrying high-capacity, high-explosive bombs of sufficient size have adequate offensive power to sink or seriously damage any naval vessel at present constructed, provided such projectiles can be placed in the water alongside the vessel." The Board doubted that "any type of vessel of sufficient strength" could be built to withstand the destructive force inherent in bombs carried from "shore bases or sheltered harbors." Future naval operations against an enemy coast defended by aviation would be extremely hazardous. On the other hand, fleet operations out on the high seas could still be built around the battleship because no existing carriers could launch airplanes with bombs big enough to sink them. The Board's report, then, was a compromise which leaned in Mitchell's direction. Its members had no illusions. They called for the maximum development of aviation, the rapid addition of aircraft carriers to the Navy, and the improvement of antiaircraft armament. At the same time, they viewed aviation as only adding "to the complexity of naval warfare," instead of economically solving the problems it presented, as Mitchell had claimed.[25]

Mitchell refused to take comfort in the report. After the tests, he sent the Brigade in mock raids on New York City, Philadelphia, Wilmington, and Baltimore to impress on the public the need for adequate defenses against aerial bombardment. Then he submitted his own report on the tests to Menoher. When the latter would not make it public, Mitchell's conclusions were leaked to the press and another internal Air Service crisis occurred. Mitchell categorically stated that "the problem of the destruction of seacraft by Air Forces has been solved and is finished." He could have left no doubt in the minds of those who were familiar with his tactical plan that he was trying to win maximum attention. His claims that the Brigade "would have put out of action the Atlantic Fleet in a single attack" and that "the cost of the airplanes involved was no more than that of a destroyer" only made good newspaper copy. Although he and his crews could not have operated over water without the navigational and rescue support of a string of destroyers acting as markers to the target, Mitchell claimed that the Air Force should take over all control of defense responsibilities for two hundred miles out to sea. Calling attention to the interservice friction that had gone on for the previous six months, Mitchell concluded his statement by asserting that a fundamental change in national defense policy was necessary. The end result would be a "Department of National Defense . . . with a staff common to all the services" and with "subsecretaries for the Army, Navy and the Air Force." Then and only then, he implied, could the government make the correct decisions in choosing weapons for the present and future needs of the country. Without a reorganization, he maintained, the question of which service would dominate the coastal defense mission in the aviation era could never be satisfactorily settled.[26]

The publication of this report, or "bombshell" as Mitchell called it, provoked Menoher into telling Secretary Weeks that either Mitchell or he had to go. Weeks once again supported Mitchell, whose success in the bombing tests had impressed him greatly. Menoher was removed and Mitchell then offered his own resignation admitting that he was a "source of irritation within the Air Service." Weeks refused it pending the completion of a new bombing test against *Alabama*. Many aviation enthusiasts wanted to see Mitchell in Menoher's place but Mason Patrick, the onetime Chief of the Air Service, AEF, got the post instead. When Mitchell tried to dictate his duties in the new regime, Patrick was quick to let him know who was in charge. Mitchell threatened to resign but, on further consideration, changed his mind.[27]

From the point of view of Mitchell's announced goals, therefore, the joint Navy-Army tests had gained very little for his campaign. In fact, the campaign had almost cost him his position. Viewed from another perspective, these tests that Mitchell had done so much to bring about gave an impetus to the creation of the Naval Air Service.

Admiral Moffett had won the Navy's support for aircraft carriers, but at the time of the tests, his proposals were bogged down in Congress. The sinking of *Ostfriesland* led to a compromise proposal whereby, instead of authoriz'ng new construction, the legislators would finance the conversion of two battle cruisers into carriers. At first unacceptable to the Navy, the proposal became much more attractive as the disarmament movement took hold in the country and threatened to put an end to all naval building.

On the world scene, Mitchell's success gained the attention of leading airmen, including Hugh Trenchard and Giulio Douhet. The air attachés eagerly sought as much information on the tests as they could obtain and, Guidoni, the Italian air attaché, wrote a detailed analysis of the event. Mitchell himself reported that on his subsequent European trip, military experts were well aware of the *Ostfriesland* affair and most eager to hear his ideas firsthand.[28]

V

At the end of August, Mitchell just missed playing a tragic role in American social history when Air Service bombers were alerted for use against striking United Mine Workers in West Virginia. Fortunately for all concerned, this extension of the constabulary idea to military aviation never took place. He was in an orthodox role a few days later when he directed Air Service aircraft in the sinking of *Alabama*. This time, Mitchell had a free hand in using a wide assortment of aircraft and projectiles to make his point. The prompt destruction of the *Alabama* was a repetition of his *Ostfriesland* triumph but also was a better example of his tactical thinking. As much as he publicized the power of one airplane over the battleship, Mitchell's tactical viewpoint demanded an overwhelming use of aircraft in actual naval warfare.[29]

He had an excellent platform for his views at the Washington Naval Conference which began in November. Just how much effect the tests had on the decisions of the conference remains uncertain, but Mitchell gave briefings on the tests to various foreign delegations. He claimed that the basic decision of the conference to limit battleship building drastically was "greatly facilitated" by the bombing test results. Airplane construction, however, was not restricted. The sweeping American proposal submitted by Secretary of State

Charles Evans Hughes that set the pace for the conference made no mention of airplanes. This suggested how much the meeting focused on eliminating the symbols of military power rather than the realities. Mitchell, in speaking to the aviation subcommittee with which he served, put his finger on the reason the whole conference officially accepted for not banning aircraft: "The only practicable limitation as to the numbers of aircraft that could be used for military purposes would be to abolish the use of aircraft for any purpose." The full subcommittee agreed, declaring that to limit aviation now was "to shut the door on progress." [30]

Mitchell's renewal of old friendships with foreign airmen at the conference was but a prelude to his inspection of aviation's progress in Europe. Although he had been thinking since the previous summer of making such a trip, other events made it imperative that he leave the Washington scene for awhile. The strain of duty in the capital once again had begun to tell on him. There had been a personal tragedy behind his public roles in campaigning for and executing the bombing tests, as well as in his struggle with Menoher and those who wished him removed from his position of influence. At the height of the *Ostfriesland* controversy in July, his marriage of sixteen years collapsed with his separation from his wife Caroline and their three children. The break preceded a bitter struggle that could have erupted into a major scandal. To repeat the details of that struggle would serve no significant purpose. It is sufficient to say that his difficulties were common knowledge in Washington. Whatever his share of the responsibility might have been, his marital crisis probably made it easier for his opponents to dismiss Mitchell as irresponsible and unworthy of further advancement in the Army.[31]

VI

Mitchell sailed for Europe in December, 1921, with his aide, Lieutenant Clayton Bissell, and an engineering adviser, Alfred Verville. Here began a period of comparative silence on Mitchell's part for almost two years. Patrick's firm control of the Air Service ended for the time being the freedom Mitchell had enjoyed in carrying on the first publicity campaign. That campaign bore fruit in a way unforeseen by Mitchell. The Navy leaders had now become aviation conscious. The Washington Naval Treaty had authorized the United

States to carry out the compromise proposal voiced in Congress after the sinking of *Ostfriesland*. Congress voted the money for a conversion of two battle cruisers into the carriers *Lexington* and *Saratoga*, collectively the cornerstone of American naval aviation. With these working materials, the airmen of the U.S. Navy were to create a significant element in America's military posture, but they had needed Mitchell's challenge to their superiors to get under way as quickly as they did.[32]

During ceremonies at National Air Museum, Smithsonian Institution, Washington, D.C. in 1957, a statue of General Mitchell was unveiled by William Mitchell, Jr. Here, Billy Mitchell, Jr. looks up at the statue, which was sculptured by Bruce Moore.

General Mitchell and Will Rogers after a flight at Bolling Field, April 24, 1925.

Mitchell standing by his Spad plane during World War I.

A scene taken during General Mitchell's court-martial in 1925.

General Pershing, General Mitchell, General March and aides at Bolling Field, D.C., October 21, 1920, welcoming Alaskan flyers.

General Patrick and General Mitchell watching the Pulitzer Trophy Race, October 14, 1922.

*General Mitchell is shown here standing by a V.E.7 at
Bolling Field Air Tournament, May 1920.*

General Mitchell and Eddie Rickenbacker at Langley Field, Virginia.

CHAPTER FIVE

"The First Line of Offense"

Despite Billy Mitchell's personal and official troubles, there was at least one happy experience for him during this period. General Patrick began to assign him to duties that made the best use of his talents, but for the time being, he also kept him out of further difficulties in Washington. He sent Mitchell to study European aeronautical progress, Air Service operations in the United States, and the American defense system in the Pacific. In about two years, Mitchell deepened his appreciation of the potential of aviation and made some of his finest contributions to the tactical and doctrinal growth of the Air Service. These contributions were impressive evidence of the genius that he would too often obscure by his role as a publicist.

I

Mitchell had easy access to the "Who's Who" of the military and aeronautical leadership of Europe after he returned to France on December 19, 1921. The fame of his work in the bombing tests

73

and his wartime reputation had preceded him. Even the aviation manufacturers were most helpful. They gave him a full picture of their progress, which Mitchell and his companions recorded in a voluminous technical report. Hospitality for a fellow pioneer, however, was not the only motive behind their openhandedness. The German industrialists, for example, were interested in entering the American market because the disarmament provisions of the Versailles Treaty denied them full scope at home. A favorable impression on Mitchell, they probably hoped, might well give them the foothold in America that they desired.[1]

His month-long stay in France set the tone for what Mitchell learned during his three-month sojourn in Europe. By a fortunate coincidence, he was in Paris during a conference of all the French military aviation experts. The chairman was Marshal Fayolle, the Inspector General of the Army and virtual chief of French aviation. The objective of the conference was to draw what lessons the participants could for the future from a retrospective study of their wartime operations.

Mitchell reported that the group agreed that the great effort put into Army support in the war could not be repeated in the future. In the next continental war, the aviators believed, the opposing air forces would battle even before their armies met. This first series of air battles could be decisive because future wars would not be won without mastery of the air. Accordingly, the airmen argued that there must be an air force ready to operate independently at the outbreak of war. This air force, then, was "the first line of offense" against the two major powers and potential enemies bordering on France. The aviators were well aware that key German targets were no more than two hours away from the French side of the Rhine. England, toward whom Mitchell noted the French were growing increasingly cool, had cities less than forty minutes from the French coast. Nevertheless, Mitchell realized that the beliefs of the airmen were a long way from the realm of reality. They might well understand the new problems presented by aviation in warfare, but they still lacked significant influence even in their own service. They found little sympathy among their senior officers, assigned by the army to give administrative stability to the air arm. The leaders of the French army and navy also blocked their aviators. In the case of the French navy, the aviators had challenged its effectiveness with bombing tests on a smaller scale than in America. The aviators were quite in agreement with the lessons which Mitchell had drawn from the *Ostfriesland* experience and went even further than he did by doubting the effectiveness of the aircraft carrier. The decks of the carriers, they argued, were too vulnerable to attack.[2]

While Mitchell found France to be the strongest military nation in Europe, he believed Italy, the next stop on his trip, to be the weakest major power. Potentially, in the team of Caproni and Douhet, Italy had the technical and theoretical ability to be an aeronautical leader. Mitchell knew Caproni and probably saw him again during this visit, but ten years passed before Mitchell ever mentioned having had "frequent conversations" with Douhet. Mitchell probably was referring to Caproni and Douhet when he reported meeting "more men of exceptional ability in Italy than we did in any other country." It is also possible that Mitchell may have become familiar at this time with the main points of the classic work published in 1921 by Douhet, *Il Domino dell'Aria,* translated many years afterward as *The Command of the Air*. This book seemed like a response to Trenchard's appeal in 1920 for a summary of the common principles held by airmen of the world, such as Admiral Mahan had made for seamen everywhere in his *The Influence of Seapower Upon History*.[3]

Mitchell never attributed any special influence on his thinking to Douhet. If he had heard nothing about *The Command of the Air* while he was in Italy, he nevertheless became aware of its main points a few months later. Lieutenant Colonel A. Guidoni, the Italian Air Attaché in Washington, sent an Italian aviation journal's summary of the book to Air Service Headquarters and to Lester Gardner, the editor of *Aviation* magazine. Gardner discussed the piece with Mitchell, called attention to it in his journal, and planned to publish a translation of the entire book. In a letter to Douhet, Guidoni quoted Gardner as saying that Mitchell was greatly impressed by the ideas of Douhet. Gardner, Guidoni continued, had noted the possible parallel between this work and that of Admiral Mahan. The translation promised by Gardner never appeared, perhaps because Guidoni soon returned to Rome for reassignment in the spring of 1923.[4]

Whenever Mitchell actually learned what Douhet advocated, he recognized that their ideas had been similar since the war. At that time, primarily British and French airmen had educated Mitchell in an outlook shared by many of the airmen of Europe. Mitchell undoubtedly knew that Caproni, Douhet's associate, had helped to shape the thinking of other American aviators, particularly the members of the 1917 Bolling Mission. In this light, any Douhetan influence on Mitchell was at best indirect and dated from World War I. Mitchell most likely regarded what he knew of the ideas of Douhet as only another argument for his point of view. This allegedly was Mitchell's reaction when he was told that Douhet had persuaded Benito Mussolini in December, 1922, to establish a separate air force under a Ministry of National Defense in the new Fascist government.[5]

In 1922, Mitchell and Douhet held many similar views. Both men accepted the premise that they lived in an era of total war; both sensed the rapid pace of aviation development; both sought independent air services under a Ministry of National Defense in their countries; both believed in the power of chemical attacks; and both stressed the importance of civil aviation as a peacetime base for wartime needs.

In one fundamental respect, however, Douhet was more advanced than Mitchell. While the two men agreed that future wars would begin with a struggle for air supremacy, Douhet was more radical in discussing the next phase of aerial warfare. Indeed, Douhet wrote, as he had in 1917, in terms of a national strategy which used control of the air to destroy "the vital centers" of the enemy, or his will to fight and industrial backbone. Although he could not say so openly at this time, Douhet believed that the destruction of the "vital centers" required the use of all the aerial strength of his nation. In his view, no aviation would be allotted to the army or navy. Consistently enough, Douhet also went beyond Mitchell in his claims for the power of the offensive over the defensive. Mitchell had much greater confidence in air defense than did Douhet, who argued that: "We must resign ourselves to the offensives the enemy inflicts upon us, while striving to put all our resources to work to inflict even heavier ones upon him." There is little doubt that the economic weaknesses of Italy greatly influenced Douhet. His country could not afford an aviation development broad enough to cover offensive and defensive preparations, nor to equip the army and navy with aircraft.[6]

Douhet also thought that his country could not afford to invest in airships, and he argued that German dependence upon the Zeppelin during the war had been a gigantic blunder. Mitchell, by contrast, joined with other Italian flyers in continuing to believe in the possibilities of such craft. Aeronautical engineers in Italy were then experimenting with dirigibles as airplane carriers and had developed the so-called semirigid airship. One of these, the *Roma*, had already been sold to the United States. It crashed while Mitchell was in Europe and added another page to the disastrous history of the airship. Another Italian experiment helped to explain somewhat why Douhet could be so confident about the air offensive. Then in progress was the testing of aerial torpedoes, that is, of radio-controlled unmanned aircraft loaded with explosives. Launched against targets from a distance sufficient to challenge the utility of strong local air defenses, the possibilities of the aerial torpedo made a lasting impression on Mitchell.[7]

Both Douhet and Mitchell were also very much in agreement about a different problem—the likelihood of a German comeback. At the end of February, Mitchell visited Germany after returning to Paris from Italy and then visiting French air bases en route to the American station at Koblenz in occupied Germany. His interview in Berlin with General von Seeckt, the leader of the German army, convinced him that the "German mind is still militaristic." Von Seeckt "complained bitterly" to Mitchell about the restrictions of the Versailles Treaty on German aviation. Just the same, Mitchell met a group of former aviators on von Seeckt's staff who supposedly were working in army specialties other than aviation. Actually, they formed the nucleus for a future German air force. They had even circumvented the Versailles Treaty's restrictions on flying by taking up the sport of gliding. Although the Allies had banned the sport just before Mitchell arrived, the former aviators were undaunted. Mitchell found them to be thoroughly conversant with worldwide aviation progress. Despite their present difficulties, they were confident that the traditional scientific competence of their nation would prevent its falling too far behind the rest of the world in aviation. Also, there were other military aviation veterans who were not in the army, but still active in German aeronautics.

Mitchell met many of these men, including Ernst Udet and Hermann Goering, at a memorable meeting of the German Aero Club in Berlin. The entire group of aviators formed a pool of talented leadership for the military revival Mitchell thought was highly possible. Meanwhile, noted German aircraft manufacturers such as the Junkers firm were staying in business by making consumer goods and plowing their profits into aviation research. Junkers, as well as the Dornier organization, had already devised ideas about big bombers and aircraft engines which prompted Mitchell to urge his superiors to keep in touch with both organizations. And still at the top of the international airship field was the Zeppelin Corporation. Mitchell found its leadership actively planning to circumvent the Versailles restrictions. He reported that negotiations were under way between the Spanish government and the company about building a plant in that country.[8]

This German aeronautical potential further underscored the problems facing Great Britain, which country Mitchell visited in early March. The British government, however, had directed its armed forces to plan in terms of no war during the 1920's. Trenchard put considerable trust in the policy of his government, and he was carrying out a long-range program which stressed building the most enduring elements of the RAF. Rather than make large-scale purchases of aircraft before technical advances had slowed down, Trenchard focused on what he called the "brick and mortar" side of the air force. He had just opened Cranwell, the "West Point" of the RAF, and Halton, a school for training a pool of maintenance personnel drawn from fourteen-year-old English youth. Mitchell was obviously impressed, the more so because he himself had been seeking a distinctive program for training the members of the American Air Service. Once again, Mitchell found that the British airmen were quite concerned about the opening phase of the next war. They too feared "a bolt from the blue" against their own country, which might knock it out of action in short order. Also, they shared his conclusions about the bombing tests and agreed that a surface fleet could not operate successfully against a coastline defended by a major air force.[9]

This consensus showed how much the military aviators of the world spoke the same language. It also reaffirmed Mitchell's conviction that the question of the defensive capabilities of the airplane against invading fleets had been settled. He was now ready to focus his attention on what the French airmen had called the "first line of offense." An air force had to be ready at the beginning of the next war, Mitchell concluded, so that a country "might not lose the campaign at once or be placed in a very embarrassing position." European airmen had once again inspired Mitchell, but he had extracted their viewpoint from a context of frequent wars and short distances. In the American setting, the political and geographical isolation of his country, to say nothing of the state of technology, initially made Mitchell's concern about "the offensive air force" a private one.[10]

II

After completing his European trip, Mitchell began to feel the full force of his relationship with General Patrick. The latter had become the head, in fact as well as in name, of the Air Service. Patrick had done so by learning to fly, keeping a tight control over the Washington office of the Air Service, and by taking up with greater political skill many of the issues for which Mitchell had fought. His control over the Air Service was apparent during a typical incident in October, 1922, when Mitchell told a reporter: "I am arranging for a 'round the world' trip with a squadron of six planes." The resulting news story immediately brought an inquiry from the Deputy Chief of the Staff of the Army to Patrick, demanding information about the flight which had not won official clearance. The reply Patrick gave showed who was running the Air Service: "By *my* direction, one of the divisions in *my* office has been giving study to possible long flights." (Italics added.) [11]

Such incidents were few, however, because Patrick kept Mitchell out of Air Service headquarters and, as much as possible, on extensive inspection visits to Air Service bases throughout the United States. In this role, Mitchell considerably influenced the tactical and doctrinal growth of the Air Service. On occasion, these duties put him in the public spotlight. In November of 1922, he captured the world's speed record in an airplane. Another Air Service pilot, Lieutenant Maughan, broke the record again the very next day, but Mitchell's achievement won him international attention. Also, he wrote infrequently for the press, but only on technical subjects. A ruling by Secretary of War Weeks that Mitchell should submit his articles for official clearance temporarily prevented him from writing any controversial pieces.[12]

While he was constantly recommending technical improvements, especially ones designed to match any superior equipment he saw abroad, Mitchell was extremely interested in two experiments. The first was the work of Lawrence Sperry in devising the techniques necessary to make airborne carriers of airplanes a reality. The initial experiments, apparently matching work Mitchell had seen in Europe, demonstrated that an airship could actually pick up light airplanes in midair. This in turn promised an extension of range for the airplane and became another factor in Mitchell's faith in the airship. Another and broader advance appeared in all-weather flying. Working with the Royal Canadian Air Force and Air Service units in the winter of 1923, Mitchell directed tests in northern United States that also anticipated the indispensably close liaison with the RCAF in the years ahead.[13]

Mitchell was most concerned with preserving the "tactical system and the spirit" attained in the war by the Air Service. Many of those who had been the leading flyers during the brief combat period overseas had not made military aviation a career. The few who remained on active duty, including Colonel Thomas Milling, Majors Carl Spaatz and Lewis Brereton, Captain Walter Lawson, and Lieutenant Clayton Bissell, worked closely with Mitchell in passing on to the new generation of flyers their World War I experiences and leading them in the development of new techniques. Nowhere was Mitchell's influence on the "tactical spirit" more evident than in his supervision of the training of Air Service personnel. He seemed never to have been satisfied with the quality level of personnel in the service. As he told Patrick, the Air Service was not drawing enough of the highest-caliber men. Mitchell was anxious to build the flying officer corps around "young men from the colleges and universities who are keen athletes and who have had excellent educational advantages." No meaningful program, however, was developed to do this; budgetary limitations and the uncertainties of a military career were sufficient reasons.

On the other hand, Mitchell strove to bring the men he had up to the highest standards of efficiency. In his inspection of various units, whether they were observation, pursuit, attack, or bombardment, Mitchell pushed them as hard as he could by presenting their members with tactical problems that he had formulated. Upon their completion of these exercises, the flyers heard Mitchell's evaluation of their performance and his requirements for the additional training necessary to bring them up to his standards. In one such case, Mitchell sent the attack squadron based at Kelly Field, Texas, on low-level missions against mock targets, representing truck columns and railroad trains. After they had finished this exercise and he had left the base, the squadron members volunteered that Mitchell had given them a grasp of their wartime mission which they had never had before.[14]

His similar activities with other types of units, especially his favorite organization, Spaatz's First Pursuit Group, suggested that Mitchell's ideas had impregnated the makeup of the fledgling Air Service. He took particular pains to pass on his experiences and those of his associates, such as Spaatz in pursuit work and Lawson in bombardment, through the manuals which described the functions and tactics of various kinds of units.

Mitchell's own manual on bombardment, which he privately distributed within the Air Service during 1923, best described the contribution he made during this period. This monograph was the basis for a conception of bombardment far ahead of the times, and thus hardly suitable for printing as an official document. The manual "Notes on the Multi-Motored Bombardment Group" used the approach a man of Mitchell's background, temperament, and experience made to the same problems with which Douhet dealt in *Il Domino dell 'Aria*. While Douhet wrote a philosophical treatise on the first principles of total war through the air, Mitchell produced a work on how to carry out that type of war.[15]

"The attack of objectives on land," Mitchell pointed out in the manual, was "the normal mission of bombardment." The aerial bomb, "a terrible reality," was only in its primitive stage; "the most formidable bombs of today may be relegated to the class of antiquity within the next ten years." He distinguished between military and civilian objectives when he asserted that the latter would be attacked only "as an act of reprisal." The military category, however, was so broad as to include civilians implicitly and also to make it clear that he was writing about wars fought for more than the immediate defense of American territory: "enemy aerodromes, concentration centers, training camps, personnel pools, transporta-

tion centers whether rail, road, river or canal, ammunition and
supply dumps, headquarters of staff commands, forts and heavily
fortified positions, trains, convoys, columns of troops, bridges, dams,
locks, power plants, tunnels, telephone and telegraph centers,
manufacturing areas, water supplies and growing grain." Furthermore, while direct attacks on centers of population would only be
reprisals rarely indulged in, the mere threat of such raids had a
"moral effect" that could cause such demands for expensive outlays
on defense arrangements as to dissipate an enemy's war effort.[16]

This type of warfare, Mitchell suggested, might shorten future
wars. Despite the current disarmament mood, despite "well-intended
efforts, more effective weapons have been devised and utilized in
each war. What the outcome will be is problematic." While offering
no opinion "regarding the use of bombardment in the back areas,"
Mitchell thought it "folly not to prepare and train for the use of this
weapon in case circumstances make it necessary." The decision
whether or not to use bombardment, he contended, did not belong
to the airman. The airman's function was to get ready "for every
possible contingency which might arise." [17]

Peacetime training should involve an analysis of how to attack
possible targets followed by practice missions. Each member of a
bombardment group had definite preparations to make as well.
Mitchell outlined the duties in which each of the key officers in the
unit should be most proficient. The entire unit, he asserted, should
strive to be as flexible and as mobile as possible so as to be able to
support a war of movement as well as a war of position. The success
of the unit depended to a large degree on the success of its supply
system. Mitchell envisioned a supply arrangement that included the
construction of a whole new class of aerial transport. To use tactical
aircraft for such work, he thought, was a serious mistake. For one
thing, the dominant characteristics of each class of aircraft were too
different. The transports required "carrying ability," a strong under-
carriage for landing anywhere, "cargo compartments so designed
that they are loaded and unloaded with dispatch," and the ability
to airlift "anything that may be needed" by a unit. Since American
commercial airlines were nonexistent, the Air Service would have to
develop its own carriers. At that time, airships seemed highly promising for such work, but Mitchell thought other methods might eventually prove superior.[18]

Combat operations, Mitchell made clear, could not proceed without the full cooperation of pursuit aircraft. Bombers could go with impunity "to any target if the United States had control of the air," but Mitchell considered absolute aerial control as a practical impossibility. He recognized that "regardless of which side has aerial supremacy, our bombardment will force a concentration of enemy pursuit at a time and place selected for an attack." The job of American pursuit was not to stay too close to the bombers but "to engage enemy pursuit when it had concentrated." In addition, he claimed that a bomber formation had an excellent defensive capability in its own "guns, steady gun platform, bountiful supply of ammunition, converging fire and the mutual support given each other by the planes in the formation." Mitchell rated an enemy's pursuit as the type of opposition most difficult to handle. The low effectiveness of antiaircraft guns in the war seemed to him a sure sign of their inadequacy. Inadequate or not, he was still thorough enough to insist that the bombardment commander select the route to and from his target along which antiaircraft fire was least likely to be effective.[19]

Mitchell tried out some of these ideas in the summer of 1923 when he led eighteen Martin bombers in maneuvers to show the mobility with which a bomber force could move to protect any point in the "heart" of the United States. The triangle formed by Boston, Norfolk, and Chicago, he said, enclosed "all of our main arteries of communication from east to west, the nation's capital, financial center, coalfields and our greatest manufacturing industries." The best protection for this concentration of national resources in case of war, he concluded, was a vigorous offensive against any threatening enemy force. During the maneuvers, Mitchell encountered many of the problems yet to be solved before his manual became practicable. For one thing, when he tried to move his force to an improvised base at Bangor, Maine, his 85-mph bombers flew into severe head winds that scattered them short of Bangor, along the upper east coast of the United States.[20]

In reviewing these maneuvers for Patrick, Mitchell remarked that any future tests would be impossible until the Air Service was in better condition. He was not exaggerating. Between 1920 and 1923, the air arm had noticeably deteriorated. The economy mood in the government and the country at large had deepened until the aviation strength levels authorized by the National Defense Act of 1920 were only happy memories. By the summer of 1923, the strength of the whole Army was less than half the peacetime force permitted by the National Defense Act. In terms of actual strength, the air arm had suffered proportionately. The National Defense Act had envisaged 1,516 officers and 16,000 enlisted men (including 2,500 aviation cadets) in Army aviation. This authorized figure soon dropped to 1,061 officers and 8,764 enlisted men (including 190 cadets). Actually, however, the Air Service only had 880 officers and 8,399 enlisted men (including 91 cadets) by March of 1923.

Compounding this personnel shortage was Patrick's refusal to bring the air arm up to authorized strength in the officer ranks by permitting transfers of senior men from other branches. Had he relented, however, men inexperienced in aviation would have been directing most of the best flyers in the service. The flyers generally had not joined the commissioned ranks of the Army until the last days of the war, or later. They now languished at the bottom of the new single list used in all promotions, which stressed seniority rather than specialty. The gravest deficiencies were in materiel. The government had relied on its war stocks to equip the Army, especially in aviation. In 1923, of the 1,970 airplanes of all types in the inventory, 1,531 had been built during the war. Within three years, if this procurement policy continued, normal attrition would cut the 1923 figures to a total of 289 airplanes, 102 from war stocks.[21]

While Mitchell normally had been absent from Washington during this period, Patrick had been trying to secure support within the government for a new aviation policy. After studying his case in March, 1923, a board of seven General Staff officers headed by Major General William Lassiter and including two Air Service men, Lieutenant Colonel Frank P. Lahm as a member and Major Herbert A. Dargue as secretary, gave Patrick their unqualified support. The Lassiter Board pointed out that: "unless steps are taken to improve conditions in the Air Service it will in effect be practically demobilized at an early date." The report of that group was by far the most progressive action taken by any such body up to that time. The Board proposed "minimum" peacetime requirements of 4,000 officers, 25,000 enlisted men, 2,500 aviation cadets, 2,534 airplanes, 20 airships, and 38 balloons. In war, this force would be expanded to 22,628 officers, 172,994 enlisted men, 8,756 airplanes, 31 airships, and 134 balloons. The Board supported Patrick's suggestion that, while certain units of the Air Service would be assigned to the direct support of Army units, the remainder were to be formed into a reserve under General Headquarters, where it might be used either in ground support or in independent operations.

To finance this monumental project, the Board suggested a ten-year development program and added its belief that both the Army and Navy should work out their aviation requirements together. Secretary Weeks concurred with the Lassiter group and forwarded its report to the Joint Board along with a potentially explosive recommendation. He followed the line the Lassiter Board had suggested by urging that Congress should consider future appropriations for Army and Navy aviation jointly, with the Army getting the larger share. The Navy's leadership wanted no part of Weeks's suggestion, probably because they saw it as a direct threat to the retention of their own aviation. As a result, the Lassiter Board report remained within the Executive Branch awaiting further action by Weeks.[22]

No price tag was affixed to the Lassiter Board recommendations, although Weeks later thought the full program would make the total cost of Army aviation as much as 496 million dollars over the ten-year span. The magnitude of that figure could be gauged by the War Department's offer to the Air Service of 13 million dollars in direct appropriations for the fiscal year 1923, while Patrick estimated that he needed 26 million. Congress finally appropriated only 12.7 million. As one General Staff officer accurately foretold about the Lassiter Board proposals, the "progress and growth of the Air Service is bound to be more or less surrounded with conservatism on the part of the appropriating power of the Government."

To add to the difficulties which Patrick and the Air Service men could anticipate, they suddenly found themselves in a new Administration. President Warren G. Harding's premature death brought Calvin Coolidge of Massachusetts into the White House. The new President replaced a weak-willed man who allowed too many executive branch figures to do as they pleased. Coolidge, on the other hand, was a disciplinarian who tightly ran the executive branch. His commitment to rigid economy in government offered little room for any improvement in aviation. Coolidge's attitude and the difficulties encountered by the Lassiter program were deadly blows at

Mitchell's hopes of seeing an air force in being before he retired. Before he could act, however, a personal matter occupied his attention.[23]

Divorced from his first wife in 1922, Mitchell married Elizabeth Trumbull, a Michigan socialite, in October of 1923. After the wedding, he and his bride began a honeymoon trip through the Pacific. This trip was at the same time an inspection by Mitchell of the American security position in that area. Once again, Patrick probably had acted to keep his stormy subordinate out of Washington, when the failure of the Lassiter Board recommendations signaled another round in the struggle for a fuller recognition of aviation in the American military establishment.[24]

III

Mitchell's original itinerary through the Pacific from December, 1923, to July, 1924, included visits to the Hawaiian and Philippine Islands, India, China, Manchuria, Korea, and Japan. The War Department, however, ordered him not to visit Japan in an official status, believing that such a visit might further damage already strained relations between that country and the United States. Once again, feeling was running high over American immigration restrictions against Asiatics. However, Mitchell briefly visited Japan as a tourist in June, 1924. Before that, he had spent the last of 1923 in Hawaii; three weeks in the Philippines, a few days in Java and Singapore in January; most of February and March in India; April and May in Siam, China, and Manchuria, ending with a day or two during June in Japan. He returned to Washington on July 22, 1924.[25]

Mitchell's basic conclusion in the 325-page report which he wrote after his trip was the same as that after his tour of duty in the Far East in 1909–11. Mitchell thought a war between the United States and Japan was inevitable. He believed Japan was now the dominant nation in Asia and ready to do battle against the United States over grievances shared by all Asiatics. America's basic strength was so great that the Japanese could hope to defeat the United States by using only the most advanced methods possible. For Mitchell, these methods centered about aviation. Other American military men shared Mitchell's belief in a future war with Japan. For example, a Marine officer, Major Henry C. Ellis, died mysteriously during a 1923 visit to the Japanese-controlled Palau Islands. Ellis was the harbinger of Marine strategists who recognized that a conflict in the Pacific might revolve around the control of island bases. This idea further spurred on the Marine Corps to develop its doctrines and techniques of amphibious warfare.[26]

Mitchell also saw the islands of the Pacific as crucial objectives, but primarily because of their value as aviation bases. He looked at the entire Pacific area as a gigantic isosceles triangle with its apex in the Bering Straits, its eastern side running through Canada and the United States, and the base line across the Pacific from the Panama Canal through the Philippines. Mitchell believed that in the event of war the best way for the United States to strike at Japan was through a northern route along the eastern side of the triangle and across its apex, from Alaska and the Aleutian Islands across the Bering Straits to Kamchatka, then down to the Kuriles and Japan itself. He thought an aerial offensive from air bases along this northern route against Japan's congested and highly inflammable cities might prove decisive. In presenting his ideas on a northern advance against Japan, Mitchell said nothing about the notoriously poor flying weather in the Aleutians west of Alaska, although he subsequently recommended meteorological studies of this area.[27]

Mitchell believed any advance against Japan along a more southerly route, such as from Honolulu west, had to contend with flank attacks from Japan's mandated islands. Furthermore, Mitchell thought that operations across such an expanse would prove too costly and difficult to supply. If such an advance took place, Mitchell was certain that its success depended upon forces dominated by aviation. Finally, a southerly advance could not rely upon the American bases in the Philippines and Guam. Both were extremely vulnerable to Japanese occupation. The short distance between the Philippines and Formosa made it a simple enough matter for the Japanese to advance over the small islands between Formosa and Luzon until they were close enough for air attacks against the major military installations around Manila as well as the city itself. Once such air bases as Clark Field were destroyed, Corregidor, the island fortress guarding the entrance to Manila Bay, was open to reduction from the air. Guam's position was also difficult since it was so close to the Japanese-controlled Marianas and Bonin Islands and so far from Hawaii.[28]

Hawaii, he believed, could be defended, provided the United States reorganized its military policy. After a detailed inspection of Hawaii, Mitchell laid down certain principles to guide its defense. He thought it indispensable to consider the territory as a total defense establishment under a single commander. He also urged a substantial increase in the number of aircraft stationed there so as to meet the possible strategy the Japanese might follow in a campaign against Hawaii. He argued that after establishing a base at Midway Island, the Japanese could use submarines and an aircraft carrier to transport sufficient aircraft to the island of Niihau, the most westerly island in the Hawaiian chain. Once based there, they could launch a series of attacks against the main military installations and Honolulu itself, which he thought would break the resistance of the defenders.

In outlining this possible Japanese plan of attack, Mitchell was following his basic view that no naval force could operate close enough to any area dominated by land-based aircraft. Hence, land bases were crucial for any meaningful operation. An enormous strengthening of the Air Service in the Hawaiian Islands was Mitchell's chief hope for protection of the area. Ground defenses such as antiaircraft guns were useless, especially since massed air attacks as well as the use of two new kinds of bombs could be expected. These innovations were the gliding bomb and the aerial torpedo. The former, also based on an idea Mitchell had encountered in Italy, could be dropped from 15,000 feet against a target twelve miles away.[29]

Major General Charles Summerall, the Army Commander in Hawaii, immediately challenged Mitchell's ideas when they appeared in a preliminary report. Patrick tended to play down Mitchell's paper by describing it to Summerall as a "theoretical treatise on the employment of air power in the Pacific, which, in all probability, undoubtedly will be of extreme value some ten or fifteen years hence." Patrick recognized that Mitchell had a proven sense of aviation's potential but "the fact remains that aviation was not developed as yet to the point of employment outlined in General Mitchell's report."

Nevertheless, the leaders of the 1925 Joint Army and Navy maneuvers in Hawaii attempted to seek a solution to the problem of an enemy seizing a base in the Hawaiian area for the purpose of mounting an air attack against the main island of Oahu. Obvious deficiencies in the Hawaiian Department's aviation strength and Army and Navy aerial cooperation were noted and reported to Washington. Yet this practical evidence of Mitchell's theories seemingly had no impact on Washington.[30]

IV

During the period from February, 1922, to July, 1924, Mitchell had privately made a series of contributions to the Air Service's tactical and doctrinal growth. The most substantial of these were his bombardment manual and his study of aviation's place in Pacific strategy. The influence of the manual would not be felt for another decade, when technology had begun to catch up with his theories. His ideas on the problems of Pacific defense, publicly voiced countless times in succeeding years, had no effect upon an American military policy buried beneath the dominant isolationist attitudes of the twenties and the domestic crises of the thirties. After his Pacific trip, Mitchell made one more effort to speak out on problems such as this while he was still in uniform. The result was his second publicity campaign and the subsequent end of his military career.

CHAPTER SIX

The Second Campaign: "Treasonable Administration of the National Defense"

In the fall of 1924, Mitchell reentered the Washington political arena for the fight that ended his military career. The conditions for this contest differed markedly from those of his first campaign in 1921. At that time, Mitchell had had an issue which matched the public mood. He also had been able to dramatize the defensive capabilities of the inexpensive airplane against seaborne invasion with the tangible although unscientific bombing tests. Moreover, his chief antagonists were the leaders of the Navy who ineptly allowed him to spotlight the deficiencies of their own aviation program. The result was a net gain for aviation in national military policy and at least a draw for Mitchell.

Three years later, however, only the public mood remained unchanged. The American people seemed dedicated more than ever to "normalcy," isolationism, and economy in government. Mitchell now completely lacked an issue that matched the public mood or that even had the substance to hold public attention whenever he attracted it. His chief antagonist, whatever else historians have said about President Calvin Coolidge, was no man to tolerate internal opposition to his conduct of the executive branch of the government. But Mitchell, instead of recognizing this new state of affairs and modifying what he was doing, kept swinging harder until he himself dramatized his case with his own court-martial. Thanks largely to Mitchell's crusade, a broad aeronautical policy that led to significant progress resulted, but his very methods were to cost him his military career.

I

The pioneering phase of Mitchell's military aviation career ended on the same note on which it had begun—the gulf between his ideas and the actual performance of aviation. On September 6, 1924, Mitchell witnessed in Washington the completion of the first "Round the World" flight. Three Army Air Service crews had circled the globe by following the same island-hopping route across the northern Atlantic and Pacific which Mitchell had projected four years before. The duration of this trip—some six months—highlighted the vast technical problems still facing aviation. A month after the flight, Mitchell visited the Air Service Engineering Division in Dayton, Ohio, for the last time. He briefed its personnel on the remarkable conclusions he had drawn from his Pacific inspection trip. Once again, he could only play the pacesetter, posing through his ideas tremendous challenges for the technician.[1]

Shortly before Mitchell traveled to Dayton, the Lassiter Board proposals had floundered upon another refusal, this time by the new Secretary of the Navy, Curtis Wilbur, to accept the War Department plan for a single appropriation for all military aviation. Secretary of War Weeks tried to change Wilbur's mind, but he could not overcome the prevalent fear in the Navy that a single appropriation would ultimately cost that service control over naval aviation. As Mitchell later admitted, the Lassiter program was the closest thing to an "aeronautical policy" that the Army Air Service had known so far. How to bring that program to reality was the question besetting

Patrick and Mitchell. Patrick, whose own aeronautical ideas were becoming more like those of Mitchell, judiciously decided to keep working within normal channels. Mitchell, however, acted upon his deep conviction that "changes in military systems are brought about only through the pressure of public opinion or disaster in war." He therefore took it upon himself to launch a one-man effort to force a new policy into being. The ultimate effect was that Mitchell ran a bone-crushing interference for Patrick, the Army Air Service, and all others who wanted to move American aviation out of its doldrums.[2]

Mitchell quickly began his second publicity campaign in October after Wilbur's decision on the appropriation issue. Thanks to his appointment as the personal reprsentative of President Coolidge to the National Aeronautics Convention, Mitchell had an extraordinary starting point. He delivered a "daring" speech to the delegates in which he divulged his long-hidden ideas on the concept of strategic bombardment. His public discussion of the subject made him the first American to present such views openly. Previously, only visiting British airmen had ever done so before the American public. For example, in 1918, Sir Sefton Brancker had annoyed Secretary Newton Baker because of his advocacy in the American press of strategic bombardment. Some nine months before Mitchell spoke, General P. R. C. Groves had reintroduced the subject in an article for the *Atlantic Monthly*.

Underlying Mitchell's speech was the assumption that, in the future, the United States would fight another major power overseas. "If we are required to act against an enemy on land," he asserted, "we may so smash up his means of production, supply and transportation by bombardment, that there is a great probability that the armies will never come into contact on the field of battle." To such a claim, he added his usual prediction that surface navies were doomed. The aerial threat, Mitchell thought, would force all naval operations under the sea. Indeed, he continued, the United States could never transport another army to Europe as it had in the recent war, if she faced an enemy that possessed a powerful air force.[3]

Mitchell was careful in the speech to lavish praise on Coolidge, who had appeared highly interested in aviation during the welcoming ceremonies for the returning "Round the World" flyers. Coolidge's interest may have inspired an unmilitary maneuver by

Mitchell to keep his campaign going. Secretary Weeks, it will be remembered, had previously directed Mitchell to submit all his articles for War Department clearance. Mitchell circumvented this by going directly to Coolidge for permission to write a new, and undoubtedly explosive, series of articles. Coolidge sidestepped the issue and, apparently without seeing the articles, consented to their publication on the condition that Mitchell's superiors in the War Department gave their consent. Mitchell interpreted the evasive ruling to mean that he needed only the approval of Patrick, who later denied that he had ever given Mitchell his permission. In any case, Mitchell boldly sent five articles to the *Saturday Evening Post*.[4]

Appearing between December, 1924, and the following March, the articles were in the familiar vein of much of Mitchell's earlier writing. Collectively, the articles were a broadside at all who disagreed with him. The editors of the *Post* added a generous sprinkling of the most sensational pictures available of the bombing tests. On the other hand, when the articles were read closely, they afforded some penetrating insights into the problems presented by military aviation as it moved from infancy into adolescence.

The opening article, for example, contained the fullest exposition of the potential of strategic bombardment yet unfolded before the American people. Mitchell began by asserting that the time-honored method of winning wars by the defeat of the enemy army in the field had lost its significance in the face of a strategic revolution. Aviation promised quick victory by insuring the destruction of an enemy's war-making potential. Now, no one could "cut a limb out of a tree or pick a stone from a hill" and make it his primary weapon. Mighty industrial centers were the key to waging war and, at the same time, targets vulnerable to air attack. Wars carried on through the air, Mitchell asserted, promised to make war briefer, more humane, and less expensive because industries once destroyed could not be replaced in the course of "modern wars." Indeed, Mitchell went so far as to say that such a war might enable "a special class" like "the armored knights in the Middle Ages" to do all the actual fighting. Only enough of a nation's population "to man the machines that are most potent in defense" might be needed.

Despite his suggestions of a complete future military revolution, Mitchell thought that armies were in a period of arrested development and navies were in a period of rapid decline and change. Soldiers and sailors, he asserted, were dependent for inspiration on the Cannaes and Trafalgars of the past and were "psychologically unfit" either to appreciate the meaning, or to direct the growth, of aviation. He carefully pointed out, however, that the resolution of any war ultimately took place on the ground. Furthermore, the strategic bombardment idea varied in its applicability to each nation's geographic position, implying a corresponding variation in the value of sea and ground forces. Thus, "an island country must completely dominate the air" to invade an adjoining continent. If a continental enemy controlled the air, that enemy "can cut off all the insular country's supplies that come across the sea; they can bomb its ports and its interior cities and with their air forces alone, bring the war to a close." If two adjacent nations were to go to war, their armies might come into contact only "if the air forces did not act quickly enough."

Nevertheless, Mitchell pointed out, air action by either belligerent could lay waste its enemy's entire country. There was a strong possibility that control of the air by one side would mean victory over the other. In a third case, that of a self-sustaining country which was "out of ordinary aircraft range," like the United States, an aerial standoff was conceivable. The United States could only act defensively from its home bases. To defeat any major enemy, it would have to send its air forces abroad via the step-by-step island routes connecting North America and Asia or Europe. "Comparatively small numbers of troops" could hold each island base as long as sufficient air forces were available to stop any seaborne or air attacks.

Although Mitchell did not say so, any enemy wishing to attack the United States obviously would have to reverse this procedure. He also never stated directly that America herself should use strategic bombardment. Later, when challenged in a congressional hearing as to whether he thought his country should do so, Mitchell sidestepped the question. He seemed to content himself with saying that strategic bombardment was a new facet of warfare which each nation had to take into consideration. Just how quickly the world should take this new concept of warfare into account, Mitchell did not say. He certainly left the impression in his *Saturday Evening Post* series that the idea of strategic bombardment was of immediate consequence relative to a nation's geographic position. In succeeding articles, however, he made certain statements which exposed aviation's present limitations. For example, three of the bombers used in the battleship test of July, 1921, he claimed, broke a long-distance flight record for aircraft of this type in traveling from Texas to Virginia. To use existing aircraft against targets far out to sea, Mitchell declared, was "to take a chance." [5]

The remaining *Post* articles also had their merits, but Mitchell's prime objective was controversy. As each piece appeared, he hit harder. By January, he was accusing the Navy of letting water into the *Ostfriesland* to equalize her list "so that she would not roll over" after being attacked with only light bombs. Loose charges in the press were bad enough, but Mitchell went even farther. He carried his sensationalism into congressional hearings and broadened his attack to include the War Department.[6]

Two more investigations were then in progress. In the spring of 1924, the House had appointed a special committee to study alleged monopolistic practices in the aviation industry. The inquiry, under its chairman, Representative Julian Lampert, expanded into a lengthy investigation of all aviation. Another set of hearings followed the introduction of a bill for a unified aviation service by Representative John F. Curry of California in December, 1924. Mitchell had every chance to present his views before both hearings, but he misused his opportunities. After all, the War Department had shown a new awareness of aviation through its Lassiter program. The Navy now had its own organized aviation effort under Admiral Moffett. To charge both departments, as Mitchell did, with blocking the progress of aviation was far less valid than similar charges would have been three or four years before. He never mentioned those decisive factors, aptly summed up by a *New York Times* feature writer as "peace and penury," which had caused the pitiful condition of aviation.[7]

When Secretary of War Weeks called him to account for his attacks on the War and Navy Departments, Mitchell even then would not let up. He challenged the integrity of the Navy's leadership by saying to Weeks: "In my opinion, the Navy actually tried to prevent our sinking the *Ostfriesland.*" He was in trouble when he charged before the Lampert Committee that witnesses for other viewpoints were "in some cases" responsible for "possibly a falsification of evidence, with the evident intent to confuse Congress." What was more, he said that officers who could have spoken in his behalf would not do so because they feared retaliation by their superiors. When queried on these points by Weeks, Mitchell could only show that there had been inaccuracies or differences of opinion, but no falsehoods. Similarly, he could not produce any evidence of the intimidation of witnesses, although there undoubtedly were officers who shared his objectives but did not come forward.[8]

In provoking this controversy, Mitchell could not always control the course it took. In the heat of the moment, he may have made statements to the Lampert Committee that severely damaged his credibility, even though, at a later and cooler time, he could have corrected them for the final record of the hearings. For example, both the Lampert Committee and Weeks understood him to claim on February 6, 1925, that the United States only had "nineteen airplanes fit for war." Three days later, a *New York Times* reporter indirectly quoted him in a bizarre story about the vulnerability of New York to air attack as stating that the United States had "nineteen airplanes fit for war." In the published record of the hearings, Mitchell said "nineteen pursuit airplanes." Also, Weeks, a *New York Times* reporter, and, possibly the Lampert Committee, all understood Mitchell to say that the War Department had ignored his study of Pacific strategy.

According to the final record of the hearings, Mitchell had qualified his charge about the Pacific report with the admission that the study had "only just been submitted, I will say in all justice." Weeks granted no such qualification by Mitchell in protesting to the Lampert Committee that the Pacific report had not reached him until after Mitchell had testified. Moreover, Senator James Wadsworth, at that time the Chairman of the Senate Military Affairs Committee, recalled many years later that Weeks used Mitchell's allegedly false claim about the Pacific report to discredit him in the Senate. According to Wadsworth, Weeks appeared before an executive session of the Senate committee to stress that Mitchell's statement was additional evidence why his patience was almost at an end with Mitchell. He (Weeks) wanted the support of the Senate in any action he proposed to take. One possible course would be open to Weeks in March, 1925, when Mitchell's appointment as Assistant

Chief of the Air Service with its accompanying rank of Brigadier General came up for renewal.[9]

Mitchell's many other opponents were also trying to shoot him down. The Navy men, especially Admiral Moffett, were most active in this regard. Their most plausible charge was that Mitchell sought complete power over American aviation for himself. Also, Wadsworth has recalled that he mistrusted Mitchell ever since the latter allegedly had confided political ambitions to him. There can be little doubt that Mitchell wanted to carve out a major role for aviation in the American defense establishment before he retired, or that he often toyed with the idea of following his father and grandfather into politics. It would be wrong to imply therefrom that Mitchell had been motivated solely by his own ambition in these aviation controversies. Men dominated by personal ambition are not likely to act as Mitchell did. They are much more careful to protect their position at any given moment. Mitchell knew that by continuing to speak out, he had ruined any possibility of even holding on to his position as Assistant Chief of the Air Service and his rank of a general officer. News dispatches from Washington had reported Mitchell's downfall as a likelihood on February 5, but on February 7 he was still pounding away.

Later that month, Mitchell wrote to Patrick and the Lampert Committee that Weeks had threatened him with the loss of his position, if he did not stop making "statements." It would seem more reasonable to believe, therefore, that Mitchell had allowed his vision of the potential of aviation to cost him his perspective. In Trenchard's memorable comment, Mitchell tried "to convert his opponents by killing them first." Once battling to realize his vision, he could not draw back. What was more, he became the slave of the publicity which he had used to attract attention. To hold his place in the headlines, he made progressively more reckless statements which he could never specifically prove.[10]

His own conduct assured the dire outcome. Weeks told Coolidge in early March that he could not recommend the reappointment of Mitchell. Weeks outlined his position in a letter that was, in large measure, a defense of the Administration. Contrary to what Mitchell had said, the War Department had created an aeronautical policy through the Lassiter program. "We have not reached the goal," Weeks wrote with too much innocence, "because of the lack of sufficient appropriations to do so." In fact, he argued, Mitchell and Patrick shared the responsibility with the Administration for defects in the Air Service. They had permitted their men to fly the very planes that they had thought dangerous. Weeks took the greatest offense at the charges hurled by Mitchell that the air arm was not ready for war and that the airmen had been muzzled. The Secretary possibly was unfair in blaming Mitchell for protesting that the country had only nineteen aircraft fit for war, and he certainly glided too quickly over the quality differences in the 1,592 airplanes in the inventory. Weeks was on better ground in pointing to the directives that officers were free to express their own opinions in congressional testimony, as long as they specified that they were voicing their personal views. Mitchell's conduct goaded Weeks into saying that his "whole course had been so lawless, so contrary to the building up of an efficient organization, so lacking in reasonable teamwork, so indicative of a personal desire for publicity at the expense of everyone with whom he associated that his actions render him unfit for a high administrative post such as he now occupies. . . ." [11]

At the end of March, Mitchell reverted to his permanent grade of colonel and received a transfer to Fort Sam Houston, San Antonio, Texas, as the Aviation Officer for the Eighth Corps Area. He kept up a brave front before his friends saying: "We have had a very interesting time here and have planted seeds that are growing well." Undoubtedly denied any chance of future advancement, Mitchell told another friend that he would stay in the Army for "another year or two." Then, perhaps he would go into politics. If he were to remain in the Army for two more years, Mitchell would be eligible for retirement. His "defiant" speech at a farewell luncheon given him by his Washington friends, however, dimmed any prospect that he would remain quietly in Texas long enough to earn retirement. [12]

During the tumult Mitchell had created, Patrick made his own move. In December, he submitted to the War Department a plan calling for the immediate implementation of the Lassiter program and the creation of an Army Air Corps, similar to the Marine Corps in its semi-independent status within the Navy. As Patrick saw it, the Air Corps would represent one step along the road to ultimate independence. Behind his request was a theory much like that Mitchell had voiced publicly: "We should gather our air forces together under one air commander and strike at the strategic points of our enemy—cripple him even before the ground forces can come into contact. Air power is coordinate with land and sea power and the air commander should sit in councils of war on an equal footing with the commanders of the land and sea forces." Patrick's proposal also included a plan for remedial action on the many minor complaints irritating airmen since the war. The General Staff, however, merely studied his letter, but sent no reply down the chain of command to Patrick until Mitchell forced that response.[13]

Another witness to the uproar over Mitchell then made his moves. Calvin Coolidge apparently realized that an aviation policy was badly needed and possibly also recognized that he had not heard the last of Mitchell. Four days after Coolidge concurred with Weeks's recommendation not to reappoint Mitchell, he alerted Dwight Morrow, his lifelong friend, and a partner in the J. P. Morgan firm. He told Morrow that he planned to have his own aviation inquiry and wanted Morrow to lead it. "Suppose you think this over," Coolidge said, "and think who you would wish to join with you in case I call on you." Both "civilians and military men" might be included.

Morrow was no expert on aviation and, indeed, had expressed his ignorance of the subject when he had been invited to testify before the Lampert Committee on the financial aspects of the aviation industry. After Coolidge wrote him, however, Morrow began studying the aviation problems covered by the Lampert group. Morrow and his inquiry would wait in the wings for the right moment. Just when that would be was up to Mitchell. As Coolidge said to a friend some eight years later about matters such as these, "public administrators would get along better if they would restrain the impulse to butt in or to be dragged into trouble. They should remain silent until an issue is reduced to its lowest terms, until it boils down into something like a moral issue." [14]

Meanwhile, Coolidge addressed himself to some of the minor but still irritating problems of the airmen. Was West Point familiarizing its cadets with the problems of aviation, he wanted to know? To what degree was the desire of the airmen for a different uniform a matter of the vanity that his New England conscience abhorred? Of course, the solution of these problems offered the twin advantages of relaxing tensions and not increasing the federal budget very much. Coolidge seemed primarily interested—perhaps obsessed would be the better word—with keeping costs down. He could not "view with equanimity an increase in the War Department budget for 1927," he told Dwight Davis, the Assistant Secretary of War, in May. Rather, he had hoped that "further study of our national defense might point the way to additional reduction without weakening our defense but rather perfecting it." When Davis later warned of adverse publicity if the War Department cut its requests, Coolidge angrily drafted a comment: "Your department should make its budget estimates such that there would be no criticism if they were public." The actual reply was softened but his point remained. Coolidge would do only what could be done without undue cost. His attitude was a decided factor in the frustration which helped to push Mitchell into his irrevocable act.[15]

II

From his post in San Antonio, Mitchell kept his campaign going with occasional outbursts. In August, he published another book, *Winged Defense*. By his own admission, this book was a "hastily compiled collection" of previously published articles and statements before Congress. This made *Winged Defense* a repetitious and disorganized piece of work. The publisher, supposedly without Mitchell's knowledge, had made the book a polemic by illustrating the inside covers with a collection of newspaper cartoons lampooning Mitchell's opponents, Weeks in particular. Since Weeks was then seriously ill, the use of the cartoons was poorly timed, even in the opinion of those close to Mitchell. He tried to reduce the damage the cartoons caused by saying in a press interview: "I imagine that they made Secretary Weeks laugh as much as anybody else." [16]

While War Department officials were closely scrutinizing *Winged Defense,* two naval aviation disasters occurred in close succession in early September. The PN-9 aircraft disappeared in the Pacific during the first flight between the West Coast and Hawaii. Then the dirigible *Shenandoah* crashed after running into severe weather over Ohio. Both disasters offered ample grounds for controversy. Professional flyers could justifiably question the advisability of trying a flight along a route where the prevailing westerly winds, even thirty years after the PN-9 flight, seriously limited the range of most aircraft. Also open to question was whether or not a dirigible should have gone into that part of the United States during the thunderstorm season.

Mitchell's concern, however, was more than that of the professional airman. He called in several reporters in San Antonio and handed them his biggest bombshell. His prepared remarks, contained in a nine-page mimeographed statement, had all the earmarks of a calculated attempt to force a showdown with his superiors. The crux of his first statement on September 5 was a blistering indictment of "the incompetency, criminal negligence, and almost treasonable administration of the National Defense by the Navy and War Departments." Further signs of premeditated conduct appeared in his prompt negotiations with David Lawrence of the Bell Syndicate and the editors of *Liberty* magazine for articles on the crisis he fully expected. Four days later, he called back the reporters to announce: "Let every American know that we are going to better our National Defense, that we are on the warpath and that we are going to stay there until these conditions are remedied." [17]

Mitchell had given Coolidge the "moral issue" he wanted. Some two weeks elapsed while the War Department went through the customary investigation before announcing the decision to court-martial Mitchell. Only later was it announced that Coolidge himself had preferred the charges. Within six days after Mitchell made his first statement, the service secretaries "asked" Coolidge to undertake a new investigation of aviation. Coolidge agreed, and Dwight Morrow came onstage. Apparently Coolidge was not going to allow the court-martial to be the focus of attention that Mitchell would have tried to make it. He directed Morrow and his group to produce a report by the end of November. That report presumably would take the sting out of the almost certain punitive action resulting from the court-martial.[18]

For this aviation inquiry, Coolidge and Morrow had selected a group of men certain to inspire the confidence of the American people, and in particular, the Congress, the military, and the aviation community. Serving with Morrow were Judge Arthur C. Denison of the Sixth Circuit Court of Appeals (as vice-chairman); Doctor William F. Durand of Stanford University, and also the National Advisory Committee for Aeronautics (as secretary); Senator Hiram Bingham of the Military Affairs Committee; Representative James S. Parker, of the Interstate and Foreign Commerce Committee; retired General James G. Harbord, Pershing's Chief of Staff for much of the war and now president of the Radio Corporation of America; retired Admiral Frank F. Fletcher, an early supporter of naval aviation; and Howard E. Coffin, longtime figure in the aviation industry. Assisting the Morrow group was an unofficial committee of technical advisers that included Doctor Edward Warner of the Massachusetts Institute of Technology, Major Leslie MacDill of the Army Air Service, and Commanders Jerome Hunsaker and H. C. Richardson of the Naval Air Service.[19]

The Morrow Board held its first public session on September 21, five weeks before the court-martial began. As chairman, Dwight Morrow set the tone for an investigation that was to be a model of propriety. The group first heard testimony for a month from ninety-nine witnesses, and then retired for private deliberations and the writing of its report. Essentially, the Morrow Board worked the same vein of material that the long line of investigations since 1913 had mined. Accordingly, only one relatively new solution to the problem of organizing military aeronautics appeared. On the first day of the hearings, Patrick outlined to the committee his nine-month-old request for an Air Corps. He suggested a similar status for naval aviation and the erection of a new division in the Department of Commerce to supervise all civil aviation.[20]

In less than a week after Patrick had testified, the War Department directed him to submit in five days a complete plan for the implementation of the Corps idea. In addition, the heads of each Army branch whose functions supported the Air Service had the same brief period in which to make their comments on the impact of an Air Corps upon their own activity. Each objected, mainly on the grounds that an Air Corps on the model of the Marine Corps would upset coordination between the various branches of the Army.[21]

The renewed interest in an Air Corps indicated the direction of the Morrow Board's recommendations. Despite this development, Mitchell's position as he expressed it to that group on September 29 and 30 admitted of far less compromise. He firmly adhered to the idea of a reorganization of the defense structure, providing an Air Force coordinated with the Army and Navy under a Department of National Defense. As to various modifications in his position, a naval witness later dismissed them as "bait." Mitchell now made no mention of civil aviation and stipulated that the Army and Navy should control their own aircraft. He proposed a total force of 2,600 first-line planes (one-half in reserve and not including training ships) and 25,000 officers and men. Some 600 aircraft would be allotted to the Army and Navy. Two thirds of the remainder would be pursuit planes, the rest bombardment and attack ships.

This new "Air Force," in Mitchell's view, would have complete charge of the aerial dimension of warfare, including the defense of the United States and its possessions for some 200 miles out to sea or to the perimeter of the airplane's range. The naval aviation would be based on the carriers and catapults of the fleet, while the Navy would possess only a few coastal training stations. To support these proposals, Mitchell could muster very little solid evidence. Speaking with due regard for the limitations imposed by isolationist sentiment, he could talk only about possible attacks against the United States. The best he could do was to argue that England, acting in concert with other powers, had the capability to attack the United States. Admitting that this was highly inconceivable, Mitchell was at an immediate disadvantage in trying to make his theories tangible.[22]

Dwight Morrow skillfully handled Mitchell's appearance before the group. In fact, Mitchell may have fallen into a trap, because he spent his first four hours in the witness chair reading entire chapters of *Winged Defense* into the record. Morrow merely let Mitchell read until he was exhausted. Then Morrow adjourned the hearings until the next day. By not challenging what Mitchell was saying, Morrow and his group had stopped him from striking any more sparks.

General Henry H. Arnold recalled years later that he and the few other partisans of Mitchell in the audience wanted to yell: "Come on Billy! Put down that damned book! Answer their questions and step down, that'll show them!" The next morning, Mitchell returned to the witness chair for an hour and a half of questions by the committee. Unquestionably, however, his opportunity to make an effective appearance had disappeared the day before.[23]

The Morrow Board had ended its public hearings by the time the court-martial got under way on October 28. Mitchell's judges included: Major Generals Charles P. Summerall, Robert L. Howze, Fred W. Sladen, Douglas MacArthur, William S. Graves, and Benjamin A. Poore; Brigadier Generals Albert L. Bowley, Edward K. King, Frank R. McCoy, Edwin B. Winans, George Le R. Irwin, and Ewing E. Booth.

As was his privilege, Mitchell promptly challenged Generals Summerall and Bowley on grounds of "prejudice and bias." Summerall, as the commander in Hawaii, allegedly had taken personal exception to Mitchell's views on the conduct of the defense of that post, and Bowley supposedly had made an anti-Mitchell speech. Mitchell then used his peremptory challenge against General Sladen to remove him also from the court.

One can only surmise the reaction of the remaining judges to the unpleasant prospect of trying a comrade-in-arms of twenty-eight years' standing. General Leonard Wood, then retired from the Army and serving as Governor-General of the Philippines, probably was expressing some of that sentiment when he wrote General McCoy: "I do not envy you your detail on the court. Mitchell has been a gallant, hard-fighting officer but with always a turn for overstating things." Both Wood and General Pershing, also out of Washington on a special mission to Chile, privately conceded that there were grave defects in the air arm which had to be remedied. The course Mitchell had taken, however, was no solution. Pershing thought that his conduct was symptomatic of a kind of "Bolshevik bug" at work in the Army which had to be stamped out.[24]

The court-martial began and essentially remained a test of whether or not Mitchell was guilty of conduct prejudicial to "good order and military discipline [and] . . . conduct of a nature to bring discredit upon the military service." His civilian defense counsel, Representative Frank Reid of Illinois, at first pleaded that Mitchell had been only exercising his right of free speech. In his opening statement, Reid made the outlandish claim that "anyone who read Colonel Mitchell's statement would recognize that it is a free play of words that really means nothing."

When the court, and presumably the Administration, permitted Mitchell to introduce all the evidence he could muster in support of his views, their decision obscured the legal point at issue. The result was to lengthen the trial by many weeks and turn it into a legally irrelevant discussion of Mitchell's ideas. General McCoy humorously reported to Mrs. Leonard Wood that he had planned only on a short stay with friends in Washington but that the trial dragged on until he had to find new accommodations. He thought Mitchell and Reid were handling the publicity aspects of the "case so well that to the public the War Department is on trial instead of the festive Bill."

As always, the press was most responsive to Mitchell's efforts to focus attention on the trial. Although they helped to build the case into one of the sensations of the decade, most of the same newspapers took the editorial stand that Mitchell had gone too far. There were signs of some public support for Mitchell. The American Legion, then in its annual convention at Omaha, was supposedly considering electing Mitchell as their next commander. Whether the Legionnaires understood the implications of Mitchell's views must be open to speculation. Many of those former "doughboys" may have been more interested in seeing Mitchell challenge the "brass hats" they had learned to dislike during the war.

Nothing more solid developed to help Mitchell. First he, and then the War and Navy Departments, displayed their familiar points of view in the courtroom and for the press. The disciplinary issue won out as it had to, and, on December 17, the court decreed that Mitchell was "Guilty." [25]

Mitchell still regarded his trial as a "necessary cog in the wheel of progress, a requisite step in the modernization and rehabilitation of the national defense of the country." As with much of what Mitchell said, there was a great amount of truth in his remarks. His final campaign and court-martial, whatever else might be said about them, had forced the Administration to consider aviation as it had not done before. [26]

Two weeks before the court-martial verdict, the Morrow Board submitted a report that ably dealt with the solid elements in Mitchell's position. Backed by the prestige of its members, the report at once reassured the nation and also mobilized the support of Coolidge and the Congress for a series of legislative actions that added up to America's first broad aeronautical policy. The premises of the report were both implicit and explicit. Implicitly, the Board recognized America's commitment to isolationism. Explicitly, the Board declared that: America was safe from aerial attack; there should be a clear separation between military and commercial development; agencies other than the federal government should bear much of the responsibility for development; and finally, that its recommendations had been made with an "eye to the budget."

The report then proceeded to specify that: the Army and Navy should retain control over their own aviation; a Department of National Defense was unnecessary, unwieldy, and too costly; a separate service could not be justified on the grounds of the possibility of independent, decisive action on its part, "certainly not in a country situated as ours." In a sleight of hand, Patrick got his Air Corps, but in name only, and then "to avoid confusion of nomenclature between the name of the Air Service and certain phases of its duties." The semi-independent arm he wanted obviously would be too expensive; so would the realization of the Lassiter program. As Weeks told Morrow, "the broad, sound economic policy of the Government prohibited such expenditures at this time."

In place of the Lassiter program, the Morrow Board advocated a less ambitious five-year buildup of the two service air arms. This meant that the aviation industry would have the basis for orderly development sufficient to attract private capital. The personnel situation was to be alleviated by offering a greater number of temporary promotions to the flying officers who were selected for command positions. To give aviation more of a voice in the government and some special direction, assistant secretaries for aviation should be added to the War, Navy, and Commerce Departments. The appointment to the latter organization would support another major proposal, that the Department of Commerce would foster and regulate civil and commercial aviation.[27]

Thanks in part to the continuing interest of Dwight Morrow and General Harbord in realizing this program, significant legislation resulted in early 1926. Morrow testified before Congress and occasionally served as an intermediary between the Administration and the proponents of the various bills. The Navy and Army Air Corps Acts, along with the authorization of the five-year development program, became law in early 1926. The work of the Morrow Board also gave new momentum to the Air Commerce Act of 1926. That legislation, coupled with the Kelly Act of February, 1925, which had already put the airmail in the hands of private operators, gave American commercial aviation the impetus it needed.[28]

In this overall progress there was another reminder of the role

Mitchell had played. Admiral William Moffett, the head of the Bureau of Aeronautics, advanced the cause of naval aviation under the cover of Mitchell's campaign. After the hopeful start implied by the opening of the Bureau of Aeronautics and the authorizations of the carriers *Lexington* and *Saratoga*, Moffett had been having difficulties with the top-ranking battleship advocates in the Navy. Only after Mitchell had forced the Administration to act, did Moffett find his superiors receptive to further improvements in naval aviation. He dusted off the plans he had been holding for this favorable moment and saw them translated into the Naval Air Corps Act and the five-year expansion plan. In moving the legislation to final passage, Moffett and his ally, Representative Carl Vinson of the Naval Affairs Committee, frequently turned to Dwight Morrow for advice and his intercession with the Administration.[29]

Before the legislative package for aviation materialized, however, Mitchell found his military career at an end. The court-martial sentence—five years' suspension from active duty without pay or allowances—probably had no precedent in American military justice. Upon reviewing the sentence, Coolidge made it five years' suspension at half pay.

The effect the Administration desired was obvious: to force Mitchell out of the Army but not by dismissing him and making him a martyr. He saw no recourse but to resign and did so on February 1, 1926. By his action, of course, Mitchell was denied any claim to retirement benefits. He described his resignation to friends, such as Trenchard, as the result of his disgust with conditions in the service and his decision to become a civilian in order to campaign more effectively for his views. The court-martial was not mentioned then or ever again in any of his future writings. In treating the subject as a closed issue, he may well have provided the final evidence that he had deliberately brought on the whole matter.[30]

The punishment meted out to Mitchell outraged his handful of allies in the House. No senators came to his defense, possibly because of his alleged difficulties in early 1925 with Wadsworth's Military Affairs Committee about his report on Pacific strategy. Three days before the announcement of the court-martial verdict, the Lampert Committee had submitted a final report endorsing Mitchell's proposals. At issue here may well have been the fear of

its membership that his outspokenness to them had led to his downfall at the hands of the Executive. The Lampert report, however,
could only have been a gesture; the Morrow report too neatly met
the needs of the moment.

After the announcement of the court-martial verdict, several
congressmen made some zany moves. Fiorello La Guardia of New
York, in many ways the congressional counterpart of Mitchell,
introduced a bill to curtail the authority of courts-martial so that
Mitchell could not receive any punishment exceeding thirty days.
Thomas L. Blanton of Texas was even wilder. He called for the
abolition of all peacetime courts-martial and the restoration of
Mitchell to his rank of brigadier general. Also, Blanton contradic-
torily sought the five-year suspensions from active duty of two of
Mitchell's highest-ranking enemies in the Army, Generals Hugh A.
Drum and Dennis G. Nolan, as well as two of his judges, Generals
Graves and King. This legislative byplay, however, quickly died.[31]

III

After resigning from the Army, Mitchell made plans for the
future. He stayed close to Washington by establishing himself as a
gentleman farmer and horse breeder in Virginia. For a time, he
seriously considered running for the Senate in his native state of
Wisconsin. His friend, Joseph E. Davies, tested the sentiment there,
but evidently made an unfavorable report. Mitchell made no further
mention of the project and, instead, concentrated on becoming an
author and lecturer on aviation.[32]

Mitchell started poorly. His national lecture tour in February and
March enjoyed an uneven success. Possibly one reason could be
found in a report from his publisher on the sales of *Winged Defense*.
Only 4,500 copies had been sold between August, 1925, and
January, 1926, the time span when the sensationalism of the court-
martial was at a real peak. The defects of the book undoubtedly
were important, but its poor sale still suggested that Mitchell had
not reached many informed Americans. Indeed, the praise showered
upon Dwight Morrow in personal letters to him from leaders in all
walks of life tended to confirm this suspicion about the effectiveness
of Mitchell's message. On the other hand, Mitchell kept a gigantic
audience in the popular press. The Bell Syndicate and *Liberty*

initially handled his output. In time, the Hearst papers took up his case and absorbed most of his writing in the daily press. A wide range of popular magazines, especially the aviation journals, shared his magazine output with *Liberty*.[33]

The year 1926, therefore, marked a watershed in Mitchell's life. Cut off from his commanding place in military aviation, he could speak only from the sidelines. After the court-martial, General Harbord recognized with relief something that Mitchell apparently had not begun to realize: the court-martial would cloud his reputation and hurt his influence with the press as well as the American people. The men on active duty in the War Department hoped that, if they ignored him, Mitchell's influence would die altogether. The ideas with which he was associated, however, were too important for this to happen. He still had a role to play and before an audience of millions.[34]

CHAPTER SEVEN

"It Is Difficult
to Get Them Stirred Up"

$\mathbf{M}$ITCHELL used his costly freedom to little immediate effect during the next eight years. His effect on the American scene depended on his work as an uninhibited publicist whose massive output reached millions. The theme of his writing was an increasingly stark concept of strategic bombardment, coupled with one of the earliest warnings to the American people that German militarism and Japanese imperialism could threaten the postwar settlements. In advocating strategic bombardment, he spoke for a number of Army Air Corps flyers who themselves dared not engage in any public controversy. Those flyers continued the work Mitchell had begun of laying the groundwork for the Army Air Forces of World War II. Their efforts, as well as those of Mitchell, took place under circumstances which worsened with the onset of the depression.

I

The day after the War Department accepted his resignation trom the Army, Mitchell set the tone for much of his writing for the next decade with an article in *Liberty* magazine. Previously, he had been careful to act only as a reporter of the strategic bombardment concept. Now freed of any official restraint, he began an outspoken campaign for its incorporation into national military policy. Traditional military doctrine, he noted, had prescribed the destruction of the enemy's army as the key to victory. The World War had shown the futility of depending upon this method without incurring unacceptable losses. Mitchell argued that aviation now made it feasible to jump over the enemy army and strike at the enemy's "will to resist." This objective "is accomplished only by reaching the enemy nation's vital centers, paralyzing them and making it impossible for the population to carry on in war or to live in peace."

Actually, Mitchell's "vital centers" theme was not new. Douhet had voiced similar ideas in 1917 and had even used the same phrase "vital centers" as the key to his arguments. Mitchell was familiar with the main points of Douhet's book, *Il Domino dell 'Aria,* that continued the "vital centers" argument. Mitchell, however, also had a very clear and fresh statement of the same view available to him in English. Some four months before his article appeared, Captain Basil Liddell Hart, the British publicist, brought out his book entitled *Paris: Or the Future of War.* The work, simultaneously published in New York and London, was one result of Liddell Hart's search for a method whereby his country could avoid a repetition of her disastrous losses in the recent war. His view of strategic bombardment was not original in his own country, as witnessed by the role of Jan Smuts and others in the founding of the RAF in 1917–18. What *was* of interest in *Paris: Or the Future of War* was the neatness of his argument and the forthrightness of his attack upon the waste of life in the war.[1]

Whatever his inspiration, Mitchell vigorously solicited assignments from newspaper and magazine editors to write articles built around the "vital centers" rationale. Within the next two years, some ten million subscribers read his ideas in the Hearst publications, *Liberty,* the *Saturday Evening Post, Colliers,* and *Outlook.* Even

Atlantic Monthly and the *Annals of the American Academy of Political and Social Science* accepted one article apiece. The most popular of these publications illustrated his material with drawings that enhanced the radicalism of his views. For example, the editors of *Colliers* set his article against a background picture of the New York skyline collapsing under an air attack.[2]

Although he was now out of the Army, Mitchell was the public exponent of what Patrick and others dared talk about only privately. Patrick had used Liddell Hart's book as the basis for a private lecture to the Army War College in November, 1925. Any public statement by him would conflict with the official doctrine laid down as recently as January, 1926. The Army-imposed Training Regulation 440-15 reaffirmed the subordinate role of the air arm to the needs of the ground forces. "The fundamental doctrine" permitted the airmen was "to aid the ground forces to gain decisive success." Some recognition was given to a striking force, the General Headquarters Air Force, which could aid the Army by "carrying out special missions at a great distance from the ground forces." The GHQ Air Force concept was not far removed from the British GHQ Brigade or the French *aviation de combat* of the war.

Whenever they had a chance, the more daring of the airmen demonstrated that the ideas Mitchell advocated were still at work in the air arm. In April of 1926, some unidentified officers at the Air Service Tactical School published an unofficial textbook called *Employment of Combined Air Force,* which treated the air arm as equal to the Army and Navy. The unknown authors insisted, as Mitchell himself had, that the object of war was to break the will of the enemy to resist. The destruction of his armed forces was only one of several means toward that end. Air attack offered the method most quickly available at the beginning of a conflict. This method, the manual asserted, "is a means of imposing a nation's will by terrorizing the whole population of a belligerent country while conserving life and property to the greatest extent." To the airmen, strategic bombardment was "a means of imposing will with the least possible loss by heavily striking vital points rather than by gradually wearing down an enemy to exhaustion." [3]

The state of technology and of public opinion, of course, still made discussions of strategic bombardment largely academic. Mitchell, however, kept trying to change public opinion. He tried to do so not only through his articles, but also by creating an organization known as the United States Air Force Association. As the name implied, he and his associates, Edward J. Rickenbacker, the famous wartime pilot, and J. Edward Cassidy, a publicist and consulting engineer, sought the creation of a service whose mission would be strategic bombardment. The new organization had no immediate success, but in that summer of 1926 Mitchell almost gained control of the only solid American aviation organization. He looked like a highly probable choice to be the president of the National Aeronautics Association—until a behind-the-scenes battle finally forced Mitchell to withdraw. Also in 1926, he unsuccessfully tried to win the endorsement of the American Legion at its annual convention in St. Louis. He remained confident that he would eventually secure the backing of the Legion, but obviously he had gone as far as he could with publicity alone. More tangible evidence of the potential of aviation was needed.[4] It was Charles A. Lindbergh who provided that evidence in May of 1927. His historic nonstop flight from New York to Paris captured the attention of the American people in a way in which previous exploits, almost unanimously military in their direction and accomplishment, had not done. The Morrow Board had given aviation the benefit of an overall national policy, but that policy depended on increased private initiative. The Lindbergh flight spurred public interest in aviation investments and in commercial flying. At long last, American aviation seemed to be on its way.[5]

This new public enthusiasm renewed Mitchell's role as a publicist. One enterprising publisher wanted Mitchell to write a story debunking the significance of the Lindbergh flight, but, instead, he sold the Hearst organization a piece that praised the accomplishment and predicted the advent of regular transatlantic flying. The Hearst editors, ever alert to any new public interest, accepted Mitchell's proposal to write a series on European aviation progress. This assignment dovetailed with his plans to try again for the endorsement of the American Legion at its convention in Paris that September.[6]

II.

Mitchell's trip to Europe was a short one, for in a bare five weeks he visited France, Italy, Germany, Russia, and England. Still, his reputation in the international aviation community had stayed potent enough to give him prompt entrée to whatever he wanted to see. He was able to write a series for Hearst that conveyed the acceptability of the "vital centers" theme among European airmen and his uncertainty that peace on the Continent would endure.[7]

At the end of August, 1927, Mitchell inspected French aeronautics before he set out on a hurried trip so as to return to Paris in time for the opening of the American Legion Convention on September 23. In France, he detected signs of official concern prompted by English coolness and evidence of a possible German military resurgence. After visiting Germany, Mitchell had to admit that the 100,000-man force permitted her by the Versailles Treaty was only "a core for future development." This prospect, he realized, more than justified the French insistence on maintaining the largest standing army in the world. In fact, he found out that the French airmen were also believers in strategic bombardment, but were handicapped like their American counterparts by army control. He praised the French procedure of concentrating experimentation, communications, weather services, and airport maintenance under one agency. To him, this was at least progress in the direction of unification. Nevertheless, Italian aviation was in his view even more progressive.[8]

The ideas of Douhet obviously were having some impact on his country. Douhet had expanded his 1921 version of *Il Domino dell 'Aria* to take an even more radical stand. He now argued that Italy should deny its army and navy any aviation and should not spend any more money on air defense. Every resource, he contended, should go into the aerial offensive, carried on by all-purpose "battleplanes" which would accomplish the normally separate functions of the fighter and bomber. Marshal Italo Balbo, the head of the air force, had not gone as far as Douhet had wanted. Balbo still allocated aircraft to defensive work, but in case of war, Mitchell said, Balbo intended to devote the main effort against the "vital centers of the enemy." In describing maneuvers for this strategic force to Mitchell, Balbo asked the American to observe that "these operations involved neither soldiers on the ground nor ships on the sea." Mitchell concluded: "With a good military air force, Italy can very easily control communications by vessels or ships across the Mediterranean Sea because they have the central position and a narrow stretch of ocean to guard by which all the shipping has to pass." Likewise, aerial operations gave Italy her "best means of defense against attacks coming from the North, down from the Alps."

The Fascist movement also caught Mitchell's attention. He came away from an interview with Benito Mussolini believing that the dictator "stands as one of the greatest constructive powers for good government that exists in the world today." [9]

Proceeding to Berlin, Mitchell put the American Military Attaché, Colonel A. L. Conger, in a difficult position. Although the War Department's policy was to ignore Mitchell, Conger still felt obliged to assist the many German airmen and industrialists who wanted to meet him. In spite of his court-martial, Conger explained to Washington, Mitchell was regarded "as a leading American authority on aviation." For his part, Mitchell confessed himself thoroughly impressed by German aeronautics. His contacts with the officials of the national airline, *Lufthansa,* and with Dr. Hugo Eckener of the Zeppelin corporation, as well as his inspection of Tempelhof Airport in Berlin, convinced him that "in aerial passenger and express traffic," the Germans "unquestionably lead the world." This commercial capability, plus her vast chemical industry, gave Germany the "most formidable potential in Europe" for bombardment with toxic gases. "Germany, now, in case of a great war, might be able to bring about one of the greatest military surprises in history with her air force." Mitchell quickly declared his belief "in the average German's desire for peace," but warned: "With each new generation, however, the lessons learned in the one just past are forgotten." [10]

Mitchell then flew to Moscow for a two-day visit via the Russo-German airline operating between the two cities. The close relationship between German and Russian aviation, not only in commercial operation but also through the activity of firms like Junkers which were manufacturing aircraft in Russia, did not escape Mitchell's notice. He was most enthusiastic about the *Ossoviakim,* the Russian national organization encouraging interest in aviation. To Mitchell, this organization was one way of developing interest at the grass roots. By marked contrast, his own United States Air Force Association had enjoyed little tangible success. He remarked that, militarily,

Russian aviation would have a great importance through immediate, massive strikes against an invader before the latter penetrated very far into that vast country. Mitchell's judgment did not hold with the long-standing Russian tradition of dependence on its army, but Mitchell may have gained the idea from Russian airmen. Like all the European aviators Mitchell met, the Russians had ideas similar to his, but they had also managed to make as little progress.[11]

The most meaningful exception to this rule was the RAF. After a bitter postwar fight, Trenchard had managed to preserve the independence of the air arm. When Mitchell visited England, after again failing to win Legion endorsement in Paris, he acknowledged his admiration for Trenchard in a way that he had never praised any other airman: "Air Marshal Trenchard commanding the British Air Force, is not only one of the greatest airmen that the world has produced, but also is one of the outstanding figures of the war, whether on land, sea, or air." Mitchell found RAF thinkers still preoccupied about sudden aerial attack against their nation. The aerial torpedo, a radio-controlled airplane packed with explosive, Mitchell noted, would be an excellent weapon for an enemy to use against the crowded island. He was certain that England could never survive any future war without control of the air. Mitchell also approvingly pointed to signs of widespread interest in flying, gained through aviation clubs.

In addition, the controversial American thought highly of the Imperial Defense College and its unified education of Britain's high-ranking leaders in joint air, sea, and ground operations. This military activity, he recognized, had to be measured against the faith of too many Englishmen in disarmament conferences. Mitchell was sure that "conferences of this kind will fail, when the people sent to them are professionally paid Army and Navy officers who do not want to work themselves out of a job." This kind of sour comment flowed from Mitchell's presumption that the officers of the armies and navies of the world were obstacles to progress and airmen were not. How much this approach only stimulated the pacifistic thinking Mitchell deplored was open to speculation.[12]

Just the same, the Hearst articles marked Mitchell as one of the few Americans who understood that the "Great War" had not solved the basic problems affecting world peace. Also, he was the first American to warn his countrymen so resoundingly of the impact aviation would have on future conflicts or to show them how wide-spread was the idea of strategic bombardment among the airmen of the Western world.

Actually, his European trip had inspired no major departures in Mitchell's ideas, but had only served to confirm his position. He continued to publish articles on strategic bombing, with a repetitiveness that must have exhausted any faithful reader. At the same time, he also tried to broaden the range of his activities by writing three book-length manuscripts.[13]

The first was an expansion of his World War memoirs, "From Start to Finish of Our Greatest War," which *Liberty* magazine partially serialized during the spring of 1928. His draft was in the genre of the two leading British critics of the conduct of the war, Liddell Hart and Major General J. F. C. Fuller. Like those men, Mitchell attacked the wastage of life in the war because of the employment of outmoded strategy and tactics. His criticism of the frequent inability of the average American professional officer to adapt to the fighting in France and his comments on American deficiencies in aerial leadership undoubtedly reflected his own thoughts when the events took place. His introduction of a well-developed strategic bombardment thesis, however, was hindsight, and turned the diary into a memoir, for he failed to distinguish between the "vital centers" idea of 1925 and what were only its first indications in 1917–18. His indulgence in personalities, notably his recital of his difficulties with General Foulois, served little purpose either. Nevertheless, the manuscript was a contribution to the limited literature on the American conduct of the war. To the degree that his comments were valid, his work was a reminder to his pacifistic-minded countrymen that they should reexamine American military policy.[14]

Another manuscript, "The Opening of Alaska," never enjoyed publication in his lifetime. He described therein his exciting experiences as a member of the Signal Corps team struggling to develop the Alaskan communication system in 1901–3. His purpose was more than storytelling, because he wanted to drive home to his readers the importance of Alaska in the air age. That territory now surpassed the Panama Canal in importance, he said, as the Canal drew its significance from "the old theory" of sea power. In the air age, "aircraft"—and here he probably meant dirigibles—could now fly round trip "with one charge of fuel to New York or to Peking, China" from Alaska. The radius of action for a dirigible operating from an Alaskan air base covered "all the vital centers of the United States and of Eastern Asia, including Japan." He defined "vital centers" in a manner somewhat reminiscent of his 1922–23 manual on bombardment: "cities, power plants, water supplies, and agricultural areas." However, he had treated cities in the manual only as targets of reprisal. To those who with very good reason might object to Alaska as a base of operations because of its weather conditions, Mitchell replied in what should have been futuristic terms. "With modern means of transportation in the air, we are no longer afraid of cold, fog, rain, and snow, or any other climatic condition." New techniques could permit the operation of aircraft in minimal flying conditions and, once airborne, aircraft could move "into the so-called stratosphere where conditions are always the same and navigate with precision and assurance." The value of Alaskan bases was nowhere more apparent to Mitchell than in Pacific strategy which he described in a third manuscript, "America, Air Power and the Pacific." [15]

He repeated the position he had taken in his report following his study of the Pacific in 1923–24, but then went on to reemphasize the role of Alaska as the key to American strategy in the inevitable war with Japan. The threat of strategic bombardment of her highly vulnerable cities from Alaskan bases was the best way, Mitchell claimed, to protect America's isolated outpost in the Philippines. Also, he repeated his warning that Japan might launch a combined air and submarine attack against Hawaii. Mitchell seemingly never tried to publish this manuscript. The same ideas, however, appeared in articles for the popular press at the end of the twenties.[16]

In February, 1928, Mitchell tried another venture—the creation of the United States Aeronautical University in Washington, D.C. Announcing plans for a $10,000,000 fund drive, he described the school as a center for aeronautical research and the training of civilian flying personnel. Closely allied with his ideas about the school were Mitchell's plans to step up the activities of his Air Force Association, the objective of which was avowedly "political." The entire project died for lack of support.[17]

More successful was Mitchell's third effort to win the backing of the American Legion for legislation providing for a Department of

Defense directing the activities of the Army, Navy, and an Air Force. The October, 1928, meeting at San Antonio, Texas, unanimously supported the proposal at a moment when Mitchell was hoping for a favorable change in the Administration. He evidently thought that the Democratic party would bring about changes from above, which the American people had not demanded from below. The trouble so far had been, he told the British publicist Admiral Murray Sueter, that "our people . . . consider themselves so far removed from possible aggression that it is difficult to get them stirred up on any improvement in our national defense." [18]

Mitchell devoted part of the fall of 1928 to campaigning for a change from the top through the election of Governor Alfred E. Smith of New York. His work for Smith began after a breakfast meeting at the governor's home in Albany. Mitchell was active primarily in his native state of Wisconsin, where he belabored Coolidge for throttling efficiency in government, especially in the aeronautical program. In his usual "no holds barred" fashion, Mitchell told one friend that a vote for Smith was "but a question of coming out for straight-going honest Americanism." [19]

Herbert Hoover's resounding defeat of Smith made clear, among other things, the satisfaction of the American people with the existing order, and left Mitchell, once again, on the losing side. There was no assurance, of course, that even a Smith victory would have helped Mitchell. The year 1928 was also the year of the Kellogg-Briand Pact, an expression of the naïve but still very real belief of the American and other people of the world that peace could be had by wishing for it. Overlooked in the general rejoicing about the attainment of another step to permanent peace were the interpretations the signatories had managed to affix to their actions, without any real understanding by a naïve public. Those interpretations enabled the signatories to refuse to arbitrate any dispute affecting their national interest. [20]

IV

The future of Mitchell's post-court-martial career as a publicist must have seemed particularly bleak in 1929. President Herbert Hoover brought no new military plans into office. Indeed, after lunching with his wartime Chief of Staff, Colonel Thomas Milling, Mitchell wrote that: "The Army men are down in the mouth at the way Hoover was cutting down." The start of the depression in the fall of 1929 guaranteed further cuts in the appropriations required to implement the Morrow recommendations. The economic turndown hit Mitchell very hard financially. Earlier in the year, there had been some approaches made to him about his coming into commercial aviation. The collapse of the stock market ended such talk; aviation stocks shrank in value from one billion dollars to some fifty million four years later. Writing became a crucially important source of income, but he found declining interest in his output.[21]

Some American publishers had become wary of publishing material by Mitchell. One publisher believed that his methods hurt the sales possibilities of his war diary. His injection of propaganda and his attacks on the Army and Navy, in that publisher's view, detracted from what could have been an important account. Mitchell flatly refused to change the book, saying that he wanted it to be read "a hundred years hence." He was confident that his views would prevail; a department of defense would be a reality "sooner than many realized." To Mitchell, "a work of this kind has no value whatever if it appeals to the ordinary, popular conception of things as propagandized by bureaucratic systems."

The *Saturday Evening Post* then rejected his Alaskan manuscript but, in this case, simply said that there was a glut of such material already in its files. Mitchell reacted to these rebuffs by swinging harder than ever and trying some new topics. He wrote pieces on flying, on hunting, and then a book for laymen on aeronautics. Such unlikely magazines as *Woman's Home Companion* now bought this new material and by 1930 he had secured a publisher for his aeronautical textbook, *Skyways*.[22]

The book was an excellent survey of all phases of aviation in its theoretical and technical aspects. The work showed his intimate acquaintance with the field, but especially how he had stayed in touch with developments. His Army Air Corps friends had seen to it that he had information; so had his old engineering adviser Alfred Verville and men in the industry such as Frank Russell of Curtiss Wright. A continuing source was John F. Victory of the National Advisory Committee for Aeronautics, whose organization was the federal clearinghouse for information on technical developments and the sponsor, through its basic research activities, of many breakthroughs in the aeronautical sciences.[23]

Skyways was full of remarkable predictions about the future of aeronautics. In dedicating it to the children of his second marriage, Lucy and William, Jr., Mitchell predicted that they "in their lifetime will see aeronautics become the greatest and principal means of national defense and rapid transportation all over the world and possibly beyond our world into interstellar space." At one point in the text, he noted the fantastic potential of aircraft once scientists could "transmit energy without resistance" and "apply the rocket principle of propulsion." Possibly "substances such as radium which are constantly active within themselves" possess the key to obtaining "a constant source of power." [24]

In this same book, he also demonstrated a range of aeronautical interests that extended beyond strategic bombardment. He praised the virtues of the attack plane which could be used against nations whose chief reliance was on armies rather than air forces, or on irregular or partisan troops. Mitchell wrote at length on the defensive arrangements England had employed in the world war against bombardment. He improved on these by describing a warning and defensive system of the future—a network of dirigibles, aircraft carriers, and submarines deployed as much as a thousand miles from the "vital centers" of the nation. Their purpose was both to warn of an approaching air raid and to launch pursuit aircraft to engage an oncoming enemy. He emphasized that these defensive arrangements could never be a guarantee against air attack. The concealment possible in the vastness of the sky, and the altitudes bombers could attain, made the task of air defense systems very difficult. Implicit here was a belief held by many airmen at the beginning of the 1930's that bomber development would outstrip fighter advances. Also, Mitchell argued that the offensive would continue its advantage when future bombers avoided flying directly over a target and its defenses, but instead launched aerial torpedoes from one hundred miles away or gliding bombs from distances of some fifteen miles.[25]

In the larger context of world affairs, Mitchell was equally perceptive. In one of his few radio addresses, he warned in 1929 that while the Allied victory had given the United States many advantages in the world, "History shows that each time a nation becomes rich, it attempts to work out a system to retain these gains without asserting itself." That system might include "schemes to limit armaments and all sorts of self-deluding agreements."

World events, in fact, soon began to lend some substance to what Mitchell said. The Japanese occupation of Manchuria in 1931, in spite of protests from its wartime allies, marked a decisive turn in international politics. Few Americans were able to escape the delusions encouraged by the previous decade. Most prominent among these men was Henry Stimson, the Secretary of State in the Hoover Administration, and formerly the Secretary of War under Taft, during the abortive effort to create an army that could back up foreign policy. When Stimson repeatedly wanted to impose economic sanctions on the Japanese, Hoover would not support him, particularly because America was militarily powerless. From the sidelines, Mitchell saw that "the Japanese are just putting it over on an incompetent European world, and this includes ourselves."

In previous crises, Mitchell wrote that America "by dint of tremendous exertion and untold pouring out of lives and treasure" had been able to succeed in getting out of trouble. He was insistent that "conditions have changed so that our former practical isolation is now merely a myth." Since future wars could "come suddenly and possibly without warning," America must "strike at the enemy's heart with our own air force before he can hit us." To prepare for the next war, the United States should not only reorganize the military establishment, but also streamline the whole government. The proliferation of bureaus had robbed the federal government of its efficiency, he believed, and had added so heavily to the cost of government as to deepen the current depression.[26]

In July, 1931, Mitchell met Franklin D. Roosevelt. Here was the man, Mitchell declared, who could bring about a reorganization of the government. Mitchell proceeded to work actively in lining up the support of Virginia Democrats for the nomination of Roosevelt at the convention in 1932. Although he found common cause with Roosevelt in a broader issue, Mitchell faced many difficulties in winning his support for his views on aviation. Roosevelt, he should have remembered, had been the first government official to attack Mitchell's views publicly. During the controversy which had led to the court-martial in 1925, Roosevelt indicated to his son James his reluctance to accept the claims of aviation enthusiasts. More importantly, so great a domestic issue as the depression tended to make every other problem seem minor.[27]

This view of solving the depression first enjoyed widespread support. The Hearst organization, for example, told Mitchell to tone down his claims about an inevitable war with Japan. The average newspaper reader had enough to worry about in his struggles with the depression. Mitchell seemed to consent, saying, "I thought you wanted a good deal of fire" in the articles. The editors of *Liberty*, however, were not so sensitive and featured two pieces by Mitchell in January and June, 1932, "Are We Ready for War With Japan?" and "Will Japan Try to Conquer the United States?"

In the first article, Mitchell emphasized that a strategic bombardment campaign against Japanese cities would destroy her industrial backbone and knock her out of any war. To do this the United States had to create a bomber force with a range of 5,000 miles and a ceiling of 35,000 feet, which could be based at Midway Island and in Alaska. The contribution of the Navy should be a submarine campaign against the Japanese oil and tin supply lines to the Dutch East Indies.

Mitchell's second article appeared in the most sensational graphic arts setting thus far—on a bloody red background in the magazine. In it, he warned that Japan would try to conquer the United States. The conquest of Asia would give her the resources to do this. The only effective American response could be a modernized military establishment. He derided aircraft carriers as being largely "a delusion and a snare," and apparently ignored the fact that these ships offered the best early hope of using aircraft in the Pacific.[28]

To win the modernization of the armed services for whatever lay ahead, Mitchell threw himself into the successful Democratic campaign of 1932. His work for the new President encouraged the belief that Mitchell might have an active role in the new Administration. He certainly shared that belief, because he confidently told the victorious Roosevelt in December, 1932, that he was ready to discuss with him his plans for a reorganization of national defense. The stage, then, seemed to be set for an end to Mitchell's exile.[29]

V

These years after the court-martial must have been especially galling to an active person like Billy Mitchell. In the only way open to him, that of a publicist, he futilely tried to evoke a national demand for a change in military policy. Most Americans adhered, however, to their traditional policy of reacting only to definite crises. His efforts to point to the future with alarm antagonized some and bored most. The chief effect of Mitchell's work may well have been, in the long run, to begin the preparation of the millions of Americans who read his articles to accept both a potential relationship between foreign policy and air power, as well as a kind of warfare such as they had never known nor would have countenanced before.

CHAPTER EIGHT

"The End of a Long and Tortuous Road"

Mitchell plainly hoped that the "New Deal" of Franklin Roosevelt would include him among its beneficiaries. In so hoping, he was doubtless "playing a long shot." While Roosevelt may have owed something to Mitchell politically, he was nevertheless on record as being fundamentally opposed to what Mitchell represented. Time, however, was on Mitchell's side in that technical advances and the deteriorating world situation argued an eventual reassessment of aviation progress by the Administration. Although that reassessment came unexpectedly in two major investigations, Mitchell failed to benefit. His years of crusading had had their effect, because he seemed hopelessly committed to an uncompromising radicalism.

I

The year 1933 marked the last concerted effort by Mitchell and his followers to win a united air force. Mitchell auspiciously began that effort when fellow Democrats such as Joseph E. Davies and the leaders of the party in Wisconsin, Michigan, and possibly Virginia, supported his candidacy for the post of Assistant Secretary of War for Air in the new Administration. This new strength then seemed confirmed when he played a leading part in the inaugural arrangements. His prospects even caused many of his old associates in and out of the Army to rally around him. Mitchell, however, had his eye on bigger game than any "stopgap" position, as he described the Assistant Secretary post. He was determined to bring about a complete reorganization of national defense. On occasion, his preference for this total solution apparently wavered, but his temperament won out and finally prevented him from focusing on the more realistic goal.[1]

His "all or nothing" approach was apparent when he sought the help of his Hearst and *Liberty* editors in pressuring Roosevelt through new articles on strategic bombing. He claimed that this was the only way to move the President away from his attachment to the Navy and the *status quo*.

When Hearst and *Liberty* hesitated, Mitchell tried a new outlet. He formed an alliance with Earl Findley, the editor of *U. S. Air Services* magazine, and also retired Colonel Charles de F. Chandler, an old associate in the original Operations and Training Group of 1919. Together, the three men undertook the promulgation of the strategic bombing thesis for which Mitchell had been fighting for years, but wisely chose to give it an author generally unknown to Americans, Giulio Douhet. The references to Mitchell in *U. S. Air Services* as America's "outstanding leader in aeronautical thought" and as "our dishonored son" suggested that Douhet's name was but a fresh label for a familiar package. In January, Mitchell told one airman, Major Charles B. Oldfield, that he had written "a good deal from time to time" on the same things as Douhet. Mitchell even "had in mind a book which will deal with most of those things." He urged Oldfield to obtain a translation of an excerpt from Douhet's principal works published in 1932 by the magazine *Les Ailes* as *La Guerre de l'Air*.

Chandler published a summary of the French article in *U. S. Air Services* in May, 1933. He claimed that the assistant military attaché in Paris, Colonel Frank P. Lahm, had called his attention to the

Les Ailes piece. Several unnamed "friends in Washington," who probably included Mitchell, were already familiar with Douhet's approach and had urged Chandler to publish the French article. In surveying what Douhet had said, Chandler stressed concepts which Mitchell had already advocated, including his insistence on the strategy of hitting the vital centers of an enemy through the air at the beginning of a war. Also, those ideas of Douhet never fully accepted by Mitchell were in evidence, such as his view of the all-purpose combat aircraft, the "battleplane," and his emphasis on an unrestrained offensive in preference to any defensive measures. Indeed, the airman readers of the magazine showed their familiarity with those ideas and, possibly, their ready acceptance of them, by debating only the question of the merits of the battleplane versus the escort fighter. The most prominent participants were fighter pilots such as Captain Claire Chennault and bomber champions such as Lieutenant Kenneth N. Walker.

Chandler finally intervened with a reminder that Douhet's primary emphasis was not on the tactical question of the merits of the fighter versus the battleplane, but rather on the strategical question of a new approach to war. Chandler's "friends in Washington" found other uses for the French version of Douhet. Captain George C. Kenney, another Mitchell follower, had a translation made of *La Guerre de l'Air,* which he placed in the Air Corps library and sent to the Tactical School, then in Montgomery, Alabama. The Chief of the Air Corps, Major General Benjamin Foulois, also saw to it that summaries of the translation went to key congressmen.[2]

This activity had its greatest significance at the Tactical School, where faculty members like Walker and Major Harold L. George were openly advocating in their lectures a doctrine of strategic bombardment. These men had the touch of reality behind their remarks which Mitchell had heretofore lacked. After 1930, the Air Corps had a limited number of promising bombers in its inventory such as the B-9 and the B-10. The B-10 embodied major technical improvements in almost every aspect of its design. Its top speed was more than twice that of the MB-2 with which Mitchell had worked in the early twenties. The B-10 could operate at almost 200 mph at 21,000 feet, with a range of 500 miles and 2,000-pound bombload.

By 1934, a far better airplane was on the way. The Boeing Airplane Company produced plans for a four-engine airplane capable of 225 mph at 30,000 feet with a range of 2,200 miles and up to a 4,000-pound bombload. The prospect of the B-17 gave the airmen, and especially the Tactical School faculty, a tremendous boost which excited a considerable exchange of ideas between the faculty members like George and Walker and such men in the field as Major Carl Spaatz and Lieutenant Colonel Frank Andrews.[3]

Mitchell's role at this ripe moment certainly was not what he would have wished it to be. When he was on active duty, he had given the new theorists a starting point for their work with his bombardment manual. One of the Tactical School faculty, Laurence Kuter, then a lieutenant, later went so far as to say that the manual was the "basis for instruction at the Air Corps Tactical School since its inception." Undoubtedly, Mitchell's manual was most instructive to the new generation; the remarkable parallels between Mitchell's manual and the tactical aspects of subsequent American bomber operations suggested his influence. Mitchell and the theorists, however, seemed to have had little direct contact. He was a personal friend of Spaatz, Andrews, and George, who had been junior to him in the early days. These men were among those marked for the highest command positions in the next conflict. To a large degree, however, these officers—and particularly the younger group that included Kenny, Walker, and Kuter—took the rather primitive concepts Mitchell and others had advocated in the twenties and elaborated and systematized them.

Thus, the Tactical School men developed the daylight precision bombardment idea during the early thirties. They, in effect, sought to define what Mitchell and others called the "vital centers"; that is, they planned to discover and then to destroy by determined bombardment those elements in the economic structure of an enemy that were essential to his war-making power. The high altitude and daylight factors in their theory represented tactical considerations. They hoped to find security for their bomber formations at altitude and they knew that their bombardiers had to be able to see their targets in order to hit them. Likewise, they were well aware, as Mitchell had been in his most careful work, such as the bombardment manual, of the hostility of their countrymen to what Newton Baker had called the "promiscuous bombing" of civilian populations. The daylight precision bombardment theory, then, was their sophisticated response to the challenge presented by the long-awaited technical breakthroughs of the 1930's. Their confidence in the technical superiority of the bombers and their preoccupation with bringing their theory to fruition in the face of limited funds, however, carried them away in some respects.

Thus, the theorists scrapped Mitchell's insistence on a balanced air force in which control of the air by fighter aircraft was a fundamental prerequisite to effective bomber operations. Andrews and George kept Mitchell abreast of these new trends. For a while in 1933 and 1934, Mitchell corresponded with George. He sought to encourage the men at the Tactical School through George, and reminded him that they were working on the very same ideas he had fought for ten years before. If he had been successful in creating a strategic bomber force then, Mitchell remarked, "the Japanese would not be quite so cocky." [4]

While Mitchell never wrote the book on strategic bombardment that he had in mind, there were signs that he was aware of the refinements in what the new theorists were accomplishing. In one unpublished manuscript in 1933, he pointed to the economic importance of the northeastern United States and claimed that if an enemy destroyed "seven of the largest cities in this area, seventeen of the large power plants that distribute electricity, seven great reservoirs and aqueducts, such as the water supply of New York, and if the network of railroads which goes through Sandusky, Ohio, were neutralized by a tremendous accumulation of gas, this country would be in a desperate condition." His use of the numbers seven and seventeen was an arbitrary way of achieving effect, but his discussion of these precise targets indicated a new direction in his thinking. Furthermore, he made his own comments about the Douhetan belief in putting every aeronautical resource into the offensive. The offensive was superior in Mitchell's view, because of the variety of approaches a bomber force might make to a target, the difficulties any defense system might encounter in locating attacking aircraft in the vastness of the sky, and the defensive fire generated by a bomber formation. Mitchell, on the other hand, would not go as far as Douhet. He refused in the same manuscript to shut the door on pursuit development. Also, like other American airmen such as Spaatz had recognized years before, Mitchell realized that exclusive emphasis on the air offensive represented a politically impossible view. The American people would demand that a defensive effort be made.[5]

In spite of the definite signs that American military aviation was making progress, however slow, Mitchell seemed glued to an unyielding radicalism. In mid-1933, he had begun to charge privately that the aviation industry was responsible for retarding progress. Its control of the basic patents on aircraft, he said, enabled the industry to concentrate on profit-taking rather than spending money on the dramatic advances he thought were perfectly possible. His charges may have had a connection with the experiences of his friend Harold E. Hartney, a wartime "ace" and for a while one of his associates in the old Training and Operations Group. Hartney charged that stock market speculators had squeezed him out of the industry just before the 1929 crash. In February, 1933, he urgently asked Mitchell to visit him for a discussion of the industry. Although Mitchell at first declined to see Hartney, he soon began writing letters to congressmen and to other publicists, in which he attacked the manufacturers.[6]

The only segment of the industry with which he remained on good terms was the Goodyear Zeppelin Corporation. That company had been trying to start an airship program in the United States on the German model. A new disaster, however, struck another blow at public confidence in the dirigible. On April 3, 1933, the Navy airship *Akron* crashed. Among the victims was Admiral Moffett, Mitchell's old antagonist. The tragedy spurred public demands that the government abandon the airship altogether, as Great Britain had finally done the year before. Mitchell had never lost hope in the dirigible as a bombardment as well as a commercial vehicle. For years to come, only the dirigible could have the range to satisfy his ideas about bombing Japan from Hawaii, Midway, and Alaska. He unsuccessfully advised Goodyear officials to bring top German experts like Dr. Hugo Eckener to the United States as friendly witnesses before the congressional investigation of the *Akron* crash. The opposition to the dirigible on the grounds of its "maneuverability, vulnerability, and general construction" received additional momentum a year later with the crash of another Navy ship, the *Macon*. These disasters left the field open to Germany, which was pouring money into the construction of a new and also ill-fated dirigible, the *Hindenburg*.[7]

Mitchell's association with the luckless airship was but one symptom of how misfortunes began to snowball for him during the last half of 1933. The full effect of the depression hit him financially, as it did most Americans. After three years on the market, his book *Skyways* had not sold well enough for him to pay off his advance from the publisher. Moreover, Hearst and *Liberty* began to show signs of wearying of his material. Despite his repeated efforts to convince Roosevelt, the President remained noncommittal about Mitchell's national defense goals. In his letters to his friends, at least, Mitchell remained optimistic that the Administration would soon act in his behalf. Admittedly, as he told another Air Corps contact, Major Walter Weaver, the road to success was a "long and tortuous" one.[8]

When a new Army Board, headed by Major General Hugh Drum, declared in October that aviation still belonged under Army control, Mitchell and his friends came out fighting. The Drum Board had met to restudy the national defense picture but still would only prescribe the roles for aviation that the Lassiter Board had advanced in 1923. Aside from its ground support and reconnaissance functions, some aviation might be employed in a General Headquarters Air Force. At the discretion of the Commander in Chief, this aviation would either support ground operations, attack the communication lines of the enemy army, or destroy important enemy installations. When Weaver, Mitchell's friend in the office of the Chief of the Air Corps, promptly wrote so strong a reply for *United Air Services* that it could not appear under his signature, Earl Findley, the editor, asked Mitchell if he would introduce the article. He did so, and rewrote Weaver's conclusion "to give it more punch." The entire article was one more plea for a separate air force; it argued, as its title indicated, that "Air Power Has its Own Theatre of Operations." Weaver, and in effect, Mitchell, called attention to the views of Douhet as well as those of less well-known airmen in Great Britain and France.[9]

This kind of activity seemed to be doing nothing for Mitchell. He was helpless until Postmaster General James A. Farley announced in February, 1934, that he had found evidence of improprieties in the awarding of airmail contracts. His cancellation of those contracts threw the job of carrying the airmail to the pilots of the Air Corps. The result was a fiasco in which ten pilots died within three weeks. A streak of particularly bad weather was a major cause, but so were the inadequate airplanes the pilots had to fly. The failure provoked the kind of public outcry which Roosevelt understood. He promptly called Newton Baker back to public service as the chairman of a new investigation of the state of American aviation. Congress, in the Air Mail Act of 1934, began its own inquiry under Clark Howell, the editor of the Atlanta *Constitution*. Both the Baker Board and the Howell Commission were unexpected opportunities for Mitchell to try again.[10]

II

During 1934, Mitchell's fortunes went into a nose dive from which they never recovered. Throughout his career, he had been flexible enough to adapt himself to new conditions, however radical the views were that he had entertained. In 1917 and 1918, he had successfully distinguished between the dreams and actual capabilities of his European teachers when he conformed with the desire of Pershing for ground support. In 1919, after he had returned from France, he attempted for almost two years to work within the existing governmental framework in trying to sell his point of view. When he went to the public in 1921, he had successfully gauged its temper, his opposition, and the capabilities of the aircraft available for the battleship test. By 1925, however, he had gone so far that he would not, and perhaps could not, pull back to take advantage of the new conditions of 1933 and 1934.[11]

During the uproar over the airmail debacle, Mitchell took the side of the flyers but condemned their equipment. He publicly and forcefully exclaimed that profiteering had devoured most of the money the government had spent on aviation since the Air Corps Act of 1926. A congressional investigation turned up some evidence of very large profits by the industry on military contracts and a Washington, D.C., grand jury studied the matter. Nothing substantial resulted, but Mitchell kept up the attack. He found himself in a $200,000 libel suit when he charged in March, 1934, that neither of the two giants of the industry, Curtiss-Wright nor United Aircraft, had ever "been responsible for the introduction or adoption of any actual improvement in aircraft or aircraft engines." A battery of lawyers headed by Joseph E. Davies assured him that he had not violated the libel laws, but Mitchell found the case to be a tremendous financial drain. He was hard pressed enough to ask Arthur Brisbane, the Hearst columnist, whether he thought his organization would sponsor a fund-raising campaign in his defense. Ultimately, an aircraft industry representative suggested through Walter Weaver that the matter be dropped. As far as is known, Mitchell never replied to his suggestion, but the case did not go to trial.[12]

In April of 1934, the Baker Board convened. Its twelve-man civilian and military membership included four ground officer members and veterans of the Drum Board, Major Generals Hugh A. Drum, George S. Simonds, and John W. Gulick, and Brigadier General Charles E. Kilbourne. There were three airman members, General Foulois (now Chief of the Air Corps), former Colonel Edgar Gorrell, and former Lieutenant James Doolittle.

Not surprisingly, the Baker Board took the line established by every board created by some agency of the Executive Branch since the 1919 Dickman Board. Baker and his colleagues, with only Lieutenant James Doolittle dissenting, denied that Army aviation had any claim to independence. Such a status would violate the principles of unity of command, the Board declared. Its report supported the GHQ Air Force which the Lassiter Board had accepted in principle in 1923 and which the Drum Board had just reaffirmed. During the hearings, there had been an attempt by several airmen to win what Patrick had wanted in 1924 when he asked for an Army Air Corps. He had obtained only a new name, but nothing of the semi-autonomy enjoyed by the Marine Corps with its separate staff, budget, and promotion list. The Baker Board scored the unanimity with which the airmen seeking this Corps status had presented their case. In fact, the Board relegated them to the same limbo with those who stood by the separate service concept.[13]

Mitchell attacked the report of the Baker Board as "just another whitewash." His inability to enlist Hearst and *Liberty* in publishing his attacks on the Board's conclusions suggested a widespread public confidence that the New Deal was making progress with aviation. The prompt creation of the GHQ Air Force in December, 1934, and then the announcement by Roosevelt of support for a stepped-up procurement program, blunted Mitchell's attacks. His last hope was the Howell Commission which, like the Lampert Committee in

1924–25, was a congressional product and very ready to give him a full hearing. By way of preparation for the investigation, its chairman, Clark Howell, had even made a personal survey of European aeronautical organizations. This may have been the reason why the recommendations of the Baker report were in force before the Howell Board delivered its findings in March, 1935.

In his appearances before the Commission, Mitchell was suddenly alone in his insistence on a separate service. Airmen like Lieutenant Colonel Henry H. Arnold who had unhesitatingly supported Mitchell in earlier times, now declared themselves willing to go along with the GHQ proposal. These airmen had wearied of the struggle for complete independence and had come to see that progress to their ultimate goal must be slow. Some may have agreed with the charge made in an unsigned article in *United Air Services* the previous November that Mitchell's claims actually hurt their cause more than helped it. The Howell Commission evidently agreed with the new attitudes of the airmen on active duty and recommended that the GHQ Air Force be given a two year trial.[14]

In a rage, Mitchell called the Howell decision "a sellout" to the aircraft industry. Describing himself as "fed up" with Franklin Roosevelt, he claimed that he told James A. Farley in March, 1935, that he "was going to open up" on the President. By the end of the year, he publicly charged that the President's son Elliott was a lobbyist for the aircraft manufacturers. Elliott Roosevelt quickly denied Mitchell's allegation as "a vicious libel." [15]

The fact seemed to be that Mitchell had become so much the crusader that he did not know the meaning of compromise. He now had no public allies among the airmen on active duty. Nor could he hope any longer for political support after he had attacked Roosevelt's own family. To complete his estrangement, he also lost his sounding board in the popular press. The refusal of the Hearst papers to print his charges against the Baker Board ended their relationship. The editors of *Liberty* told him that he had worked the mine of aviation material to the point where there was nothing new to say. His warnings about the Japanese threat were so unpopular that *Liberty* refused to print any more material on the subject in the fear that his articles hurt their circulation.

Rather than prudently stand back from the controversy for a while, Mitchell irrevocably damaged his relationship with Hearst and *Liberty* by charging that they had succumbed to the influence of the aircraft industry in their decision to turn down his articles. This prompted Fulton Oursler, the editor of *Liberty,* to tell Mitchell rather bluntly that the public had lost interest in his material. Moreover, a rejection from *Field and Stream* magazine on one of his sporting articles in 1935 showed how much of a toll his difficulties were taking of him. The editor noted that the article lacked Mitchell's usual vigor and any new content.[16]

Mitchell may have recognized this because he tried to change his pace. He undertook a biography of General Adolphus Greely, the onetime Chief of the Signal Corps and his former patron. He also decided to begin writing his reminiscences "after the first of January" in 1936. That decision may have signaled his own sudden realization that the past had become more important than the future. He never started those memoirs, for in January he fell ill with influenza, complicated by heart trouble.

On the same day that he went to the hospital in New York from his Virginia farm, the House Military Affairs Committee considered a bill to restore him to the retired list as a colonel. While many of the members deemed themselves personal friends of Mitchell, they felt compelled to vote against the proposed legislation. Their action spotlighted the dilemma facing so many of his contemporaries. They recognized his real services to the nation, but could not honor him without seemingly approving his methods.

III

The unfavorable action of the Military Affairs Committee may have been the last disappointment Mitchell could endure. His illness took a turn for the worse and he died on February 17, 1936. His burial followed in Milwaukee, Wisconsin. Those who saw him in his last days reported that he remained adamant to the end.

Epilogue: An Interpretation

BILLY MITCHELL was dead less than five years when the American people began to discover awesome validity in what he had said. The audacious success of the Japanese at Pearl Harbor, followed a few days later by their sinking of the two British warships *Prince of Wales* and *Repulse* in the Gulf of Siam, confirmed some of his most famous predictions. Another prediction came true at the conclusion of the Pacific phase of the war when Japan finally collapsed before a combined American air and submarine offensive.

In Europe, the Nazi successes just before and during the early part of the war vividly dramatized much of what Mitchell had foreseen. Three years before Pearl Harbor, the threat of German air power had helped to paralyze the resolution of the democracies at Munich. Air power then spearheaded the German conquest of Poland, the Low Countries, and France. Fortunately for the future history of the world, German air power was oriented to the support of the army and could not accomplish the strategic mission of knocking England out of the war.

By 1941, World War II had become the conflict in which air power was indispensable. To describe air power as decisive would be to overstate its role. Often throughout the war, other weapons were also indispensable. Although Mitchell had too readily dismissed aircraft carriers after having unwittingly spurred their development, those vessels made victory possible in the Pacific. At Midway, carrier aircraft won a battle that must rank with Stalingrad as one of the two most important battles of the war. Moreover, Marine and Army infantrymen won the bases essential to the B-29 bomber operations which administered the knockout blow against Japan. Before the B-29 force could burn out most of the major cities of Japan, mine her harbors, and atomize Hiroshima and Nagasaki, submarines had mutilated her lifeline to her sources of raw material.

In the European theater, tanks and infantrymen shared the credit for the triumph with the airmen. Not to be overlooked either was the gigantic logistical effort that supported both the Army and the Army Air Forces across the submarine-infested waters of the Atlantic. The airmen were not able to put their strategic bombardment campaign into high gear before 1944. Not only had too few bombers arrived in Europe before then, but the airmen had first to reshape the hothouse theories formulated in the Air Corps Tactical School. Most notably over Schweinfurt, they learned the lesson that World War I operations had taught Mitchell and many other airmen. Control of the air was the fundamental prerequisite to any sophisticated bombing effort. American bombing missions, immensely aided by the rediscovery of the escort fighter, had to be air battles which finally wore out the German defensive fighter force. These battles paid the priceless dividend of landings unopposed from the air at Normandy and eventually led to the unimpeded destruction of the German transportation system and oil industry.

The nuclear climax at Hiroshima in 1945, however, pointed to the realization of the strategic bombardment thesis which Mitchell had first advocated to the American public twenty years before. At last, the key judgment of the Dickman Board of 1919 and the many subsequent investigating committees and boards could be satisfied. The mating of the ever improving bomber and the ever more powerful nuclear weapon gave aviation the decisive capability in war which it had previously lacked. The birth of the United States Air Force as an equal partner of the Army and Navy under a Department of National Defense could no longer be delayed. In 1947, eleven years after Mitchell had died, the Air Force came into being.

The leaders of the new Air Force had the freedom, so desperately sought by Mitchell, to pursue the doctrinal and technological objectives of their choice. The post–World War II international situation soon gave them resources on a scale far surpassing anything known in Mitchell's time. With freedom and resources, they could vigorously exploit technology until they had given deeper meaning to many of the ideas of Mitchell.

Technology, of course, knew no national boundaries, so Mitchell's forecast that a future war might begin with a sudden massive attack through the air against the United States became a realistic part of its defense planning. The birth of the intercontinental missile only added to the potential swiftness and effectiveness of a surprise attack.

Conversely, the cold war threat led the United States to create a Strategic Air Command. Perhaps the most popular label for the political-military justification for this command is "deterrence." Deterrence, the means to carry it out, and its acceptance by public opinion, owe something to Mitchell's ideas. He was the first to suggest that a parallel policy of deterrence might control Japanese adventures in the Far East. His bombardment manual and other writings which called for an elite group of airmen, intensively trained to deploy their aircraft anywhere in the world, describe the essence of the Strategic Air Command. It was Mitchell who took the lead in preparing American public opinion to accept the concept of strategic bombardment.

During the limited wars of Korea and Southeast Asia, the Air Force consistently employed an expanded version of the offensive principle that Mitchell borrowed from Trenchard in France. In those wars, the spiritual descendants of Mitchell sought the destruction of enemy aircraft, missiles, and supporting systems as relentlessly as they could within political restraints.

Similar restraints prohibited the full application in Southeast Asia of the strategic bombing idea with its emphasis on attacking the vital centers of the enemy. Not yet available is the entire story of the Linebacker II B-52 bombing strikes against North Vietnam in December 1972 which apparently were part of a diplomatic-military offensive to force a conclusion to the war that was acceptable to the United States. When the full story becomes available, perhaps the Linebacker operation will become one more example of the attacks on vital centers advocated by Mitchell.

Far clearer to the historian at this writing is the flexibility shown by aircraft, both manned and unmanned, in the Vietnam war. The striking successes of aircraft in ground support, reconnaissance, airlift, rescue, and air refueling have handsomely vindicated Mitchell's call for balanced development of air power. This same flexibility is the key to the assignment of the long-range bomber as a member of the strategic Triad along with land-based and sea-based missiles.

Whatever the future will bring, the airmen of this generation, both in the United States and abroad, can still find inspiration and instruction in the story of Mitchell and his work. He and his fellows, operating with fantastically limited means by the standards of today, laid the foundation for a conception of air power which has well served the United States and its allies.

This achievement should not imply that Mitchell was an original thinker; he borrowed his ideas largely from an international community of airmen which he joined during World War I. The airmen of today as well as their civilian superiors, however, might profitably remember that the conception of air power which Mitchell and his fellows brought to the United States from France in 1919 was an all-encompassing one. Those pioneers sought the exploitation of the full potential of the third or aerial dimension to warfare. Over the next fifty years, both Mitchell, his contemporaries, and afterward, their immediate successors, settled on strategic bombardment by manned aircraft as the primary method of their art.

To the airmen of today and their civilian superiors, the end of the era dominated by that method should mean only the conclusion of one more phase in the history of war. The exploitation and conquest of the aerial dimension to warfare must still remain fundamental objectives in the defense programs of the United States and of all its allies. Especially instructive to airmen everywhere as they pursue new approaches to these objectives must be the mistakes Mitchell made. He erred in believing that the realization of his vision would justify his tactics. Those tactics included his denial of the integrity of an often equally dedicated opposition, his substitution of promises for performance, and his failure to sustain the kind of day-to-day self-effacing effort that builds any institution, whether military or otherwise.

The dichotomy between Mitchell's vision and his tactics has blocked every effort of his family and friends to win his full vindication. On August 8, 1946, the United States Congress voted Mitchell a special medal in recognition of his "outstanding pioneer service and foresight in the field of American Military Aviation." His son, William Mitchell, Jr., received the medal from General Carl Spaatz, the first Chief of Staff of the Air Force, on March 27, 1948. The presence at the ceremony of many of the highest officials in the government demonstrated how the times had caught up with Mitchell's ideas.

Eight years later, however, William Mitchell, Jr., and the U. S. Air Force Association unsuccessfully petitioned the Secretary of the Air Force, James Douglas, to set aside the court-martial verdict. It seems safe to assume that the matter underwent a searching investigation by those most likely to be sympathetic to Mitchell. Just the same, the passage of time had not healed the split between his contributions and his methods.

Finally, Mitchell's story should have its interest for all Americans. They might remember that Mitchell was one of a handful of Americans who labored to give their nation a pitifully small but worthy nucleus of military strength in the years between the world wars. Americans might well regard Mitchell as one of the extraordinary men in their history, one who employed some remarkable gifts and unusual energy in trying to alert his countrymen to the promise of aviation. Indeed, every age has had its crusaders—men like Mitchell whose relentless insistence on the correctness of their beliefs ultimately destroyed them. In the interim, however, their zeal also sustained them in combating the antagonism of the shortsighted. To deny Mitchell a significant place in American history would be to deny the realities of the contemporary world and to ignore history's duty of providing perspective for the age in which it is written.

Appendix: Additional Insights

Some additional insights into the story of General Mitchell and his ideas are now possible, thanks to new scholarship, my recent access to materials closed to me in 1963, and my own wider and deeper study of the sources on air power. These new insights, I believe, only reinforce the essential validity of my original thesis and conclusions.

When Mitchell entered the career Signal Corps in 1901, he joined an organization which, in spite of its miniscule resources and limited aeronautical experience, was in closer touch with international thought about military aeronautics than I first understood. Perhaps two interrelated examples from the history of the Signal Corps before 1901 will suffice.

In 1892, Brigadier General Adolphus Greely, the Chief Signal Officer, and the man whom Mitchell later credited with making him and all in the Corps conscious of aeronautics, cautiously cited in his *Annual Report* the ideas of French and British inventors and theorists, including those of Major J. D. Fullerton, a member of the British Royal Engineers and an aeronautical pioneer in his own country. Greely noted Fullerton's description of a "satisfactory war balloon" as one that could carry three to four passengers, explosives, and machine guns.[1]

In 1893, Fullerton was among the military experts from England, Mexico, Germany, France, and Sweden who joined Greely and other U.S. Army specialists in the sub-conference on military engineering of the International Engineering Congress at Chicago's World Columbian Exposition. In a striking paper, "Some Remarks on Aerial Warfare," Fullerton declared that the ongoing advances in aeronautics meant the coming of "as great a revolution in the art of war as the discovery of gunpowder in the past." The threat of aerial bombardment would force changes in the design of naval ships, the dispersal of armies on battlefields, and construction standards for fortresses. Future wars were likely to start with a great air battle, whose winner would then carry out naval and ground attacks. "The arrival of the aerial fleet over the enemy capital will probably conclude the campaign." Fullerton ended his paper with seven propositions about the impact of aeronautics on warfare. Among them were his beliefs that the speed of the air vehicle (he favored the coming airplane over the existing dirigible) would make it necessary for all nations to be ready for a lightning war; and sea and land warfare would be possible only when "a nation has command of the air."[2]

As host for the conference, the United States War Department put Fullerton's remarks immediately after Greely's unpretentious paper in the proceedings of the military engineering session. The British theorist's paper was probably the first of its kind to have appeared either under War Department editorship or in professional military literature in the United States. However prematurely, Fullerton's paper clearly foreshadowed the work of Mitchell and his contemporary air theorists.[3]

Mitchell may never have heard of Fullerton's work. That work, so far, can only be evidence of Signal Corps consciousness of foreign aeronautical thought before 1901 and an indication of the climate of opinion Mitchell encountered upon entering the Signal Corps. On the other hand, Mitchell had many direct contacts with George O. Squier, the officer who continued Greely's work of making the Signal Corps conscious of aeronautics. The first, and very recent, biographer of Squier has documented his extensive work in aeronautics from 1905 through 1918, climaxed by his role as the primary instigator of the unsuccessful effort to create an Army air arm overnight after the United States entered World War I.[4]

In 1905–6, Mitchell was an assistant to then Major Squier, the Commandant of the new Signal School at Fort Leavenworth, where Squier vigorously promoted the study of aeronautical theory in his own school and in the Staff college. Mitchell's earliest known paper on aeronautics, his forward-looking 1906 lecture on military balloons, was part of a lecture and seminar program created by Squier at the Signal School.[5]

In December 1908, Squier staked his clearest claim to be the leading theorist on aeronautics in the American military when he addressed the annual meeting of the American Society of Mechanical Engineers. His paper, fully indorsed by the Chief Signal Officer of the moment as the position of their Corps on the matter, was published both in the United States and in England. The fifteen-page bibliography accompanying the published version of the paper emphasized European over American sources and showed Squier's grasp of international thought on his subject.[6]

Squier carefully stressed in his paper the enormous technical problems yet to be solved if aeronautics were to become militarily useful. He left no doubt of his conviction that those problems were solvable and went on to anticipate tactical and strategic roles for aeronautics which Mitchell, his contemporaries, and their successors would emphasize. In 1908, the dirigible surpassed the airplane in reliability, range, and carrying ability, so Squier gave lighter-than-air equipment the most difficult tasks. To one type of dirigible, he assigned the tactical job of bombing bridges, fortifications, and supply depots adjacent to the battlefront. Much large strategic dirigibles would vault over and beyond an enemy's ground forces to strike his "base of supplies; to destroy his drydocks, arsenals, ammunition depots, principal railway centers, storehouses . . . and the enemy's navy itself." These aircraft would be, to use the current phrase, highly cost effective against far more expensive enemy navies, and would make possible attacks against the enemy capital. The threat of attacks on the capital would "deter" precipitate action by the leaders of an enemy nation since "now for the first time" they would be "in immediate and personal danger after the declaration of war." In the overly sanguine manner which has characterized most air theorists,

Squier anticipated that the advent of air forces would help "to make war less likely in the future than in the past."[7]

Mitchell could not have been a stranger to Squier's ideas after their service together at Fort Leavenworth. As a keen and ambitious officer, Mitchell could be expected to be familiar with a paper so strongly indorsed by the Chief of his Corps. That these ideas had no immediate, perceptible impact on Mitchell is understandable, largely because Congress firmly refused to finance a meaningful aviation development until shortly before the United States entered the World War.

Squier went to London as military attaché in 1912, before Congress got around to shaping any aviation policy. Mitchell was a ringside witness to the Congressional decision-making, since he was serving with the General Staff. It was not until 1914, some six years after the Army contracted for its first dirigible and first airplane, that Congress decided to create only a tiny Signal Corps Aviation Section, merely to keep the United States Army "abreast with the experiments which are being made in aviation." Congress expected the European powers to bear the gigantic costs of developing aviation and, by implication, the theories of a Squier.[8]

As the only Signal Corps officer on the General Staff, Mitchell was that organization's point of contact for the limited aviation role authorized by Congress. In this assignment, Mitchell was exposed to many ambitious ideas about aviation both from American and European sources. He was in occasional, but not always amicable, contact with the young Army fliers who asserted in 1916 their near-unanimous determination to control their aviation's future, once Congress ended Signal Corps control of their work and loosened the strings of the national purse. Both Mitchell and the Army airmen seem to have gotten much of their information on European aviation from the various Army attachés abroad.[9]

After World War I began, Squier seems to have been the Army's best source of information among its attachés in Europe on the conduct of the war. In air matters, Squier apparently enjoyed a special relationship with British aviation leaders from the outset of his service in London. He knew well two officers who must be counted among the founders of the Royal Air Force: Brigadier General David Henderson, the Director-General of Military Aeronautics, and Lieutenant Colonel Frederick Sykes, the first commander of the Military

Wing of the Royal Flying Corps. Since Squier was intensely interested in the creation of the National Advisory Committee for Aeronautics (NACA) in the United States, he most likely knew the aeronautical theorist and engineer, Frederick Lanchester, who was a top member of the British model for the NACA.[10]

Through a report from Squier, for example, Mitchell had at hand a 1913 forecast by Sykes that offensive action would be essential to maintain control of the air. Sykes cited the experience of the participants in the Balkan Wars and maneuvers in England and France to support his view that "the side which loses command of the air will labor under all the disadvantages of defensive action."[11]

Before Squier returned to the United States in 1916, he sent Mitchell's office in the General Staff a copy of Lanchester's influential *Aircraft in Warfare,* with an introduction by Henderson. The book was largely a compilation of articles Lanchester had written as early as 1914. He discussed such now familiar concepts as "air power," "command of the air," "strategic and tactical uses of the aeronautical arm," and the "independent air fleet."[12]

Squier found Mitchell temporarily in charge of the Aviation Section when he returned to Washington to become its Chief. Congress was now ready to expand its support, and Mitchell's decision to cast his lot indefinitely with aviation as Squier's deputy signalled his own recognition that the great opportunity he had sought throughout his career had arrived. Benjamin Foulois, a bitter enemy, has recalled that Mitchell did not prosper as Squier's deputy because of his inexperience in aviation and got his assignment to Europe as an observer only after Squier became dissatisfied with his work. Even if Foulois were correct, Mitchell now had a role he had long wanted and one better suited to his talents.[13]

In Europe, Mitchell's speedy perception of the key doctrinal issues posed by the air war suggests that his previous exposure to these issues in the United States had helped to prepare him to be able to react so quickly. The multiple influences he encountered in Europe, directly from French and British airmen and indirectly from Giulio Douhet through Gianni Caproni, are matters of record. He seemed most attracted to Trenchard and his ideas, if only because Trenchard had been markedly successful in doing what Mitchell had to do if he were to succeed in France. Although the radical theory of bombing the nerve centers of Germany had strong British sponsors, such

as General Henderson, both Trenchard and Mitchell had their hands
full with immediate realities while they were assigned to direct
support of their armies.[14]

Mitchell's recollections of his own aerial experiences in France
often seemed to reflect the influence more of the case he was trying
to make for a separate service in 1919 and for strategic bombardment in 1926, rather than the facts of the situation he handled so
well in 1918. As a subordinate Army commander, Mitchell's primary
tactical assignment was to try to control the airspace over the battlefield area through aerial action within 25,000 yards in front of Allied
ground forces. His strategic assignment was not that sought by radical
theorists. His job in this regard was to conduct pursuit and bombardment work beginning at the 25,000 yard mark and with the objective
of preventing the enemy from throwing all his resources into the
ground battle. During the St.-Mihiel battle, for example, his aircraft
went no more than thirty-five miles beyond the front.[15]

During his four-month visit to Europe in 1921–22, Mitchell encountered widespread acceptance among airmen in France, Italy,
and England of the radical strategic bombing thesis which the still-
born Inter-Allied Air Force never had the chance to test in 1919.
While Mitchell was in Italy in January and February, 1922, he probably saw Caproni and may have met Douhet. In March of that year,
and perhaps at Mitchell's request, the United States military attaché
in Rome sent two copies of Douhet's basic work, *Il Domino dell'Aria,*
to the War Department General Staff. Translations of a five-page
extract of the famous book promptly went to the Air Service Plans
Division. A translation of the first 100 pages of the book appeared
fourteen months later in the library of the Air Service Field Officers
School at Langley Field.[16]

That Mitchell was aware of the viewpoint of Douhet is a matter of
record. In the light of the preparatory work of Greely and Squier and
the entire experience of the Air Service, AEF in World War I, Douhet
must rank as no more than one of the multiple influences on Mitchell,
his colleagues, and their successors, as they slowly evolved a strategic
bombardment doctrine that was sensitive to the American political
and military tradition. Douhet's central emphasis on unrestrained,
all-out aggressive warfare, conducted primarily through the air, was
not at all sensitive to that tradition. Indeed, when Mitchell spoke out
as early as 1924 about strategic bombardment, he acted contrary

both to that tradition and to the facts of his country's geographical position. His primary motive appears to have been to meet the insatiable demands of his publicity campaign for a separate service. The same motive seems to have led to Mitchell's collaboration with Colonel Charles de F. Chandler and others in publicly advocating Douhet's views in 1933. The starkness of Douhet's thought made it grist for the publicity mills of that era, while the comprehensiveness of his thought has made it a too convenient reference for anyone who would ascribe the origins of American ideas on strategic bombardment to a single, overriding influence.[17]

The now public transcript of the court-martial shows that the proceedings had deeper meaning than I originally suspected. In allowing the trial to go beyond an examination of the charges, the War Department may have gained more in the long run than it could have lost to Mitchell in any short-term effort to capture public opinion. Under strong cross-examination on both the charges and unrelated matters, Mitchell did not leave a record which would help his cause.[18]

The prosecution made several efforts to destroy Mitchell's credibility during his cross-examination. In the one instance where a foreign theorist's name and work were mentioned, the prosecution even tried to suggest that Mitchell had not read Liddell Hart's influential *Paris, or The Future of War,* before indorsing it to a radio audience. The relentless and flamboyant Assistant Trial Judge Advocate, Major Allen W. Gullion, scored most heavily for the War Department in forcing Mitchell to admit that the statement which led to his court-martial was based on opinion and not on fact; and that Mitchell, as a former leader of the Air Service, could not escape a share of the responsibility for the conditions in the air arm which he had condemned in his statement to the press. In matters not directly related to the charges, Gullion also scored telling points. For example, he forced Mitchell to admit that while he had championed dirigibles, he had never flown in one.[19]

Mitchell's difficulties at the trial appear not to have been entirely his own fault. His chief counsel, Congressman Frank Reid, does not seem to have represented his client well. For example, Reid's fruitless cross-examination of a veteran of Air Service AEF bombardment operations put into the record a detailed refutation of Mitchell's claims about the ineffectiveness of German antiaircraft fire in World War I. In refuting the claims, the veteran, a reservist at the time of the trial, made the point that he and other bomber crew members had to fly within the effective range of enemy antiaircraft guns in order to accomplish their missions. Also, the latest biographer of Mitchell has suggested that he was not well during the trial. Whatever the explanation, Mitchell's personal performance at the trial seems to have been as ineffective as his appearance before the Morrow Board.[20]

Whatever historians might say about Mitchell, his glamour and style will always make him a great subject for popular myths. One such myth appeared in a 1968 Congressional publication which included him among Medal of Honor winners and described him as a retired major general. When read closely, the publication made it clear that his heirs received only a special Congressional medal and not the Medal of Honor. As to his place on the retired list, the publication probably referred to a 1947 bill which failed in Congress.[21]

Mitchell still has no official tie with the Army. Rather, his tie will always be with the Air Force which he did so much to help found through his combat leadership in France and through his farsighted grasp of the unlimited potential of the aerial or the third dimension to warfare. The most recent evidence only reinforces the thesis that he was not an original thinker, but rather a highly effective spokesman for a point of view which an international community of airmen and civilians now appear to have shared even before World War I.

Abbreviations Appearing in Notes and Bibliography

I
(Mitchell Items)

WM William Mitchell.

WM mss. William Mitchell Papers. Unless otherwise attributed, all manuscripts cited are from this collection in the Library of Congress, Washington, D.C.

CB "Career Brief on William Mitchell," United States Air Force Academy Library, Colorado.

"War Memoirs" "From Start to Finish of Our Greatest War," mss. recently published as *Memoirs of World War I* (New York, 1960), WM mss., Box 1 and (polished version) Box 22.

II
(Manuscript Collections)

All collections listed are in the Library of Congress, unless otherwise noted.

Andrews mss.	Papers of General Frank Andrews.
Arnold mss.	Papers of General Henry H. Arnold.
Baker mss.	Papers of Newton D. Baker.
Coolidge mss.	Papers of President Calvin Coolidge.
Fullam mss.	Papers of Admiral William Fullam.
Gardner mss.	Scrapbook collection of Lester Gardner, Library of Institute of Aerospace Sciences, New York, N.Y.
Gibbs mss.	Papers of General George C. Gibbs.
Greely mss.	Papers of General Adolphus Greely.
Harbord mss.	Papers of General James Harbord—Library of Congress or New York Historical Society, as specified.
La Guardia mss.	Papers of Fiorello La Guardia, Municipal Archives, New York, N.Y.
McCoy mss.	Papers of General Frank McCoy.
Morrow mss.	Papers of Dwight Morrow, Amhurst College Library, Massachusetts.
Patrick Diary.	Diary of General Mason Patrick, United States Air Force Academy Library, Colorado.
Pershing mss.	Papers of General John J. Pershing.
Roosevelt mss.	Papers of President Franklin D. Roosevelt, Hyde Park, N.Y.
Spaatz mss.	Papers of General Carl Spaatz.
Wood mss.	Papers of General Leonard Wood.

III
(National Archives Material)

All items cited are in the Old Army Records Division, unless otherwise attributed.

AG	Army Adjutant General
CAS	Chief of the Air Service
CSO	Chief Signal Officer
GS	General Staff
NA	National Archives, Washington, D.C.
RG	Record Group
WCD	War College Division

IV
(Oral History Papers)

All items cited are in the Oral Research History Office, Columbia University, N. Y.

Arnold OHP	The Reminiscences of Mrs. Henry H. Arnold.
Douglas OHP	The Reminiscences of Donald Douglas.
MacReady OHP	The Reminiscences of Colonel William MacReady.
Prinz OHP	The Reminiscences of Leroy Prinz.
Verville OHP	The Reminiscences of Alfred Verville.
Wadsworth OHP	The Reminiscences of Senator James Wadsworth.
Wilson OHP	The Reminiscences of Gill Robb Wilson.

V
(USAF Historical Materials)

H.D.	Historical Division document, USAF Historical Archives, Montgomery, Alabama.
USAFA	Library, USAF Academy, Colorado.

VI
(Interviews)

Foulois Interview	Interview with Major General Benjamin D. Foulois.
Victory Interview	Interview with Doctor John F. Victory.

Notes

(To improve the readability of the text, the publishers have changed the original paragraphing. Thus, each footnote often applies not only to a particular paragraph, but also to one or more preceding paragraphs.)

INTRODUCTION and CHAPTER ONE

1. The published works on Mitchell include: Isaac Don Levine, *Mitchell, Pioneer of Air Power* (New York, 1943 and 1958) (hereafter cited as *Mitchell*); Emile Gauvreau and Lester Cohen, *Billy Mitchell, Founder of Our Air Force and Prophet Without Honor* (New York, 1942); Roger Burlingame, *General Billy Mitchell, Champion of Air Defense* (New York, 1952); Ruth Mitchell, *My Brother Bill* (New York, 1953); Arch Whitehouse, *Billy Mitchell* (New York, 1962).

2. Portions of this chapter appeared in my article "Young 'Billy' Mitchell and the 'Old Army,'" *Airpower Historian* VIII (Jan., 1961), 28–38.

3. *Biographical Directory of the American Congress 1774–1961* (Washington GPO, 1961), 1339, 1341; Levine, *Mitchell*, 9–15; Horace S. Merrill, *Bourbon Leader: Grover Cleveland and the Democratic Party* (New York, 1957), 51; Robert M. La Follette, *Autobiography* (Madison, 1913), 20–21; John L. Mitchell, *Against the Annexation of the Hawaiian Islands* (Washington, 1898), 1–12.

4. Levine, *Mitchell*, 12–16.

5. Cf., the several hundred ltrs., WM to mother, in WM mss.

6. WM's grade reports from Racine; Mrs. S. Schwall to Mrs. Mitchell, Apr. 8, 1890; Rev. H. D. Robinson to Mrs. Mitchell, Oct. 24, 1892, and Dec. 20, 1893; ltrs., WM to mother between Feb. 3, 1894, and May 23, 1894.

7. WM to father, Dec. 9, 1899; CB, 11.

8. WM to father, Aug 8, 14, 20, 1898; WM to mother, Sept. 11, 1898.

9. WM to mother, July 11, 22, Sept. 11, 1898.

10. Senator Mitchell to General Greely, Feb. 7, 1899, Greely mss.; WM to father, Aug. 14, 20, 25, Oct. 13, Dec. 24, 1898. Mitchell temporarily lost

his first lieutenant's rank on Apr. 17, 1899, during a reorganization of the volunteer forces, but regained it on June 8, 1900.

11. WM to father, Jan. 2, Apr. 11, 1899; WM to mother, July 6, 1899.

12. WM to father, Sept. 20, Dec. 24, 1898, Jan. 5, 14, 1899; WM to mother, Jan. 11, June 14, 1899; from mother, Apr. 16, 1899.

13. WM to father, July 13, 23, 29, 1899; father to mother, Aug. 25, 1899.

14. WM to father, Sept. 11, 1899; WM to mother, Dec. 28, 1899, May 7, 1900; WM to uncle, Jan. 7, 1900.

15. CB, 13; WM to father, Dec. 8, 1899, Jan. 12, Mar. 10, 1900; WM to mother, Mar. 22, June 1, 1900.

16. William R. Braisted, *The United States Navy in the Pacific, 1897–1909* (Austin, 1958), 33–42, 57–63; WM to mother, June 1, 1900; William A. Ganoe, *The History of the United States Army* (New York, 1943), 411–414.

17. Philip C. Jessup, *Elihu Root* (New York, 1938), 215–268; Emory Upton, *The Military Policy of the United States* (Washington, 1912), X–XV.

18. Richard G. Brown, "General Emory Upton: The Army's Mahan," *Military Affairs* XVII (Fall, 1953), 127–130.

19. WM to mother, July 7, Sept. 11, Nov. 5, Dec. 15, 1901, Feb. 21, 1902; to father, Jan. 17, 1902; WM, "Building The Alaskan Telegraph System," *National Geographic,* XV (Sept., 1904), 357–362.

20. WM to mother, Apr. 5, July 18, Nov. 23, 1903; on Signal Corps activities, cf., the *Annual Reports CSO* for this decade.

21. Oliver L. Spaulding, *The United States Army in War and Peace* (New York, 1937), 394–398; *Annual Report CSO* (Washington, 1905), 32.

22. Correspondence between WM and Greely, 1905–6, AGO file 88426, NA; WM, "The Signal Corps with Divisional Cavalry and Notes on Wireless Telegraphy, Searchlights and Military Ballooning," *U.S. Cavalry Journal* (Apr. 1906), 669–696 (hereafter cited as "The Signal Corps With . . ."). Essentially the same article appeared as *Field Signal Communications* (*Second Lecture*) (Fort Leavenworth, 1906).

23. Juliette Hennessy, *The United States Army Air Arm, April, 1861 to April, 1917,* USAF Historical Studies No. 98 (Montgomery, 1958), 1–19 (hereafter cited as *The United States Army Air Arm*).

24. "The Signal Corps With . . .," 694–696.

25. U.S. Army War College, *The Signal Corps and Air Service* (Washington, 1922), 30–31.

26. Henry Schindler and E. E. Booth, *History of the Army Service Schools* (Leavenworth, 1908), 23; *Annual Report of Commandant, Army Service Schools* (School of the Line) (Leavenworth, 1908), 10, 24–33; *ibid.*, (Staff College) (Leavenworth, 1909), 55–60.

27. Cf., correspondence on WM's transfer AGO file 88426, NA; WM to Capt. George S. Gibbs, undated ltr. and Nov. 23, 1909, Gibbs mss.

28. WM, "Report of Observations in Manchuria, Korea and Japan," NA, GS Report 7027–1, Jan. 2, 1912 (hereafter cited as "Report of Observations"), esp. 77–80; "Report to the Adjutant General, U.S. Army," NA, Report 7027–2, Mar. 22, 1912, 75; Outen J. Clinard, *Japan's Influence on American Naval Power 1897–1917* (Berkeley, 1947), 2f.

29. "Report of Observations," 75–78; C. Joseph Bernardo and Eugene H. Bacon, *American Military Policy* (Harrisburg, 1955), 319–325; Hermann Hagedorn, *Leonard Wood* (New York, 1931), II, 115–116.

30. Entry for Mar. 1, 1912, "Diary of Leonard Wood," Wood mss.; WM to mother, Mar. 6, 16, May 9, 1912.

31. WM to mother, May 9, 1912.

32. *Ibid.*, Oct. 20, 1913; Jan. 4, 13, Mar. 16, Apr. 1, 1914.

33. *Ibid.*, Oct. 20, 29, Nov. 12, 1913, Jan. 4, 22, 29, June 24, July 23, 30, Sept. 5, ltr. marked "Monday," all 1914.

34. WM "Military Organization of the United States," *Infantry Journal* X (Nov.-Dec. 1913), 350–392; WM to mother, Feb. 25, 1914.

35. WM, *Our Faulty Military Policy* (mimeographed, Army War College, 1915), 7; "National Organization for War," unpub. and undated mss., 12.

36. WM, Memoranda for Chief, WCD, GS, July 22, 23, 1913, NA, RG 18, File 321.9; "Notes Concerning a Proposed Aeronautical Branch, Signal Corps, U.S. Army," unpub. and undated mss.

37. U.S. Congress, House Committee on Military Affairs, *Hearings in Connection With HR 5304*, 63rd Cong., 1st Session, 1913, 77, 84, 88, 91; WM to mother, Feb. 25, 1914; Hennessy, *The United States Army Air Arm*, 109–110.

38. WM to mother, July 30, c. Sept. 8, Dec. 21, 1914, May 25, 1915.

39. Arthur S. Link, *Woodrow Wilson and the Progressive Era* (New York, 1954), 179–196; Bernardo and Bacon, *American Military Policy,* 340–346; U.S. Congress, House Committee on Military Affairs, *Bill to Increase the Efficiency of the Military Establishment,* 66th Cong., 1st Sess. Jan. 6 to Feb. 11, 1916, 130–131.

40. *Military Aviation,* War Dept. Doc. 515, Army War College (Washington, 1916), 6, 18; the National War College Library's catalog credits Mitchell with the authorship of this pamphlet; Hennessy, *The United States Army Air Arm,* 156.

41. *The Signal Corps and Air Service,* 31–32, 41; Hennessy, *The United States Army Air Arm,* 233.

42. WM to mother, Mar. 6, 1914, Jan. 19, 1916; CB, 15–16.

43. Levine, *Mitchell,* 87–88; cf., bill for Mitchell's training to Aviation Section, Mar. 1, 1917; CB, 11, 13; the orders rating Mitchell as a pilot in Sept., 1917, were backdated to July 19, 1917.

CHAPTER TWO

1. "War Memoirs," Apr., 1917, 13–17; James G. Harbord, *Leaves From a War Diary* (New York, 1925), 57.

2. Cablegram, WM to WCD, GS, Report 10,050–4, Apr. 27, 1917, NA, RG 165, Box 460; Irving B. Holley, *Ideas and Weapons* (New Haven, 1953), 42, n.6, 37; Hiram Bingham, *An Explorer in the Air Service* (New Haven, 1920), 25–28.

3. "War Memoirs," Apr., 1917, 176. However, see the Bibliography.

4. *Ibid.,* 16, 31–32; May, 1917, 49–50.

5. Andre P. Voisin, *La Doctrine de l'Aviation Francaise de Combat, 1915–1918* (Paris, 1932), 1–43, esp. 12–13 (hereafter cited as *La Doctrine*). For British development, cf., H. A. Jones, *War in the Air* (Oxford, 1937), II, 164–168, 472–475.

6. "War Memoirs," Apr., 1917, 157–159; Voisin, *La Doctrine,* 20–43, esp. 23.

7. "War Memoirs," May, 1917, 29,33; Andrew Boyle, *Trenchard* (London, 1962), 95–219.

8. "War Memoirs," May, 1917, 21, 29–30, 41; Boyle, *Trenchard*, 298–299; cf., Trenchard's views on the air offensive in Jones, *War in the Air*, II, 472–475; *ibid.*, VI, 23.

9. "War Memoirs," May, 1917, 25–28, 44–46; Jones, *War in the Air*, II, 199; III, 370; V, 482; Sir Philip Joubert, *The Third Service* (London, 1955), 35, 37.

10. "War Memoirs," May, 1917, 29; also see polished version in WM mss., Box 22, p. 28; Boyle, *Trenchard*, 219; Joubert, *The Third Service*, 67–68; Holley, *Ideas and Weapons*, 58; Frederick Palmer, *Newton D. Baker, America at War* (New York, 1931), II, 267–269 identifies Brancker as a strategic bombing advocate in 1918. For Smuts's report, cf., Jones, *War in the Air*, Appendix to VI, 8–14.

11. "War Memoirs," May, 1917, 49–50; WM to WCD, GS, Report 10,050–48, "French Estimates of the Aeronautical Aid Required from the United States," May, 1917, NA, RG 165 Box 460; Holley, *Ideas and Weapons*, 41–46, esp. 43, n.7.

12. "War Memoirs," July, 1917, 63–69; Jones, *War in the Air*, II, 349–354, 451–453; III, 78–79; IV, 69–74; VI, 385.

13. "War Memoirs," July, 1917, 48.

14. *Ibid.*, 48; John J. Pershing, *My Experiences in World War I* (New York, 1931), I, 11–12, 26 (hereafter cited as *My Experiences*); Pershing to George O. Squier, Aug. 10, 1916, Pershing mss.

15. Memo., WM to Pershing, "Air Policy in France" and "Aeronautical Organization in France," July 13, 1917, quoted in "War Memoirs," June, 1917, 81–83; Holley, *Ideas and Weapons*, 46–47.

16. "Proceedings of a Board of Officers," June 19, 1917, in "1917 Aviation Program in Europe"; Jones, *War in the Air*, VI, 4–7; cf., Harbord, *Leaves From a War Diary*, 124, on Pershing's caution; Army Air Forces Historical Studies No. 25, *Organization of Military Aeronautics* (Washington, 1944), 32 (hereafter cited as *Organization of Military Aeronautics*).

17. Holley, *Ideas and Weapons*, 52–53, suggests the implications of the Bolling Mission's one-month delay; Memo., WM to Chief of Staff, AEF, "United States Aeronautical Commission," July 22, 1917, quoted in "War Memoirs," June, 1917, 79–80.

18. Holley, *Ideas and Weapons*, 55–59; Thomas Greer, *The Development of Air Doctrine in the Army Air Arm* (Air University, 1955), 9–13 (here-

after cited as *The Development of Air Doctrine*); J. L. Boone Atkinson, "Italian Influence on the Origins of the American Concept of Strategic Bombardment," *Air Power Historian*, IV (July, 1957), 143; William G. Key, "Some Papers of Caproni di Taliedo: Controversy in the Making?" *Pegasus* supplement, XXV (1956); Giulio Douhet, *Scritti Inediti*, ed. Antonio Monti (Milan, 1951), 114–131, esp. 125, 206–207; H.D. 168, 661–36 through 73, esp. 48, 49.

19. Holley, *Ideas and Weapons,* 57–58; 65–117.

20. Boone L. Atkinson, "The Caproni Museum and Archives," *Air Power Historian*, IV (Oct., 1957), 187; Memo., WM to Ass't Chief of Staff, G-2, Aug. 7, 1918, NA, RG 120; "War Memoirs," Nov., 1917, 151–153 (polished version, Box 22); Palmer, *Newton D. Baker*, II, 184; Henry H. Arnold, *Global Mission* (New York, 1949), 52; "Principles Underlying the Use of the Air Service in the Zone of Advance," quoted in CB, 16; cf., also par. 5, General Order 19, Hqs. Air Service First Army, Oct. 21, 1918, WM mss.

21. Edgar Gorrell, *The Measure of America's World War Aeronautical Effort* (Northfield; 1940), 5 (hereafter cited as *The Measure*); Petain to Pershing, Dec. 29, 1917, *U.S. Army in the World War 1917–1919* (Washington, 1948) 127–130; Memo., WM to General Biddle, Nov. 3, 1917, NA, RG 120.

22. Gorrell, *The Measure*, 30–32; Greer, *The Development of Air Doctrine*, 9–13.

23. "War Memoirs," Nov., 1917, 149–150; Jan., 1918, 150; May, 192–193; June, 1918, 217–218; Patrick, *The United States in the Air*, 16; Edgar Gorrell, ed., "History of the Air Service AEF," 120–140, Series A, I, NA; Memo., General Fox Conner to Pershing, Oct. 22, 1919, Pershing mss; entry for Mar. 24, 1919, Patrick Diary.

24. MacReady OHP, 30, 32; Wilson OHP, 73–79; Prinz OHP, 7, 23–24; WM to mother, July 19 and Aug. 20, 1918.

25. "War Memoirs," Sept., 1918, 242–243; Gorrell, *The Measure,* 58; Voisin, *La Doctrine,* 74; Douhet, *Scritti Inediti,* 173–175; Jones, *War in the Air,* VI, 101–174, esp. 164, 273–292.

26. "War Memoirs," Sept., 1918, 249–255; Gorrell, *The Measure,* 53–56; Patrick, *The United States in the Air* (Garden City, 1928), 27, 33; WM, "The Air Service at St.-Mihiel," *World's Work* XXXVIII (Aug., 1919), 360–370. The "thirty-five" mile radius is measured from the center of the St.-Mihiel salient as depicted in *Dept. of Military Art and Engineering Atlas*

(West Point, 1954), 68. Pershing's tight control is evident in Annex 3, Field Order 9, Sept. 7, 1918, *U.S. Army in the World War*, VIII, 215–217.

27. "War Memoirs," Sept., 1918, 278–279; Patrick, *The United States in the Air*, 50–51; W. Frank Craven and James L. Cate, *The Army Air Forces in World War II* (Chicago, 1948), I, 15; Annex 4, Field Order 20, Sept. 17, 1918, and Appendix III, 99–102, esp., Memo., Lt. Col. W. C. Sherman to CAS, Army Group, 362–364, all in *U.S. Army in the World War*, IX.

28. "War Memoirs," Oct., 1918, 291, Nov., 1918, 280–281; Craven and Cate, *The Army Air Forces in World War II*, I, 15–16; J. M. Spaight, *British Aeroplanes, 1914–1918*, 277.

29. "War Memoirs," Nov., 1918, 313.

30. Baker to March, Nov. 4, 1918, Baker mss. I am indebted to Doctor Daniel Beaver for this reference.

31. "War Memoirs," Oct., 290–291, Dec., 1918, 330; Arnold, *Global Mission*, 86–88; Ruth Mitchell, *My Brother Bill* (New York, 1953), 199.

32. "War Memoirs," Feb., 1919, 337–341; Boyle, *Trenchard*, 331–353.

33. Archibald D. Turnbull and Clifford L. Lord, *History of United States Naval Aviation* (New Haven, 1949), 177; WM to mother, Dec. 3, 1918; R. Earl McClendon, *The Question of Autonomy for the United States Air Arm* (Montgomery, 1954), 36–41 (hereafter cited as *Autonomy for the Air Arm*).

CHAPTER THREE

1. This view of Wilson is based on John M. Blum, *Woodrow Wilson and the Politics of Morality* (Boston, 1956), 181–197.

2. Memo. for Chief, T and O Group, June 11, 1919; Patrick, *The United States in the Air*, 74; Hartney, *Up and At 'Em*, 309; WM to Col. J. C. Morrow, Dec. 8, 1919; Greer, *The Development of Air Doctrine*, 17, 23; Westover to Menoher, July 26, 1919.

3. Cf., Menoher's testimony, U.S. Congress, Senate, Subcommittee of the Committee on Military Affairs, *Reorganization of the Army*, 66th Cong., 1st Sess., 1919, Part I, 270–273 (hereafter cited as *Reorganization of the Army*); Eldon Downs, "Contributions of U.S. Army Aviation to Uses and Operations of Aircraft," unpub. Ph.D. Dissertation, U. of Wisconsin, 1958, 148–168, 171–208 (hereafter cited as "Contributions of U.S. Army Aviation"); *Air Service Newsletter*, Apr. 26, 1919, 2; Apr. 12, 1919, 6.

4. Army Air Forces Historical Studies, No. 39, *Legislation Relating to the Air Corps Personnel and Training Programs 1907–1939* (Washington, 1945), 15–17 (hereafter cited as *Legislation and Training*).

5. Col. Townsend F. Dodd, "Recommendations Concerning the Establishment of a Department of Aeronautics—Prepared by Direction of WM," Apr. 17, 1919, 3–5 (hereafter cited as "Recommendations . . . Dept. of Aeronautics"); "Notes on General Policy of Air Service Organization Recommended By WM," Apr. 11, 1919; "Naval Aviation Policy," Apr. 3, 1919.

6. Turnbull and Lord, *History of United States Naval Aviation*, 23, 35, 54–70, 207–208; E. B. Potter and Chester W. Nimitz, *Sea Power* (Englewood Cliffs, N. J., 1960), 635; Memo., WM to DAS, Mar. 26, 1919, "Proposed Aeronautical Organization for the United States," July 15, 1919, 8; "Naval Aviation Policy," 6.

7. *The New York Times,* Aug. 29, 1920, 6:1; Feb. 5, 1921, 4:1; *Aviation,* Mar. 7, 1919, 27, 162; Col. C. de F. Chandler to WM, "Airships," Apr. 8, 1919; Memo. by Menoher, "Military Uses of Airships," Oct. 31, 1919.

8. "Internal Operations," 4–6, unsigned mss.; this document apparently was a working paper for "Recommendations . . . Dept. of Aeronautics," 4–5, where it was substantially repeated.

9. *Ibid.,* 3, 19; cf., WM's testimony, *Reorganization of the Army,* 303; "Proposed Aeronautical Organization for the United States," July 15, 1919; Memo. for Balloons and Airships Lighter Than Air Section, Oct. 31, 1919.

10. Memos., WM to DAS, Mar. 28, Apr. 14, 1919; "Naval Aviation Policy," 1, where Admiral Winterhalter noted that a carrier had been sought in 1918; cf., also the complete file on Mitchell's carrier proposal, NA, File 560, Box 1169.

11. Memo., WM to DAS, Apr. 11, 1919; Memo., Maj. H. A. Dargue to Chief, Training and War Plans, "History Rigid Airship Question in the Army," Nov. 4, 1924 (hereafter cited as "History Rigid Airship Question").

12. "Recommendations . . . Dept. of Aeronautics," 5, 12, 21–22; Col. T. F. Dodd, "General Notes of Functions of Department of Aeronautics," Apr. 8, 1919; compare *ibid.* with the description of the functions of the British Air Ministry in C. G. Grey, *A History of the Air Ministry* (London, 1940), 97–144.

13. WM to mother, Dec. 18, 1919; WM's testimony, U.S. Congress, House Committee on Military Affairs, *Army Organization,* 66th Cong., 1st Session, 1919, V, 900–901; also cf., his testimony, *Reorganization of the*

Army, 312; Foulois' testimony in *ibid.,* 1259–1298; WM, "Air Leadership —What It Meant in the Great War," *United States Air Services,* I (May, 1919), 17.

14. WM to mother, July 10, 1919; the best example of the "aura of success" is in the *Reorganization of the Army* hearings, where the records of the military witnesses had an obvious impact.

15. McClendon, *Autonomy for the Air Arm,* 43–44.

16. Franklin D. Roosevelt, "Why Naval Aviation Won," *U.S. Air Services,* I (July, 1919), 7–8; Turnbull and Lord, *History of United States Naval Aviation,* 170–171, 188–189.

17. Cf., the summary of arguments "pro and con" a separate service, *U.S. Air Services,* II (Sept., 1919), 4–5; McClendon, *Autonomy for the Air Arm,* 42–57; Hartney, *Up and At 'Em,* 306; Greer, *The Development of Air Doctrine,* 21–22; Col. O. Westover to Menoher, June 26, 1919; transcript of Newton Baker's press release on the Crowell Mission, Aug. 11, 1919.

18. "Naval Aviation Policy," 24; "Recommendations . . . Dept. of Aeronautics," 3, 21–22; *Reorganization of the Army,* 301, 312–313; cf., Roosevelt's testimony, *ibid.,* 51–52.

19. *Ibid.,* 195–209; cablegrams, Baker to Crowell, July 2, 3, 1919, Baker mss.; Hartney, *Up and At 'Em,* 307.

20. WM to mother, July 10, Dec. 18, 1919; *Organization of Military Aeronautics,* 44, n.32; Memo., WM to President of (Menoher) Board, Aug. 13, 1919; McClendon, *Autonomy for the Air Arm,* 87–89; Memo., WM to Pershing, Oct. 27, 1919.

21. Patrick to Pershing, Nov. 11, 1919, Pershing mss.; entries for Mar. 24, June 27, July 14, 1919, Patrick Diary.

22. Memo., WM to Col. Palmer, Jan. 9, 1920; *Legislation Relating to Personnel and Training,* 20.

23. Draft of ltr. by WM and Memo., W. C. Sherman to AS Exec., July 23, 1920, but also cf., Sherman to Exec., May 20, 1920, NA, RG 18, File 560, Box 1169; P. Foster to WM, Apr. 29, 1919; Memo., WM to Exec. and telegram to General Bliss, Sept. 10, 1919; Turnbull and Lord, *History of United States Naval Aviation,* 173, 249–250, 282–283.

24. WM to mother, June 10, Dec. 18, 1919, Feb. 20, 1920; Ganoe, *History of the United States Army,* 478–483.

25. Transcript of WM's press release on Transcontinental Race, Oct. 18, 1919, 1–3; Ray L. Bowers, "The Transcontinental Air Race," unpub. master's thesis, U. of Wisconsin 1960, in full; Downs, "Contributions of U.S. Army Aviation," 43–44.

26. Hartney, *Up and At 'Em,* 309; cf., the airways map dated Aug., 1919 in WM mss.; "America's First Airway," *Air Service Newsletter,* Feb. 3, 1921, 1; *The New York Times,* Oct. 11, 1919, 13:2.

27. Memo., WM to Gen. Charlton, Oct. 18, 1919; Memo., Menoher to Chief of Staff, July 13, 1920 and Russian Division, State Dept. to War Dept., July 21, 1920, NA, File 580, Box 1061; Memo., W. C. Sherman to WM, Dec. 15, 1919 suggests the problems involved in carrying out the flight.

28. Transcript of WM's press release on Transcontinental Race, Oct. 18, 1919, 3.

29. Gill Robb Wilson OHP, 74, 77–78; Donald Douglas OHP, 59; Alfred Verville OHP, 36–37; William MacReady, OHP, 29–33; WM to Bane, Feb. 10, Mar. 16, 20, 1920.

30. Cf., e.g., War Dept., Air Service Engineering Division, "Report on Program for Brig. Gen Mitchell's visit to McCook Field," Dec. 14, 1920, USAFA; MacReady OHP, 29–32.

31. Cf., e.g., ltrs. to WM from Maj. L. H. Brereton (Paris), Jan. 10, 1921; Maj. M. Hall (London), and WM to Brereton, Jan. 27, 1921; to WM from de Lavergne, Oct. 24, 1919; from Guidoni, Apr. 3, 1919; WM to Charlton, Oct. 18, 1919. Also, cf., WM's office diary, Mar. 20, Sept. 9, 1919 and Apr. 12, June 21, 1920.

CHAPTER FOUR

1. Harold and Margaret Sprout, *Toward a New Order of Sea Power* (Princeton, 1943), 104–122.

2. Turnbull and Lord, *Naval Aviation,* 1–105, 150–175. Also, cf., the draft study of this work, "History of Naval Aviation," Vol. V, Part III, 652–659, 664, 743–770, Office of Naval History, Navy Department, Washington, D.C. (hereafter cited as "Draft History").

3. *Ibid.,* 781, 792.

4. Telegram, Fullam to Sen. Miles Poindexter, c. Feb., 1921; Fiske to Fullam, Feb. 11, 1921, Fullam mss.; *The New York Times,* Feb. 5, 1921,

1:7; Elting Morison, *Admiral Sims and the Modern American Navy* (Boston, 1942), 504–505, 508; Turnbull and Lord, *Naval Aviation,* 186–190.

5. B. G. Leighton, *Possibilities of Bombing Aircraft (U.S.S. Pennsylvania,* 1919), 3, 11–13, copy in WM mss.; Turnbull and Lord, *Naval Aviation,* 193; Memo., Chief of Naval Operations to Chief, Gunnery, etc., Sept. 25, 1919, NA, Naval History Records Division file 3829–688.

6. "Naval Aviation Policy," 18–19; Memo., WM to DAS, "Development of Ordnance for Use of Army Aviation," July 17; Memo., WM to War Plans Division, "Criticism on Paper 'A Positive System of Coast Defense,' " Oct. 14, 1919 (Brereton's dictation symbol, LHB, is on the paper).

7. Memo., WM to Capt. Maxwell, Air Service, USN, Feb. 5, 1920; *Organization of Military Aeronautics,* 54.

8. Daniels to Baker, May, 1920, quoted in Turnbull and Lord, *Naval Aviation,* 184; *The New York Times,* May 4, 1920, 1:7; Jan. 29, 1921, 1:7.

9. *Ibid.,* Aug. 17, 18:1; Aug. 29, 1920, 6:1; WM's series of articles appeared in Vol. LXII, *Review of Reviews,* 1920, "Our Army's Air Service," (Sept.), 281–290; "Aviation Over the Water," (Oct.) 391–398; "Aviation Service," (Dec.), 625–632.

10. Memo., WM to DAS, Sept. 27; entry, WM's office diary, Nov. 9, 1920; *Organization of Military Aeronautics,* 54–55; Turnbull and Lord, *Naval Aviation,* 193; Levine, *Mitchell,* 208–211; "Draft History," 726.

11. *The New York Times,* Jan. 31, 1921, 8:2; *Organization of Military Aeronautics,* 55; WM to Bane, Jan. 31, 1921.

12. Daniels to Baker, Feb. 7, 1921; Turnbull and Lord, *Naval Aviation,* 186–190; "Draft History," 809–843.

13. Cf., e.g., WM to R. R. McCormick, *Chicago Tribune,* and twelve other addressees, Feb. 24, 1921; clippings of ltrs. to *New York Tribune,* Feb. 7, 25, and *Baltimore Sun,* Feb. 8, 1921, in WM scrapbook mss.; article by H. E. Hartney, "Airplanes, Battleships, How Many?" and his note on inspired editorials, Sept. 16; "Air Service, Air Force and Air Power," *Aviation,* Apr. 25, 522–523; WM, "Air Supremacy and What It Would Mean," *American Legion Weekly,* Mar. 31, 3; WM, "Has the Airplane Made the Battleship Obsolete?" *World's Work,* XLVI (Apr.), 550–555; clipping about Sykes, "Pictures Horror Aircraft Will Add to the Next War," *New York World,* Mar. 15, 1921; for the "bolt from the blue" phrase, cf., Group Captain John A. Chamier, *Strategy and Air Strategy,* Pamphlet U-557 (U.S. Air Service, 1921), 6.

14. WM, *Our Air Force* (New York, 1921), 37, 46–54, 65, 217–233; Harold and Margaret Sprout, *Toward A New Order of Sea Power*, 85–87.

15. WM to Maj. John F. Curry, June 7, 1921; *Legislation Relating to Personnel and Training*, 20–22.

16. Downs, "Contributions of U.S. Army Aviation," 11–29, 37–48; WM to E.H. Shaunnessy, July 7; Memo., WM to Hays, Mar. 26, 1921.

17. *The New York Times*, Feb. 5, 1921; 1:7; Levine, *Mitchell*, 215.

18. Daniels to Commander in Chief, U.S. Atlantic Fleet, "Destruction of Enemy Shipping in Custody of Navy," Feb. 24, 1921 (hereafter cited as "Destruction of Enemy Shipping"); Turnbull and Lord, *Naval Aviation*, 193–204.

19. Memo., Capt. Howard Douglas to Maj. Walter Kilner, Feb. 5, 1921; "Plan of Operations for Bombardment by Airplane of Single Battleship," Dec. 11, 1920, 2; Memo., CAS to Chief of Staff, "Bombing of Battleship and Auxiliary Craft," Feb. 1, 1921; second indorsement, CAS to Chief of Staff, "Bombing of Battleship and Auxiliary Craft," Feb. 1, 1921; *ibid.,* to AG, Mar. 14, 1921, 6–7; "Draft History," 680–682.

20. Jt. Board to Sec. of War, Feb. 28, 1921, 1–2; AG to CAS, "Avoidance of Publicity in Connection with Bombing Experiments," May 9, 1921.

21. Second indorsement, CAS to AG, "Destruction of Enemy Shipping," Mar. 14; *The New York Times*, July 23, 1921, 1:1.

22. "General Mitchell's Startling Testimony," *Aviation*, Feb. 7, 167; Bane to WM, Feb. 3; Memo., Douglas to Kilner, Feb. 5; Maj. Arthur Christee to WM, Oct. 28; Maj. W. N. Hensley, Jr., to WM, Feb. 3; entry, WM's office diary, Mar. 31; telegram, WM to Gen. C. C. Williams, July 23; entry office diary, July 20; all 1921; clipping, *"Parlando Col General Mitchell,"* La Gazzetta dell' Aviazione, Jan. 23, 1922, WM scrapbook; Lavergne to WM, Feb. 22, 1921; Alexander de Seversky, "Remember Billy Mitchell," *Air Power Historian*, III (Oct., 1956), 179–181; entry, WM's office diary, July 20, 1921.

23. CAS to AG, "Relief of Brigadier General William Mitchell as Ass't Chief of Air Service," July 8; *The New York Times*, May 30, 1:7, 2:14, June 10, 2:1; June 11, 12:2, June 18, 2:4; WM to mother, June 16; all 1921; Hartney, *Up and At 'Em*, 309.

24. Memo., WM to CAS, July 25, 1921; Turnbull and Lord, *Naval Aviation*, 196–200; *The New York Times*, July 22, 1921, 2:2, 6:1, Aug. 28, III, 4; conclusion, "Report of the Operation of the First Provisional Air Brigade

in Naval Ordnance Tests," Aug. 29, 1921, 23 (hereafter cited as "Report of Operation"); Vice Admiral Alfred Johnson, USN (Ret.), "The Naval Bombing Experiments—1921," May 31, 1959, H. D. 180.058-1.

25. Jt. Board No. 349 (Serial No. 159), "Report on Results of Aviation and Ordnance Tests Held During June and July 1921 and Conclusions Reached," Aug. 18, 1921, 5–7.

26. "Report of Operation," 3, conclusion; Memo., WM to CAS, Aug. 29, 1921; *The New York Times,* Sept. 14, 1:2; "Report of Brigade Commander," July 20, 1921, 21.

27. *The New York Times,* Sept. 14, 1921, 1:2; Patrick, *The United States in the Air,* 81–83, 85–89; WM to AG, "Relief from Present Duties," and Memo., Gen. Harbord to WM, Sept. 17; *Aviation,* Sept. 26, 363; WM to mother, Aug. 3, 1921.

28. Harold and Margaret Sprout, *Toward a New Order of Sea Power,* 221–228; *The New York Times,* July 23, 1921, 6:2; Giulio Douhet, *Command of the Air,* trans. Dino Ferrari (New York, 1943), 31; Boyle, *Trenchard,* 471–473; Guidoni to WM, Aug. 23, 1921; cf., correspondence Attaché Reports File, NA, WWI, RG 165; WM, "Report of Inspection Trip to France, Italy, Germany, Holland and England," Part One, 31–32, 42–43, 97.

29. Entries, WM office diary, Aug. 27, 31; Memo., WM to CAS, "Report on Bombing of Alabama," Oct. 15, 1921.

30. Harold and Margaret Sprout, *Toward a New Order of Sea Power,* 217–240; entry, WM office diary, Nov. 18, 1921; WM, *Winged Defense* (New York, 1925), 136; for aviation subcommittee's report, cf., *Aviation,* Jan. 20, 1922, 128–132; *The New York Times,* Nov. 13, 1921, 3.

31. Cf., General James G. Harbord to Mrs. William Mitchell, Nov. 25, 1921, and Apr. 19, 1922, Harbord mss., New York Historical Society, WM to mother, Nov. 25, Dec. 5, 1921; Wadsworth OHP, 324–325.

32. WM to Arnold, Aug. 21; to Bane, Nov. 4; entry, WM office diary, Dec. 10, 1921; Harold and Margaret Sprout, *Toward a New Order of Sea Power,* 236–239.

CHAPTER FIVE

1. The technical report was published as: *Report of Inspection to France, Italy, Germany, Holland and England, Made During the Winter of 1921–1922* (Technical Supplement) (Washington, 1923); Foulois (then assistant military attaché in Berlin) to WM, Mar. 13, 1922.

2. WM to Patrick, Jan. 9, 1922; WM, "Report of Inspection Trip to France, Italy, Germany, Holland and England," Part One, 1–16, 21, 24, 31–32 (hereafter cited as "Report of Inspection").

3. *Ibid.*, 38–40; WM to Maj. C. B. Oldfield, Jan. 30, 1933, Trenchard, "Aspects of Service Aviation," (a paper read at the British Air Conference), Oct. 14, 1920, 9–10.

4. Ltr., "Il Ten. Col. A. Guidoni A Douhet," Nov. 13, 1922 in Giulio Douhet, *Scritti Inediti* ed. Antonio Monti (Milan, 1951), 236–237; Guidoni, "Problems of the Independent Air Force," *Aviation,* Nov. 20, 1922, 687; *Aviation,* Dec. 18, 1922, 804; *ibid.,* Mar. 26, 1923, 348; *Air Service Newsletter,* Mar. 21, 1923, 12.

5. Douhet, *Scritti Inediti,* 236–237.

6. Giulio Douhet, *Command of the Air,* trans. Dino Ferrari (New York, 1943), 4, 6, 9, 15–20, 24–28, 34–35, 42–51, 54–58, 72–74, 80, 87–90, 93–142.

7. *Ibid.,* 26; "Report of Inspection," 44, 47–48, 70; Memo., WM to DAS, Apr. 2, 1920 (enclosing ltr. from Guidoni); *The New York Times,* Feb. 22, 1922, 1:1.

8. Douhet, *Command of the Air,* 30–31; "Report of Inspection," 53–56, 61–66; *Air Service Newsletter,* Feb. 28, 1922, 5; Verville OHP, 79–82; Foulois Interview.

9. The "bolt from the blue" phrase is from Group Captain John A. Chamier, *Strategy and Air Strategy,* Pamphlet U-557 (U.S. Air Service, 1921), 6; "Report of Inspection," 79–83, 87–88, 97–99, 102; Trenchard, "Aspects of Service Aviation," 2; Boyle, *Trenchard,* 350, 354, 361–364.

10. "Report of Inspection," 105.

11. *Air Service Newsletter,* Apr. 7, 1922, 1; Memo., Deputy Chief of Staff to Patrick, Oct. 24, 1922 and reply, NA, RG 94, File No. 580, Box 1061; Frank C. (?) to Spaatz, Mar. 6, 1923, Spaatz mss.

12. On Mitchell's international recognition, cf., *L'Ala d' Italia* (Dec., 1922) 168; Lt. Col. J. F. Chaney to WM, Nov. 28, 1922; WM, "What's the Matter With Flying in America?" *Popular Science Monthly* (Apr., 1922), 24–26; "Aviation and Geology," *U.S. Air Services,* VIII (May, 1923), 8–10; cf., Weeks' testimony on keeping WM out of controversy in U.S. Cong., House, *Select Committee on Inquiry into Operations of the United States Air Services,* 69th Cong., 1st Sess., 1925, 3020. Note also on p. 3060, Weeks' uncertainty

as to the effectiveness of his requirement that WM submit his articles for clearance.

13. WM, "Report of Inspection of Sperry Service," Mar., 1923; Office Diary entries, Feb. 19 through Feb. 23, 1923; "Report of Inspection . . . Langley Field and visit to Canadian Aeronautical Activities . . ."; copy of speech at Chateau Laurier, Ottawa, Canada, Feb. 22, 1923.

14. WM to Patrick, Aug. 3 and Sept. 21; Bissell to Spaatz, July 22, 1922, all in Spaatz mss.; "Inspection of Brooks Field," 35–36; "Inspection of First Pursuit Group, Selfridge Field," 13–25, 50–64; *Air Service Newsletter,* Mar. 5, 1923, 7.

15. Lawson to Spaatz, Feb. 8; Spaatz to Maj. B. K. Yount, Mar. 5; Memo., Spaatz to WM, Mar. 12; Lieut. H. W. Cook to Spaatz, May 1; Bissell to Spaatz, Sept. 14, 1923, all in Spaatz mss.; WM, "Notes on the Multi-Motored Bombardment Group—Day and Night" (hereafter cited as "Bombardment"); "Report on the Bangor Flight," 49; compare WM's manual with an earlier "official" view in *Aerial Tactics,* Air Service Pamphlet No. 88, July 30, 1920.

16. "Bombardment," 74, 84–85.

17. *Ibid.,* 93–95.

18. *Ibid.,* 6–13, 17, 94, 112, 118–127.

19. *Ibid.,* 70, 97–107.

20. "Report on the Bangor Flight," 4, 6, 29, 38.

21. Office Diary entry, Sept. 5, 1923; Report of a Committee of Officers ". . . to consider . . . a plan of war organization for the Air Service . . .," Mar. 27, 1923, NA, file No. 319.2, (hereafter cited as "Lassiter Board Report"); *Annual Report of CAS* (Washington, 1923), 40, 78–79; *Hearings Before the President's Aircraft Board* (Washington, 1925), 80–81 (hereafter cited as *President's Aircraft Board*).

22. "Lassiter Board Report"; *President's Aircraft Board,* 97–99, 575; Turnbull and Lord, *History of United States Naval Aviation,* 252.

23. Weeks to Morrow, no date; Memo., Lt. Col. E. A. Heinman to Gen. Heintzleman, no date, all enclosed in "Lassiter Board Report" file.

24. Levine, *Mitchell,* 293.

25. *Ibid.,* 298–299; WM, "Report of Inspection of United States Posses-

sions in the Pacific and Java, Singapore, India, Siam, China and Japan," Oct. 24, 1924, USAFA (hereafter cited as "Report of Pacific Inspection").

26. *Ibid.*, 28–30, 50; Jeter A. Isley and Philip A. Crowl, *The U.S. Marines and Amphibious Warfare* (Princeton, 1951), 25–27.

27. "Report of Pacific Inspection," 24–25, 33–40, 299–300; on the weather conditions in Alaska, cf., *Aviation*, June 16, 1924, 641; WM, speech to members of Air Service Engineering Division, Oct. 6, 1924, 3.

28. "Report of Pacific Inspection," 39–40, 43–47, 138–143, 147–155, 323–324.

29. *Ibid.*, 50–58, 80, 130, 323; WM to Sen. James Wadsworth, Jan. (date obscure), 1924, Wadsworth Family mss. I am indebted to Mr. Alan Thompson for the Wadsworth reference.

30. Patrick to Summerall, Jan. 26; Summerall to Patrick, Feb. 18, 1924; "Extracts from the Report of the Commanding General, Hawaiian Dept. on Joint Army and Navy Exercises," No. 3, July 21, 1925, paragraphs 10 and 14.

CHAPTER SIX

1. *Aviation*, Sept. 22, 1924, 1015–1021; WM, Office Diary entry, Oct. 6; speech to Air Service Engineering Division, Oct. 6, 1924.

2. *President's Aircraft Hearings*, 587–588; WM to AG, "Testimony of Brigadier General Mitchell," Jan. 29, 1925, 12; Greer, *The Development of Air Doctrine*, 19–20; Craven and Cate, *The Army Air Forces in World War II*, I, 24.

3. "General Mitchell's Daring Speech," *Aviation*, Oct. 20, 1924, 1159–1160; Palmer, *Newton D. Baker, America at War*, II, 267–268; P. R. C. Groves, "For France to Answer," *Atlantic Monthly*, CXXIX (Feb., 1924), 145–153.

4. Coolidge to WM, Nov. 12, 1924; U.S. Congress, House. *Select Committee on Inquiry into Operation of the U.S. Air Services*, 69th Congress. 1st Sess., 1925, 3020, 3059–3060, 3064–3065 (hereafter cited as *Lampert Committee*). On Patrick's role, cf., *The New York Times*, Mar. 3, 1925, 3:1.

5. WM, "Aeronautical Era," Dec. 20, 1924, 3–4, 99–101 and "American Leadership in Aeronautics," *Saturday Evening Post*, Jan. 10, 1925, 148, 153; U.S. Congress, House, Committee on Military Affairs, *Air Service Unifica-*

tion, 68th Congress, 2d Sess., 1925, 384 (hereafter cited as *Air Service Unification*).

6. WM, "Aircraft Dominate Seacraft," *Saturday Evening Post,* Jan. 24, 1925, 77; AG to WM, "Testimony of Brigadier General Mitchell," Jan. 29, 1925.

7. *Lampert Committee,* 295–297; *Air Service Unification,* 377–378; the "peace and penury" phrase is from *The New York Times,* Dec. 6, 1925, IV, 9.

8. *Lampert Committee,* 1674–1675, 1887, 3020–3023; AG to CAS, Jan. 29; Memo., WM to CAS, Feb. 5; CAS to AG, Feb. 6, 1925; AG to CAS, Feb. 7; Memo., WM to CAS, Mar. 2; CAS to AG, Mar. 11, 1925; *The New York Times,* Feb. 1, 27:6; Feb, 5, 4:3; Feb. 7, 1925, 2:6.

9. *Lampert Committee,* 1898, 1914, 3016–3017, 3022–3023; *The New York Times,* Feb. 7, 2:1; Feb. 10, 48:3, Feb. 19, 1925, 1:6; Wadsworth OHP, 327–329. This Wadsworth material should be used with some caution. E.g., Wadsworth wrongly claimed that Weeks sent WM to the Pacific immediately after his marital crisis with the first Mrs. Mitchell.

10. *The New York Times,* Feb. 3, 3:4; Feb. 4, 1:3; Feb. 5, 1:3; Feb. 7, 1:1; Wadsworth OHP, 324–325; AG to CAS, Feb. 11, WM to CAS, Feb. 16; WM to *Lampert Committee,* Feb. 28, 1925, 3; Boyle, *Trenchard,* 472.

11. Weeks to Coolidge, Mar. 4, 1925; *Lampert Committee,* 3036, 3039–3040.

12. *The New York Times,* Mar. 7, 1:8; Mar. 31, 1:4; Apr. 28, 1925, 1:2; WM to Wg. Commander W. A. Barker, Apr. 21; WM to C. G. Grey, Mar, 20, 1925.

13. Patrick to AG, Dec. 19, 1924 and Memo., War Plans Division to Chief of Staff, Jan. 6, 1925, NA, RG 94, File 580.

14. Coolidge to Morrow, Mar. 11; Randolph Perkins (*Lampert Committee*) to Morrow, Jan. 13; A. H. Springer (Morrow's secretary) to Gibbons Co., Jan. 19; Springer to Perkins, May 25, 1925, all in Morrow mss.; William A. White, *A Puritan in Babylon* (New York, 1938), 433.

15. Coolidge to Weeks, May 5; Senator Hiram Bingham to Coolidge, May 15; Davis to Coolidge, May 9 and reply May 22; Davis to Everett Sanders (Coolidge's secretary), July 30 (with note attached in Coolidge's handwriting); Coolidge to Davis, Aug. 1, 1925, all in Coolidge mss.

16. *The New York Times,* May 7, 7:1; Aug. 2, 23:4; Aug. 20, 1925,

29:7; WM, *Winged Defense* (New York, 1925) viii; Mrs. William Mitchell to WM, Sept. 2, 1925; copy of WM interview in *San Antonio Light,* Sept. 9, 1925.

17. *The New York Times,* Sept. 2, 1:1; Sept. 4, 1925; 1:4; WM, "Statement of William Mitchell Concerning the Recent Air Accidents," (mimeographed); telegram, David Lawrence to WM, Sept. 9; *Liberty* to WM, Sept. 12, 1925; copy of WM interview *San Antonio Light,* Sept. 9, 1925; WM to Commanding General Eighth Corps Area, Sept. 11, 1925.

18. *The New York Times,* Sept. 9, 1:4; Sept. 22, 1:7; Oct. 5, 16:4; Oct. 14, 16:3; Oct. 21, 1925, 1:3; Weeks and Wilbur to Coolidge, Sept. 11 and Coolidge's reply, Sept. 12, 1925, Coolidge mss.

19. Coolidge to Weeks and Wilbur, Sept. 12, 1925, Coolidge mss.; *President's Aircraft Board,* 1694.

20. *Report of President's Aircraft Board* (Washington, 1925), 2; *President's Aircraft Board,* 72–73.

21. AG to Patrick, and various branch chiefs, Sept. 23 and replies, Oct. 3, 1925, NA, RG 94, File 580.

22. *President's Aircraft Board,* 499–502, 553–559, 1370.

23. *Ibid.,* 495–633; Arnold, *Global Mission,* 119–120; Mrs. H. H. Arnold OHP, 56–59; Harold Nicholson, *Dwight Morrow* (New York, 1935), 283.

24. The transcript of the court-martial is in the National Archives, but it is sealed. Facts relating to the court-martial therefore, are from *The New York Times* in this period; *The New York Times,* Oct. 21, 1:3; Oct. 28, 27:5; Oct. 29, 1925, 1:7; entry for Sept. 8, 1925, "Diary of Leonard Wood"; Wood to McCoy, Nov. 12, 1925, Wood mss.; Pershing to Morrow, Oct. 17; Pershing to Gen. William M. Wright, Dec. 22, 1925, Pershing mss.

25. Cf., *The New York Times* for this period, but especially, Oct. 21, 1:3; Oct. 29, 1:7; Oct. 30, 1:8; Nov. 9, 1:3; Nov. 10, 1:8; Dec. 19, 1925, 1:7; McCoy to Mrs. Wood, Nov. 14, 1925, Wood mss.; copies of U.S. Army "Mid-Weekly Press Review" and "Air Service Press Review" for this period; clipping, "Declare Mitchell Could be Chosen Legion Head," *Omaha Heraid,* Oct. 6, 1925, all in WM mss.

26. WM, article marked "No. III for Bell Syndicate," written at time of court-martial.

27. *Report of President's Aircraft Board,* 1–30; Weeks to Morrow, no date, included in Lassiter Board file, NA, AG File 319.2.

28. Rep. Hicks to Morrow, Nov. 19, 1925; Harbord to Morrow, Jan. 29, 1926, Morrow mss.; *Organization of Military Aeronautics,* 71–80; Elspeth E. Freudenthal, *The Aviation Business* (New York, 1940), 73–84; Henry Ladd Smith, *Airways* (New York, 1942), 98–99.

29. Eugene E. Wilson, *Slipstream, the Autobiography of an Air Craftsman* (New York, 1950), 57–72 (Wilson was a close associate of Moffett in this period); Moffett to Morrow, Mar. 2 and Apr. 26; Vinson to Morrow, Apr. 13 and June 22; Rep. McSwain to Morrow, June 10, 1926, all in Morrow mss.

30. *The New York Times,* Dec. 19, 4:3; Dec. 20, 1925, 9:1; WM, Resignation Statement, Feb. 1; WM to Trenchard et al., Mar. 12, 1926.

31. Judge McCook to Morrow, Dec. 30, 1925, Morrow mss.; *The New York Times,* Dec. 9, 1:5; Dec. 19, 1925, 1:7.

32. WM to Harriet (his sister), Apr. 15 and her telegraphed reply, Apr. 28, 1926.

33. Correspondence between WM and tour manager James Pond, esp. telegram Mar. 12; Pond to Mrs. Edith Thompson, Feb. 19; Eugene Putnam to WM, Jan. 26, 1926 (this evidence conflicts with *Organization of Military Aeronautics,* 77, which claims a sale of 75,000 copies of *Winged Defense* by this time); Judge McCook to Morrow, and John D. Ryan to Morrow, Dec. 4; Justice Harlan Stone to Morrow, Rep. Madden to Morrow, and Herbert Bayard Swope to Morrow, Dec. 7, 1925, Morrow mss.; John W. Wheeler, *Liberty,* to WM, Mar. 13, 1926.

34. Harbord to General George Van Moseley, Feb. 4, 1926, Harbord mss., New York Historical Society; War Dept. to Maj. Henry C. Rexach, Mar. 24, 1926, NA, RG 165.

CHAPTER SEVEN

1. WM, "Let the Air Service Crash," *Liberty,* Jan. 30, 1926, 43–46; *The New York Times,* Jan. 30, 1926, 8:4; Douhet, *Scritti Inediti,* 125, and *Command of the Air,* 54–57; B. Liddell Hart, *Paris; or The Future of War* (New York and London, 1925), 26–27, 35–56, 83–85; also cf., Liddell Hart's later views in *Strategy* (New York, 1955), 363.

2. WM, "When the Air Raiders Come," *Colliers,* May 1, 1926, 8–9; the figure of "ten million" subscribers is drawn from N. W. Ayer, *American Newspaper Annual and Directory* (Philadelphia, 1926 through 1928).

3. Greer, *The Development of Air Doctrine,* 19, 40–41; Craven and Cate,

The Army Air Forces in World War II, I, 45; (author unknown), *Employment of Combined Air Force,* USAF H. D. 248. 101–7A, p. 3.

4. Levine, *Mitchell,* 377; *The New York Times,* Aug. 28, 10:8; Sept. 9, 1926, 3:5; Oct. 13, 1928, 14:4.

5. *The New York Times,* May 23, 1927, 1:4 and 20:2; cf., the issues of *Aviation* in this period, e.g., "Happy New Year," Jan. 5, 1929, 23; Earl D. Osborn, "The Industry's Progress During 1928," 24–25.

6. R. J. Brown, *Popular Science Monthly* to WM, May 21 and reply, May 25; telegrams, B. Merrill, Hearst Publications to WM and reply, May 26; WM to Merrill, June 1, 1927.

7. *The New York Times,* Aug. 15, 4:2; Oct. 12, 1927, 11:6; WM did not date his articles, hence all dates in his itinerary are approximations.

8. WM, ms. marked "French article," 5, 7, 12; "French Air Power," 5–6; "Our First Glimpse of the Germany of Today," 3–4. All mss. for the Hearst articles are in the "European Articles" folder. These mss. have been used (with two exceptions) because the New York Public Library files of the Hearst paper, *The New York American,* is in too deteriorated a condition.

9. WM, ms. marked "Article VII—Italy," 1–7; Italian Foreign Office to WM, Sept. 12, 1927.

10. Conger to Assistant Chief of Staff, G-2, Sept. 14, 1924, NA, Military Intelligence Division Report No. 51–387, 83; WM, "Our First Glimpse of the Germany of Today," 5–10; "How the Zeppelin Company is Helping Germany to Create a Great Airship Passenger Fleet," 1–9.

11. Levine, *Mitchell,* 378; WM, "Russian Aeronautics," *Forum* LXXX (July, 1928), 110.

12. *The New York Times,* Sept. 22, 1927, 4:2; Oct. 13, 1928, 14:4; WM, "How Britain is Striding Forward in the Air," *The New York American,* Nov. 20, 1927, p. E-3; "England's Air Power," 2–7.

13. On WM's repetitiveness, compare his "Let the Air Service Crash," *Liberty,* Jan. 30, 1926, 43, with "Airplanes in National Defense," *American Assembly of Political and Social Science,* CXXXI (May, 1927), 38–42 and "Look Out Below," *Colliers,* Apr. 21, 1928, 8–9.

14. WM, "War Memoirs" or "From Start to Finish of Our Greatest War," Preface, 1–2, Apr., 1917, 176; May, 29–30; Nov., 1917, 149–150; Jan., 1918, 150; May, 192–193; June, 1918, 217–218; "Leaves from My War Diary,"

Liberty, Mar. 31, 1928, 9–13 and *passim.;* B. Liddell Hart, *The Remaking of Modern Armies* (Boston, 1928) and *The Real War* (Boston, 1930); J. F. C. Fuller, *The Reformation of War* (London, 1923) and *On Future Warfare* (London, 1928).

15. WM, "The Opening of Alaska," unpublished ms., 2a–4a; "Bombard-ment," 85.

16. WM, "America, Air Power and the Pacific," 14–17, 73; ms. marked *"Aeronautics,* Nov., 1929," "Air Power Will Dominate the Pacific."

17. *The New York Times,* Feb. 8, 1928, 8:1; Levine, *Mitchell,* 380.

18. *The New York Times,* Oct. 13, 1928, 14:4; WM to Adm. Murray Sueter, July 5, 1928.

19. Levine, *Mitchell,* 380; WM to H. Chaney, Sept. 29; clipping. *Chicago Tribune,* Nov. 2; WM to Col. R. Guggenheim, Sept. 28, 1928.

20. Robert H. Ferrell, *Peace in Their Time; The Origins of the Kellogg-Briand Pact* (New Haven, 1952), 192–200.

21. WM to Capt. A. Winslow, Sept. 4, 1929; telegram, M. V. Little to WM, Oct. 15, 1928; H. E. Hartney to WM, Feb. 1 and reply, Feb. 8, 1929.

22. J. V. Jenkins, Little, Brown Co., to WM, May 23 and reply, May 28, 1929; T. Costain, *Saturday Evening Post,* to WM and reply, July 23, 1929; WM, ms. marked *"Aeronautics,* Jan., 1930," "Aircraft of the Near Future"; "Anecdotes of the Air," *Woman's Home Companion,* LVII (Dec., 1930), 30–31; "How to Know Tigers," *Colliers,* Aug. 31, 1929, 28–29.

23. WM, *Skyways* (New York, 1930), 5, 7; WM to Verville, Jan. 22; WM to Russell, Mar. 30; WM to Doolittle, Sept. 28, 1929; Victory Interview.

24. *Skyways,* 5, 299–307.

25. *Ibid.,* 262–263, 279–280, 285–289; Greer, *The Development of Air Doctrine,* 58.

26. WM, ms. of radio address, "Colliers Radio Hour," Nov. 10, 1929, 5; Herbert Hoover, *The Memoirs of Herbert Hoover 1920–1933, The Cabinet and the Presidency* (New York, 1952), 366–379; WM to A. Brisbane, May 13, 1930, Dec. 1, 1931; WM, "The Next War—What About Our National Defense," *Liberty,* July 27, 1931, 40, 44.

27. Franklin D. Roosevelt, "Why Naval Aviation Won," *U.S. Air Service,*

I (July, 1919), 7–8; F. D. R. to J. Roosevelt, Apr. 27, 1925, *FDR- His Personal Letters* (New York, 1948), II, 579–581.

28. E. D. Coblentz, Hearst Publications to WM, and reply, May 18, 1932; WM, "Are We Ready for War With Japan?" *Liberty*, Jan. 30, 1932, 7–12, and "Will Japan Try to Conquer the United States?" *ibid.*, July 25, 1932, 6–11.

29. Levine, *Mitchell*, 390–391; WM to Roosevelt, Dec. 21, 1932.

CHAPTER EIGHT

1. Joseph E. Davies to Roosevelt, Dec. 27, 1932; undated ltrs. to Roosevelt from Democratic Party leadership in Michigan sgd. by W. A. Constode, et al., and in Wisconsin by Senator-elect F. Ryan Duffy; Gill Robb Wilson to WM, Jan. 16, and reply, Jan. 30; Alfred Verville to WM, Mar. 14; Alexander P. de Seversky to WM, Mar. 30; Col. Thomas Milling to WM, May 5; Maj. William Ocker to WM, July 15 and reply, July 19; WM to T. Coleman Andrews, Apr. 25; WM to Col. Fitzhugh Lee, Mar. 9 and Apr. 29, 1933.

2. WM to Flynn, Hearst, Mar. 20; WM to E. Balester, *Liberty*, July 10 and reply, July 26, 1933; Balester to WM, Apr. 20; WM to T. Ranck, Hearst, Apr. 25, July 10 and reply, July 16; WM to Gordon Fulcher, *Liberty*, July 25; Chandler to WM, May 3, July 30; Findley to WM, Aug. 1, Sept. 12; WM to Oldfield, Jan. 30, 1933; Editorial, "Air Warfare Trends," Aug., 1933, 8–9, and Thomas R. Reed, "Another Daniel Come to Judgment?" Sept., 1933, 28, *U.S. Air Services*, XVIII (Sept., 1933); Chandler, "The Air Warfare Doctrine of General Douhet," May, 1933, 10, Editorial, "Strong Doctrine," June, 1933, 10, Walker, "A New Trend in Pursuit Development," Oct., 1933, 15, all in *ibid.;* cf., *ibid.*, XIX, for Chennault, "Special Support for Bombardment," Jan., 1934, 18–21, Chandler, "A New Deal for Old Strategy," June, 1934, 16–17, and *ibid.*, "Air Warfare Considerations," Nov., 1934, 12–15. Greer, *The Development of Air Doctrine*, 50–51.

3. *Ibid.*, 44–75; unsigned article, "The New Martin Army Bomber," *U.S. Air Services*, XVIII (Apr., 1933), 27; Army Air Forces Historical Studies: No. 6, *The Development of the Heavy Bomber* (Montgomery, 1951), 146–147; Walker to Spaatz, Nov. 23 and reply, Dec. 25; George to Spaatz, Dec. 10, 1932, Spaatz mss.; lecture by George, "An Inquiry into the Subject of 'War,'" Andrews, mss.

4. Robert T. Finney, *History of the Air Corps Tactical School* (Montgomery, 1955), 57–58; Greer, *The Development of Air Doctrine*, 44–75; WM to George, Mar. 2 and reply, Mar. 24, 1933; WM to George, Apr. 3,

1934; Andrews to WM, May 9, 1931, Sept. 12, 1931, Nov. 6, 1931, Andrews mss.

5. WM to Maj. C. B. Oldfield, Jan. 30, 1933; WM, "Aircraft in War," unpublished ms., 7, 10; *The New York Times*, Feb. 21, 1934, 10:2; Spaatz to Lt. H. W. Cook, Feb. 13, 1923, Spaatz mss.

6. H. E. Hartney, *Up and At 'Em*, 314; Hartney to WM, Feb. 4, and reply; WM to C. G. Greer, Mar. 23; WM to Boake Carter, July 29; WM to Rep. James V. McClintic, Apr. 8, 1933; WM to A. Brisbane, June 10, 1933.

7. Unsigned article, "Establishing an Airship Building Industry in the United States," U.S. Air Services, XVII (Apr., 1932), 24–26; Editorial, "The Cause of Airships is Not Lost," *ibid.*, XVIII (Apr., 1933), 7–8; unsigned article, "The World's Greatest Airship is Now Being Built," *ibid.*, XIX (Mar., 1934), 19–20; WM to Lt. Commander T. G. Settle, Apr. 19; WM to Fred M. Harpham, Goodyear Co., Apr. 29, 1933; H. Allen to WM, Goodyear Co., Mar. 19, 1934; *The New York Times*, July 2, 1933, 15:1; Feb. 15, 1935, 3:2.

8. WM to R. S. Cochran, June 6, July 19, 1933; statement to WM from J. B. Lippincott on sales of *Skyways* through June, 1933; Elliott Balester, *Liberty*, to WM, Apr. 20, June 26; T. Ranck, Hearst, to WM, July 16; WM to Roosevelt, July 4, Sept. 24, 1933 and Dec. 1, 1934, Roosevelt mss.; WM to Richard Crane, Dec. 20; WM to Weaver, Dec. 21, 1933.

9. Army Air Forces Historical Studies: No. 25, *Organization of Military Aeronautics*, 1907–35 (Washington, 1944), 90–91 (hereafter cited as *Organization of Military Aeronautics*); Findley to WM, Oct. 12 and reply, Oct. 24, 1933; "Air Power Has its Own Theatre of Operations" (with introduction by WM), *U.S. Air Services*, XVIII (Dec., 1933), 15–19.

10. *The New York Times*, Feb. 9, 1934, 1:6; *Organization of Military Aeronautics*, 92–93.

11. *The New York Times*, Feb. 9, 2:1, 2:3; Feb. 27, 9:4; Mar. 6, 4:5; Mar. 17, 7:5, 1934; WM to A. Brisbane, Sept. 4, 1934; Weaver to WM, no date.

12. *Organization of Military Aeronautics*, 90, n.13, 93–96.

13. *The New York Times*, July 24, 6:6; Sept. 23, 28:2; Oct. 3, 1934, 1:5; T. Ranck, Hearst, to WM, Jan. 30; Gordon Fulcher, *Liberty*, to WM, Feb. 15, 1935; *Organization of Military Aeronautics*, 97–100; WM to Weaver, Oct. 3, 1934; unsigned article, "Howell Board in Action," *U.S. Air Services*, XIX (Dec., 1934), 37.

14. WM to Brisbane, Feb. 6; WM to Walter Weaver, Mar. 7, 1935; *The New York Times,* Dec. 6, 1935, 7:1, on Elliott Roosevelt, cf., "Merrily We Roll Along," *U.S. Air Services,* XIX (Dec., 1934), 11.

15. WM to T. Ranck, Hearst, Feb. 12 and Mar. 25; Ranck to WM, July 1; Gordon Fulcher, *Liberty,* to WM, Feb. 15, Mar. 26, 1935; Irving L. Ricker to *The New York Times,* Oct. 14, 1934, IV, 5:5; WM, "Am I a Jingo?" unpublished ms.; WM to Oursler, *Liberty,* July 29 and Dec. 22; Oursler to WM, July 31; WM to Joseph M. Patterson, *New York Daily News,* Mar. 7; Ray P. Holland, *Field and Stream,* to WM, Dec. 3, 1935.

16. WM, *General Greely* (New York, 1936); WM to Oursler, Dec. 22, 1935; *The New York Times,* Jan. 29, 3:5; Feb. 11, 1936, 6:8; Memo., F. D. Roosevelt to Col. Watson, Jan. 25, 1936, Roosevelt mss.

17. Levine, *Mitchell,* 399–400; *The New York Times,* Feb. 20, 1936, 10:1.

APPENDIX

1. *Annual Report CSO,* 1892, 598–599. On Greely's influence, cf., William Mitchell, *General Greely* (New York, Putnam, 1936), 201.

2. J. D. Fullerton, "Some Remarks on Aerial Warfare," in U.S. Congress, 53rd Cong., 2nd Session, Senate Executive Document 119, *Operations of the Division of Military Engineering of the International Congress of Engineers* (Washington, 1894), 571–574. On Fullerton, cf., Harald Penrose, *British Aviation, The Pioneer Years, 1903–1914* (London, Putnam, 1967), 85–86, 91, 581. For good insights into this early period, cf., Russell J. Parkinson, "Politics, Patents and Planes: Military Aeronautics in the U.S., 1863–1907," unpublished Ph.D. dissertation, Duke University, 1963.

3. Apparently in 1937–38, someone at the Air Corps Tactical School noted on a summary of Fullerton's paper: "It would seem that General Giulio Douhet was forty years late." Cf., H.D. 248. 2019A, 1937–1938.

4. Paul W. Clark, "Major General George Owen Squier: Military Scientist," unpublished Ph.D. dissertation, Case–Western Reserve University, 1974, 109–169, 202–207, 219–231, 250–291 (hereafter cited as "Squier").

5. *Ibid.,* 109–126; cf., pp. 11–12, text of this book.

6. Ltr., Brig. Gen. James Allen to Col. Frank Baker, December 19, 1908, NA, RG III; Clark, "Squier," 148; George O. Squier, "The Present State of Military Aeronautics," *Mechanical Engineering,* XXX (Dec., 1908), 1571–1641.

7. *Ibid.,* 1574–1579, 1583, 1591–1592, 1614–1617.

8. Quotation from House Committee on Military Affairs Report repeated in U.S. Congress, Senate, 63rd Cong., 2nd Session, Calendar 498, Report 576, *Army Aviation Service,* 1.

9. Henry H. Arnold, *Global Mission* (New York, Harper, 1949), 37–38; Benjamin Foulois (with C. V. Glines), *From the Wright Brothers to the Astronauts* (New York, McGraw-Hill, 1968), 124–125 (hereafter cited as "Memoirs"). Foulois errs in suggesting that Mitchell had nothing to do with aviation before 1916; cf., NA, RG 165, WCD 7615, a file of actions on aviation matters handled by Mitchell and dating from 1913 (hereafter cited as "Mitchell GS File"). Attaché information of varying quality is scattered through RG 94, III and 165 for the years 1912–17. The first major survey of attaché information (1912) is U.S. Congress, House, 62nd Cong., 2nd Session, Document 718, *Military Aviation,* 5–69. From a 1916 survey, cf., RG 165, WCD 9520, in the file on the airmen's effort in 1916 to break away from the Signal Corps.

10. Clark, "Squier," 166–169, 202–207, 221–232, 237–241. For an assessment of Henderson, Sykes and Lanchester cf., Robin Higham, *The Military Intellectuals in Britain, 1918–1939* (New Brunswick, Rutgers, 1966), 119–133 (hereafter cited as *Military Intellectuals*).

11. The report is an attachment to memo, Gen. Leonard Wood to WCD, GS, April 14, 1913, "Mitchell GS File."

12. Clark, "Squier," 244; cf., index to Frederick Lanchester, *Aircraft in Warfare* (London, Constable, 1916), 215–222.

13. Foulois, *Memoirs,* 128–141. Space limitations prevent me from citing more examples of pre–World War I thinking in the United States about military aeronautics. I intend to expand this discussion in my forthcoming history of the United States Air Force.

14. Cf., pp. 24–29, 30–32, text of this book. The late Frank J. Capelluti in "The Life and Thought of Giulio Douhet," unpublished Ph.D. dissertation, Rutgers University, 1967, showed that Douhet was Gianni Caproni's mentor and not his "mouthpiece," as Higham speculated in *Military Intellectuals,* 258.

15. Cf., pp. 35–36, 179–180, text; Robert Frank Futrell, *Ideas, Concepts, Doctrine: A History of Basic Thinking in the United States Air Force, 1907–1914,* 2 vols. (Montgomery, Air University, 1971), I, 20–22 (hereafter cited as *Ideas*). Higham, *Military Intellectuals,* 140, makes an excellent point about the limited meaning of the term "strategic" in World War I aerial operations

conducted in direct support of the British Army in France. As Futrell suggests, this limited meaning also described Mitchell's conduct of American operations.

16. Cf., pp. 73–79, text; the now public file on the reports of the U.S. Army attaché to Rome, NA, RG 165, WCD 2086, show that the attaché regularly sent information on Douhet and his writings to the General Staff, beginning in March 1922; Futrell, *Ideas*, I, 38–39; the Field Officers School was the forerunner of the Tactical School; Raymond Flugel, "United States Air Power Doctrine: A Study of the Influence of William Mitchell and Giulio Douhet at the Air Corps Tactical School, 1921–1935," unpublished dissertation, University of Oklahoma, 1965, 201 (hereafter cited as "Influence of Mitchell and Douhet").

17. Cf., pp. 75–77, 92–95, 126–127, text; Flugel, "Influence of Mitchell and Douhet," argues that Douhet's influence was overriding at the Air Corps Tactical School, but I think he pays too little attention to the factors addressed in this book to sustain his case. Bernard Brodie, *Strategy in the Missile Age* (Princeton, Princeton Press, 1959 and 1965), 71–106, is more careful than Flugel in his acknowledgement of other influences. Just the same, Brodie goes beyond his evidence and ascribes too much influence to Douhet. For an excellent memoir on the Air Corps Tactical School effort to work out a strategic bombing doctrine cf., Haywood S. Hansell, *The Air Plan That Defeated Hitler* (Atlanta, privately published, 1972).

18. Cf., pp. 111–112, text; the court-martial record is in NA (Suitland), RG 153, Office Judge Advocate General, General Courts-Martial, 1812–1930, 168771.

19. *Ibid.;* the full Mitchell testimony is on 1401–1610. Cf., p. 111, text.

20. *Ibid.*, 2955–3007. The witness was Capt. H. D. Rath, USAR. Burke Davis, *The Billy Mitchell Affair* (New York, Random House, 1967), 287n. Mr. Davis was the first author to use the court-martial transcript and provided a long account of the trial, 239–329. A lawyer's extended summary and analysis of the trial is in Box 1 of the court-martial transcript: "The Trial of Colonel William Mitchell, Oct. 28–Dec. 1, 1928," by Maj. A. Goff, JAGD-Res. Goff is highly critical of Reid's conduct of the defense.

21. U.S. Congress, Senate, 90th Cong., 2nd Session, *Medal of Honor, 1863–1968* (Washington, GPO, 1968), 728 and 972. Cf., remarks of Senator A. Wiley on the failure of the bill in *Ibid.*, Senate, 80th Cong., 2nd Session, *Congressional Record*, March 29, 1948, 3579–3580.

Bibliography

I. PRIMARY SOURCES

A. *The Mitchell Papers*

One of Mitchell's manuscripts in the Library of Congress, "From Start to Finish of Our Greatest War," was published almost in its entirety in 1960 by Random House, as the *Memoirs of World War I*. The editors of this published version omitted, in the interest of readability, some of the valuable documents which Mitchell quoted in full in the original manuscript. For that reason, I have used the Library of Congress manuscript, available in draft in Box I and (in a more polished form) in Box 22 of the collection.

There are difficulties in using Mitchell's account of his World War I service. He claimed that he based his work on a diary which he kept during the war years. Unfortunately, the diary is not in the collection and apparently has been lost. The wealth of detail in his manuscript is evidence that Mitchell kept such a diary, since much of it can be corroborated by such sources as the Air Service, AEF records in the National Archives, the memoirs of other important American leaders, including Generals John J. Pershing and James G. Harbord, and a scholarly study such as Irving B. Holley's *Ideas and Weapons*. Perhaps the major complication stems from Mitchell's use in the manuscript of his fundamental argument for strategic bombardment, the "vital centers" rationale; that is, the idea that through the aerial bombardment of an enemy's "vital centers," his industries, communications, and, in certain cases, his civilian population, a nation might break its enemy's will to resist and avoid the bloodbaths of World War I. Indeed on pages one and two of the Preface to the manuscript, Mitchell seemed to be making this the theme of the work. Thus, he went to extraordinary lengths in the entry for April, 1917, in describing the disastrous results of the Nivelle Offensive, which he observed during his first month in France. Also, in his entry for May, 1917, during which he recounted his first meeting with Trenchard and other British airmen, he uses the "vital centers" language in remarking that he had found the view to be widespread among "a large portion of British military opinion."

The crux of the problem is that Mitchell kept silent on these points privately as well as publicly for the next eight years. There can be no doubt that Mitchell encountered at least the first indications of the strategic bombardment idea during World War I, that he did not begin to pursue it in earnest until after his European trip in 1921 and then only privately, and that he had refrained from mentioning the topic publicly until 1924 in deference to

178

American public opinion. There is no evidence, so far, to show that he had fully developed his "vital centers" conception until 1926.

Therefore, when tracing the evolution of Mitchell's ideas, I have been cautious in citing "From Start to Finish of Our Greatest War" or, as it has been described in the footnotes, the "War Memoirs." Indeed, I have used the "War Memoirs" as evidence for any major points only where I have been able to cite corroborative sources.

B. *Mitchell's Published Books*

General Greely. New York: G. P. Putnam's Sons, 1936.
Memoirs of World War I. New York: Random House, 1960.
Our Air Force. New York: E. P. Dutton, 1921.
Skyways. New York: J. B. Lippincott, 1930.
Winged Defense. New York and London: G. P. Putnam's Sons, 1925.

C. *Mitchell's Published Articles and Congressional Testimony*

For a rather complete treatment see *A List of References on Brigadier General William Mitchell 1879–1936*. Washington: Library of Congress, 1942.

D. *National Archives Material*

The Old Army and Naval Historical Records Sections of the National Archives, Washington, D. C., had much important material for this study. The Mitchell Papers are most helpful only for the years 1919–36. For evidence prior to that time, the National Archives holdings had to be consulted to supplement the Mitchell Papers.

Since Mitchell kept copies of so much of his correspondence, the author's searches through the Air Service files for the years 1919–25 added very little to what he had already gained from the Mitchell Papers. There were two sources which were closed to me as late as the summer of 1962: the court-martial records and most of the attaché reports in the G-2 files of the General Staff.* The few unclassified attaché reports indicated that this source might offer even further evidence both of contacts between Mitchell and foreign airmen and of his influence on foreign aeronautical developments. For general information on the years 1919–25, the files of the Air Service were indispensable. Especially helpful were such files as 041.2, Military Attachés; 319.2, Adjutant General; 333.5, Investigations; 334.7, Army-Navy Joint Boards, et al.; 360.02, Foreign Aviation; 385, Methods and Manner of Conducting War and 400.112, Tests and Experiments.

E. *Other Primary Sources*

The list of footnote abbreviations in the Notes is also a record of some twenty manuscript collections used in researching this book. While none of

---

* See Introduction and Appendix

the collections other than the Mitchell Papers contained extensive material on Mitchell, all of them at least had helpful background information. Another important background source was the Oral History research collection at Columbia University. Some caution, however, should be exercised in using the interviews. At times, the interviewees were incorrect in their recollections of dates and of the sequence of events. The worst offender in this regard was Senator James Wadsworth. The several errors in his account dilute the effectiveness of his criticisms of Mitchell.

II. SECONDARY SOURCES

A. *Books*

Army Air Forces Historical Studies: No. 6, *The Development of the Heavy Bomber, 1918–1944*. Montgomery: Air University, 1951.

Army Air Forces Historical Studies: No. 25. *Organization of Military Aeronautics, 1907–1935*. Washington: Army Air Forces Historical Division, 1944.

Army Air Forces Historical Studies: No. 39. *Legislation Relating to Air Corps Personnel and Training Programs, 1907–1939*. Washington: Army Air Forces Historical Division, 1945.

Army War College. *The Signal Corps and the Air Service, 1917–1918*. Washington: GPO, 1922.

Arnold, Henry H. *Global Mission*. New York: Harper, 1949.

Beaverbrook, William M. A. *Men and Power*. London: Hutchinson, 1956.

Bernardo, C. Joseph and Bacon, Eugene H. *American Military Policy*. Harrisburg: Military Service Publishing Co., 1955.

Bingham, Hiram. *An Explorer in the Air Service*. New Haven: Yale University Press, 1920.

Blum, John M. *Woodrow Wilson and the Politics of Morality*. Boston: Little, Brown, 1956.

Boyle, Andrew, *Trenchard*. London: Collins, 1962.

Braisted, William R. *The United States Navy in the Pacific, 1897–1909*. Austin: University of Texas Press, 1958.

Bruce, John M. *British Aeroplanes, 1914–1918*. London: Putnam, 1957.

Burlingame, Roger. *General Billy Mitchell, Champion of Air Defense*. New York: McGraw-Hill, 1952.

Caproni, Gianni. *Gli Aeroplani Caproni*. Milan: Museo Caproni, 1937.

Chamier, John A. *Strategy and Air Strategy*. Washington: U.S. Air Service Pamphlet, U-557, 1921.

Chandler, Charles de F. and Lahm, Frank P. *How Our Army Grew Wings*. New York: Ronald, 1943.

Cuneo, John R. *Winged Mars*. Harrisburg: Military Service Publishing Company, 1942.

Department of the Army. *The U.S. Army in World War I, 1917–1919*. 10 vols. Washington: Army Historical Division, 1948.

Douhet, Giulio. *Scritti Inediti*. Edited by Antonio Monti. Milan: Scuola di Guerra Aerea, 1951.

————. *Command of the Air*. Translated by Dino Ferrari. New York: Coward-McCann, 1943.

Ferrell, Robert H. *Peace in Their Time; The Origins of the Kellogg-Briand Pact*. New Haven: Yale University Press, 1952.

Finney, Robert T. *History of the Air Corps Tactical School*. Montgomery: Air University, 1955.

Frankland, Noble and Webster, Sir Charles. *The Strategic Air Offensive Against Germany, 1939–1945*. 4 vols. London: H. M. Stationery Office, 1961.

Freudenthal, Elspeth E. *The Aviation Business*. New York: Vanguard Press, 1940.

Ganoe, William A. *The United States Army in War and Peace*. New York: G. P. Putnam's Sons, 1937.

Gauvreau, Emile and Cohen, Lester. *Billy Mitchell, Founder of Our Air Force and Prophet Without Honor*. New York: E. P. Dutton and Company, 1942.

Goltz, Colmar, Freiherr von der. *The Conduct of War*. Translated by Joseph T. Dickman. Kansas City: Hudson Kimberly, 1896.

Gorrell, Edgar S. *The Measure of America's World War Aeronautical Effort*. Northfield: Norwich University, 1940.

Greer, Thomas H. *The Development of Air Doctrine in the Army Air Arm, 1917–1941*. Montgomery: Air University, 1955.

Grey, Charles G. *A History of the Air Ministry*. London: G. Allen and Unwin, 1940.

Hagedorn, Hermann. *Leonard Wood, a Biography*. New York and London: Harper and Brothers, 1931.

Harbord, James G. *The American Army in France, 1917–1919*. Boston: Little, Brown, 1936.

————. *Leaves From a War Diary*. New York: Dodd, Mead and Company, 1925.

Hartney, Harold E. *Up and At 'Em*. Harrisburg: Stackpole Sons, 1940.

Hennessy, Juliette A. *The United States Army Air Arm, April, 1861 to April, 1917*. Montgomery: Air University, 1958.

Hicks, John D. *Republican Ascendency 1921–1933*. New York: Harper and Brothers, 1960.

Holley, Irving B. *Ideas and Weapons*. New Haven: Yale University Press, 1953.

Isley, Jeter A. and Crowl, Philip A. *The U.S. Marines and Amphibious Warfare*. Princeton: Princeton University Press, 1951.

Jessup, Philip C. *Elihu Root*. 2 vols. New York: Dodd, Mead and Co., 1938.

Joubert de la Ferte, Sir Philip B. *The Third Service*. London: Thames and Hudson, 1955.

La Follette, Robert M. *La Follette's Autobiography*. Madison: Robert M. La Follette Co., 1913.

Levine, Isaac Don. *Mitchell, Pioneer of Air Power*. New York: Duell, Sloan and Pearce, 1943 and 1958.

Liddell Hart, Basil H. *Paris; or The Future of War*. New York: E. P. Dutton and Company, 1925.

Link, Arthur S. *Woodrow Wilson and the Progressive Era*. New York: Harper, 1954.

McClendon, R. Earl. *The Question of Autonomy for the United States Air Arm*. Montgomery: Air University, 1954.

Merrill, Horace S. *Bourbon Leader: Grover Cleveland and the Democratic Party*. New York: Little, Brown, 1957.

Millis, Walter. *Arms and Men*. New York: Putnam, 1956.

Mitchell, Ruth. *My Brother Bill*. New York: Harcourt, Brace, 1953.

Morison, Elting E. *Admiral Sims and the Modern American Navy*. Boston: Houghton Mifflin Company, 1942.

Palmer, Frederick. *Newton D. Baker: America at War*. 2 vols. New York: Dodd, Mead, 1931.

Patrick, Mason M. *The United States in the Air*. Garden City: Doubleday, Doran and Company, 1928.

Pershing, John J. *My Experiences in the World War*. 2 vols. New York: Frederick A. Stokes, 1931.

Raleigh, Sir Walter A. *The War in the Air*. 6 vols. Oxford: Clarendon Press, 1922–37. Vols. II-VI by H. A. Jones.

Roosevelt, Franklin D. *F. D. R.: His Personal Letters*, 4 vols. New York: Duell, Sloan and Pearce, 1947–50.

Schindler, Henry and Booth, E. E. *History of the Army Service Schools*. Leavenworth: Army Service Schools, 1908.

Sherman, William C. *Air Warfare*. New York: Ronald Press, 1926.

Smith, Henry Ladd. *Airways*. New York: Alfred A. Knopf, 1942.

Spaight, James M. *British Aeroplanes 1914–1918*. London: Longmans, 1925.

Spaulding, Oliver L. *The United States Army in War and Peace*. New York: G. P. Putnam's Sons, 1937.

Sprout, Harold H. and Sprout, Margaret. *The Rise of American Naval Power, 1776–1918*. Princeton: Princeton University Press, 1942.

——. *Toward a New Order of Sea Power*. Princeton: Princeton University Press, 1943.

Sumner, P. H. *Aircraft Progress and Development*. London: Crosby, Lockwood and Son, Ltd., 1935.

Sweetser, Arthur. *The American Air Service*. New York: Appleton, 1919.

Templewood, Samuel J. *Empire of the Air*. London: Collins, 1957.

Toulmin, Harry A. *Air Service, American Expeditionary Force, 1918*. New York: D. Van Nostrand, 1927.

Turnbull, Archibald D. and Lord, Clifford L. *History of United States Naval Aviation*. New Haven: Yale University Press, 1949.

Upton, Emory. *The Military Policy of the United States.* Washington: Government Printing Office, 1912.

Voisin, Andre P. *La Doctrine de l'Aviation Francaise de Combat au Cours de la Guerre* (1915–18). Paris: Berger, Levrault, 1932.

Weigley, Russell L. *Towards an American Army: Military Thought from Washington to Marshall.* New York: Columbia University Press, 1962.

White, William A. *A Puritan in Babylon.* New York: Macmillan, 1938.

Whitehouse, Arch. *Billy Mitchell.* New York: Putnam's Sons, 1962.

Wilson, Eugene E. *Slipstream, the Autobiography of an Air Craftsman.* New York: Whittlesey House, 1950.

B. *Articles and Periodicals*

Air Service Newsletter. 1919–26.

Army Air Corps Newsletter. 1926–36.

Atkinson, Boone L., "Italian Influence on the Origins of the American Concept of Strategic Bombardment," *Air Power Historian,* IV (July, 1957), 142–144.

———. "Caproni Museums and Archives," *Air Power Historian,* IV (Oct., 1957), 186–188.

Aviation. 1919–36.

Brown, Richard G., "Upton, the Army's Mahan," *Military Affairs,* XVII (Fall, 1953), 127–129.

Groves, P. R. C., "For France to Answer," *Atlantic Monthly,* CXXXIX (Feb., 1924), 145–153.

Hurley, Alfred F., "Young 'Billy' Mitchell and the 'Old Army,'" *Airpower Historian,* VIII (Jan., 1961), 28–38.

Key, William G., "Some Papers of Count Caproni de Taliedo: Controversy in the Making?" *Pegasus* supplement XXV (1956).

The New York Times. 1900–36.

Ransom, Harry H., "The Battleship Meets the Airplane," *Military Affairs,* XXIII (Spring, 1959), 21–27.

Seversky, Alexander de, "Remember Billy Mitchell," *Air Power Historian,* III (Oct., 1956), 179–181.

U.S. Air Services. 1919–36.

Warner, Edward P., "Douhet, Mitchell, Seversky: Theories of Air Warfare" in Edward M. Earle, *Makers of Modern Strategy.* Princeton: Princeton University Press, 1943 and 1952, 485–501.

Watteville, H. de, "Armies of the Air," *The Nineteenth Century and After.* (Oct., 1934), 353–368.

C. *Other Sources*

Bowers, Ray L., "The Transcontinental Air Race," Unpublished M.A. thesis, University of Wisconsin, 1960.

Chamier, John A. *Strategy and Air Strategy.* Pamphlet U-557. Washington: U.S. Air Service, 1921.

Craven, W. Frank. *Why Military History?* USAF Academy, 1959.

Downs, Eldon, "Contributions of U.S. Army Aviation to Uses and Operations of Aircraft." Unpublished Ph.D. dissertation, University of Wisconsin, 1959.

Emerson, William R. *Operation Pointblank: A Tale of Bombers and Fighters.* USAF Academy, 1962.

Leighton, B. G., *Possibilities of Bombing Aircraft. U.S.S. Pennsylvania,* 1919.

Mitchell, John L. *Against the Annexation of the Hawaiian Islands.* Washington: GPO, 1898.

Navy Department. "History of Naval Aviation," Vol. V. Washington: Office of Naval History.

U.S. Air Service. *Aerial Tactics.* Pamphlet No. 88. Washington: Air Service, July 30, 1920.

U.S. Joint Board. No. 349 (Serial 159) "Report on Results of Aviation and Ordnance Tests Held during June and July 1921 and Conclusions Reached." Washington: GPO, Aug. 18, 1921.

War Department. *Annual Report—Chief Signal Officer 1901–1917.*

———. *Annual Report—Chief of the U.S. Air Service 1921–1925.*

———. *Annual Report—Chief of the U.S. Army Air Corps 1926–1936.*

Index

Alfred F. Hurley,

Brigadier General, USAF (Ret.), is Professor of History and Chancellor/
President emeritus at the University of North Texas.